MAGDA GOEBBELS

Magda Goebbels
A Biography

HANS-OTTO MEISSNER

Translated from the German by
Gwendolen Mary Keeble

SIDGWICK & JACKSON
LONDON

First published in Great Britain in 1980 by
Sidgwick & Jackson Limited

Originally published in West Germany in 1978 by
Blanvalet Verlag GmbH, München, under the title
MAGDA GOEBBELS, EIN LEBENSBILD

German edition copyright © *Blanvalet Verlag 1978*

This translation copyright © *Gwendolen Mary Keeble 1980*

ISBN 0 283 98635 2

Photoset by Servis Filmsetting Limited, Manchester and
Printed in Great Britain by
Biddles Ltd, Guildford, Surrey
for Sidgwick and Jackson Limited
1 Tavistock Chambers, Bloomsbury Way
London WC1A 2SG

Contents

AUTHOR'S NOTE   7

TRANSLATOR'S FOREWORD   10

1   Early Years   13

2   Betrothal to Günther Quandt   27

3   Wife of the Multi-Millionaire   34

4   Party Member No. 8762   48

5   Magda's Marriage Falls Apart   56

6   Gauleiter Goebbels   68

7   Suitors for Magda's Hand   75

8   Sweetheart and Wife   89

9   Years of Struggle and Married Bliss   102

10   Wife of the Reich Minister   111

11   Early Shadows   129

12   Glamour and Delusion   142

13   The Festival on Peacock Island   152

14   Plots and Projects   157

15   Casanova   170

CONTENTS

16 The Baarova Scandal   174

17 Oaths and Conspiracy   183

18 Goebbels Falls into Disgrace   192

19 Interlude   198

20 An Unmitigated Scoundrel   206

21 Towards Disaster   216

22 Illusion and Reality before the Fall   222

23 Freedom Comes and Goes   236

24 Last Days   244

25 Death in the Bunker   251

26 Aftermath   274

BIOGRAPHICAL NOTES   278

BIBLIOGRAPHY   283

INDEX   285

Author's Note

From March 1920 until May 1945 my father, the almost legendary Dr Otto Meissner, was Head of the Reich Presidential Secretariat, known after Hindenburg's death as the Presidential Chancery, the pivot of the Head of State. For twenty-five years the most important papers, decisions and appointments flowed across his desk. As permanent representative of Presidents Ebert and von Hindenburg, he took part in all the important discussions and attended all Cabinet meetings – though under the Nazi regime his authority in relation to Hitler as Head of State was restricted.

Otto Meissner himself belonged to no political party, retaining the same position under Presidents Friedrich Ebert and Paul von Hindenburg and Adolf Hitler, being variously designated Privy Councillor, Head of Ministerial Department, Secretary of State, and finally Minister of State with the status of Reich Minister. To have served for a quarter of a century as head of the same official function is a hitherto unsurpassed record.

Dr Otto Meissner was acquitted by the American Military Tribunal at Nuremberg, the judgment stating, inter alia, that:

Otto Meissner has never been a member of the National Socialist German Workers' Party; he opposed the appointment of Hitler as Reich Chancellor up to the last. It is clearly evident that Meissner insofar and as often as he could exercised his position to obstruct or mitigate the harsh measures of his chief, frequently at considerable danger to himself. There exists no proof whatsoever that he committed or was involved in any offence against humanity. He therefore stands acquitted.

7

He died in May 1953 at the age of seventy-three.

I was born in Strasbourg, Alsace, before the First World War. From the age of ten until I myself entered official life, I lived with my parents in the right wing of the Reich Presidential Palace at Wilhelmstrasse 73. Close proximity to the Ebert and Hindenburg families, as well as the neighbourly relations enjoyed with the sons and daughters of the ministers and the Reich Chancellor living at the time in the Wilhelmstrasse (all the parks behind the ministries being connected with each other by garden gates), inevitably led to friendships being established which transcended all political changes.

My education, which included a period at Trinity College, Cambridge, resulted in my passing the final State law examination and qualifying for the diplomatic service where, as an attaché in the Foreign Office, I became the youngest diplomat in the Reich. I served in the German embassies in London, Tokyo and Moscow and, after being wounded as an officer in the Tank Corps in the East, was appointed consul in Milan during the final war years.

During intervening periods on various occasions spanning a few months in the Berlin headquarters of the Foreign Office, I came to know leading personalities in political, economic, literary, artistic and social circles, and to frequent their houses. Above all, as far as this book is concerned, I moved in the same milieu as Magda at the time of her marriage to Günther Quandt, and then later during her marriage to Joseph Goebbels. My connection with Ello Quandt, Magda's sister-in-law and best friend, dates from this period.

When in 1950 Ello Quandt and I again met in Munich, Ello expressed the wish that I should write Magda's biography. I had myself often met Magda Goebbels in private life. My mother, as can well be imagined, was frequently in her company on social occasions, mostly for reasons of protocol, but also because they were drawn together by their background, education and linguistic abilities. Besides, there were very few among the wives of the National Socialist leaders who had anything in common with either of them.

Other informants – employees, relatives or friends of Magda Goebbels – have contributed material for this book. Magda's mother, Frau Behrend (Frau Ritschel by her first marriage and Frau Friedländer by her second), has also made her contribution. Other relatives from both marriages who have helped me with their recollections have stipulated that they should remain nameless.

I am deeply grateful to my old friend Ernest (Putzi) Hanfstaengl, who died in 1976 in his nineties; also to Julius Schaub, who served Hitler as his personal adjutant for more than twenty-five years. Erich Kempka, for a similar length of time the Führer's personal chauffeur, and the one who at the end had to burn the bodies of Hitler and Eva Braun, was interned in the Ludwigsburg-Ossweil prison camp after the war at the same time as I was. Nobody was more qualified than he, from his own experiences at the time, to report on the deaths of Magda, her husband and the six children. I also encountered quite a number of other direct witnesses of the events described in this book behind the barbed wire, though I met yet others in more normal circumstances.

I was associated in 1951, under the pseudonym of Hans Roos (my mother's maiden name), with the writer Dr Erich Ebermayer, unfortunately long since dead, in a much less well-authenticated biography of Magda Goebbels entitled *Partner to the Devil*, published by Hoffman and Campe, Hamburg. My old friend Erich Ebermayer, in the course of long discussions on a number of occasions with Ello Quandt, has corroborated all that she told my wife and myself, for which I am more than grateful to him. The present volume is an almost completely new piece of work considerably enriched with fundamental source material and fresh illustrations. Twenty-five years ago, not long after the collapse of the Third Reich, the majority of the witnesses did not wish to volunteer any information, partly from self-protection, partly so as not to incriminate others.

In 1949 I was exonerated by the denazification tribunal, but I did not rejoin the diplomatic service. Since then I have had fifty-three books published, chiefly on travel, but also on hunting and exploration. I have not otherwise been concerned with modern history or political themes, apart from my book – *30 January 1933 – The Story of a Coup d'Etat*, published in 1958. At some future date I intend to write of my own extremely varied life, covering as it does so many turbulent years.

HANS-OTTO MEISSNER

Translator's Foreword

Vous aimez; on ne peut vaincre sa
destinée,
Par un charme fatal vous fûtes entrainée.

RACINE: Phèdre

Quand on a tout perdu, que l'on n'a
plus d'espoir
La vie est une opprobre et la mort
un devoir.

VOLTAIRE

When Hitler in 1938 was planning his disastrous State visit to Rome at the invitation of his fellow dictator, Benito Mussolini, he realized that only one of the wives of the Nazi leaders would meet with the approval of the Italian court and be able to cope with its rigid protocol: Magda Goebbels, wife of the Minister of Information and Propaganda. She, alas, was awaiting the birth of a child and so was unable to accompany them on that occasion.

Magda Goebbels was indeed the First Lady of the Third Reich. From early childhood she had moved in the best society; she was widely travelled and a talented linguist, as well as a beautiful, elegant and aesthetically conscious woman. The Goebbels' apartment in the centre of Berlin became Adolf Hitler's private headquarters, the meeting place of Party leaders where all important internal Party conferences were held, long before anyone, even the most ambitious of Party members, remotely anticipated that the party would come to power.

Magda was drawn into the vortex of the Nazi Party at a moment of crisis in her life when, following the breakdown of an early marriage, she found herself for the first time forced to stand alone and take command of her destiny. Her hitherto one-sided experience of the world had left her ill-prepared to make a true assessment of such insidious types as the leading personalities of the Nazi movement, of which Adolf Hitler and Joseph Goebbels were the dynamic inspiration. The very novelty of their apparent idealism, their driving sense of purpose and their restless energy fascinated and held her from the first. The authoritarian structure of the German empire having been swept away, the German people, oppressed by the onerous terms of the Treaty of Versailles, and confronted by mounting economic difficulties, had perforce begun to realize that only radical solutions such as those offered by National Socialism could save them from communist domination.

Magda was so fatally caught up in her second marriage by the magnetic force exerted upon her by Joseph Goebbels that in spite of repeated efforts, she was never able to break away completely.

She gradually became increasingly sensitive to his compulsive infidelities and blatant lying, however. Although he, an undoubted psychopath, frequently referred to her as a hysterical woman, their partnership was by no means a *folie à deux*. She played no active part in his cult of the barbaric and came to feel humiliated and trapped, realizing all too late that she had sacrificed herself to the Party's shameful myth.

The author's view that Magda's Buddhist beliefs were at the root of her decision to commit suicide and take her children to the grave with her seems unconvincing. One is left wondering why he did not probe this question more fully. Having lived in Japan, he might reasonably be expected to have gained a fairly comprehensive understanding of Buddhist philosophy, or at least to be able to give a more satisfactory explanation of its general influence on Magda's character and behaviour if indeed she had, as he assures us more than once, had a lifelong interest in it. Her failure to apply its precepts earlier, when misgivings about her marriage to Goebbels and Nazi philosophy in general had crystallized into downright disgust, not only with her husband but with the Party itself, would seem to call for deeper analysis. Her despairing efforts to save her marriage must, even before the final throes, have brought her face to face with her essential self and thus with ultimate principles. 'I bring you sorrow,' said the Buddha, 'and the ending of sorrow.' Herein one would like to think lay her hope and strength and, in the last resort, salvation.

Buddha lays particular emphasis upon the psychological importance of the will, exhorting his followers 'not to be morally lazy; to be
strenuous in exerting one's will is the greatest virtue'. The entire
responsibility for either bondage or freedom is placed directly upon
oneself. Buddha clearly shows the way to overcome misery and
reach the bliss of liberation. Fundamental to this teaching is the
imperative to experience the truth for oneself.

Magda undoubtedly had the key, but there is no evidence that she
found comfort or was sustained by it. Again, in the tragic dilemma
which finally confronted her, one cannot help thinking that the
Buddhist principle of reverence for all life should surely have
deterred her from taking her own life, let alone those of her children.

But at the crucial moment the mesmeric influence of Joseph
Goebbels held final sway. Her tragic situation demands our utmost
compassion. We know little of her inner life, her emotional travail,
in those last few weeks in the Berlin bunker, but the scale of her
tragedy is of a high order, calling to mind that of Racine's *Phèdre*, one
of the great tragic figures of world literature. Both women were
caught in the toils of their own destiny, were predestined to perdition.

G.M.K.

1

Early Years

It took thirty years for Magda Ritschel, later Magda Friedländer, later still Magda Quandt, to acquire the name which was to bind her disastrously to the most sophisticated fiend of her time. But from the moment when they first met, the lovely woman fell completely under the spell of the crippled man.

Magda, née Ritschel, and Joseph Goebbels exercised a magnetic attraction for each other. This attraction between the dark-haired undersized man of the petite bourgeoisie and the beautiful blonde of the haut monde was so powerful that the bond between them could never be broken. So, inexorably, on that sombre night of 1 May 1945 in the underground bunker, they died together.

At that same hour, the fools' paradise, the make-believe greatness of the Thousand Year Reich, lay completely shattered.

Maria Magdalena Ritschel was born on 11 November 1901 in the Bulowstrasse, Berlin. Her father, a highly qualified engineer, was an urbane, elegant man, slender and well-groomed; he wore a monocle, that supreme, if highly caricatured, mark of distinction, in his left eye. Dr Ritschel was well-to-do, eminent, well-connected, cultured and much travelled, fully appreciative of the pleasant things in life, intellectual as well as material. Bending tenderly over his little daughter, he made up his mind to surround her with everything he had to offer.

Her mother, just twenty years old, came from a homely background. It was said later that she had at one time been a chambermaid in a grand hotel on the Rhine. She was no match for her husband in intellectual vigour and breeding, but she was perfectly cut out for looking after a home; above all, she was more warm-hearted and affectionate than her husband.

The marriage of such contrasting personalities was only satisfying to both in the early stages, the difference between their social status soon proving too great for true companionship. He had little time for his young wife and she suffered from his neglect. Putting his business interests before everything else, he was obsessively determined to succeed; he was always conjuring up fresh inventions and making new plans. His wife, however, still cherished the romantic notions of marriage and happiness of a young woman of a century earlier, and was consequently doomed to one disappointment after another. Finally, some three years after Magda's birth, learning of an act of adultery on the part of her husband, she did something that was most unusual at that time and applied for a divorce.

Dr Ritschel now proved himself a true gentleman. He pleaded guilty without more ado, relinquished custody of the child in favour of his wife, much as it hurt him to do so, and undertook to provide for both on a nobly generous scale. With his wife's approval, he also made himself responsible for the future direction and supervision of Magda's upbringing. Until his daughter married Joseph Goebbels, her father's guiding hand continued to protect her; it was only then that Dr Ritschel passed out of her life.

Frau Ritschel, as a divorced woman, was much too young and attractive to live alone for long. Just two years after the divorce she married again, becoming Frau Friedländer. Once again her husband was a wealthy man. Thus Magda, later the wife of Joseph Goebbels, the arch Jew-baiter, acquired a Jewish stepfather. Although he did not supplant the real father, Friedländer was indeed a second father to the child. As far as little Magda was concerned, the two fathers were friends. What Friedländer lacked in general education, he made up for in practical shrewdness and knowledge of human nature; above all he radiated the personal warmth and kindness which the more superior but cool Ritschel lacked. The little girl loved father Friedländer with all her heart, to which he responded fervently, all the more so as he and his wife had no children.

Joseph Goebbels was not born into a well-to-do family. There were no soft lights, antique furniture and deep carpets in his world, no children's nurse with a little white cap to attend to him. His background was not so clearly defined as Magda's. While hers was unequivocally upper-class, the Goebbels belonged to that hybrid social stratum not impoverished enough to vegetate apathetically, but on the other hand so ill-paid that they never had quite enough money for their needs.

Goebbels' father was neither of the working class nor yet of the middle class. As foreman in a textile factory, he had by his ability worked his way up above the body of manual workers. But the Goebbels family could never enjoy the middle-class standard of living to which they aspired. Though they owned the small house in the Prinz-Eugen-Strasse, in Rheydt, the Rhenish textile town in which they lived, this hardly lifted them above the general level of the many who owned nothing whatever. The longing for greater security, for some capital and income, still persisted. The children would need to better themselves, especially Joseph, the youngest son, born on 29 October 1897, who was said to be afflicted from birth with a club foot.★

It soon became apparent that Joseph was an unusually bright child, the pride and joy of his parents. In spite of his disability, he would succeed in rising above the smoke-blackened, drab, miserable surroundings of his birthplace. However great the sacrifice, his parents determined that he should go to the grammar school. His father, in his wildest dreams, even dared to think of being able to arrange for his clever son, perhaps by means of a scholarship, to go to university.

The youngster did not find things easy at school. Because he was odd, he was despised and jeered at by his healthy schoolfellows and his two brothers – his sister Maria was born much later. Joseph smarted under an acute sense of inferiority; daily, hourly, he was the butt of their remorseless ridicule.

The reaction of the misfit is understandable. He started off by despising and hating everybody, and this hatred he nourished all his life. Joseph swore to himself, at the age of ten, that one day he would

---

★In spite of the most zealous efforts, the author has not been able to confirm whether Joseph Goebbels was born with a club foot or, as Curt Riess in his biography (*Joseph Goebbels*, Baden Baden, 1950) states, he was a healthy, normal young man up to the age of seven, when he suffered from bone marrow inflammation, which necessitated an operation on his left thigh, leaving his left leg some 8 centimetres shorter than the other one. Ello Quandt, sister-in-law of Magda Goebbels, to whom I am indebted for so much essential information, was also unable to answer this question with any certainty. It appears that Goebbels never spoke about the cause of his infirmity either to his wife or to his relations.

show people who he really was. He would do better than the rest of them, the healthy lot, his tormentors. He would show them.

But to begin with all he could do was to take refuge in solitude. He sought consolation in books, his best and only friends, becoming more and more estranged from his family, his parents, his brothers and more particularly his schoolfellows. In the depths of that withdrawal, the prodigious energy began to be built up which, a quarter of a century later, was to convulse the world.

When she was five years old, Magda, at the insistence of her father, was sent to Belgium, where Ritschel meanwhile had gone to live. Two years later the Friedländers also moved to Brussels. Magda flourished between the attention of her two fathers, who rivalled one another in their love for her. Two gentlemen, both men of the world, of breeding and worth, they ignored the minor tensions which joint responsibility for bringing up the child engendered. Through them Magda was early able to acquire the feminine skill of adjusting to different mentalities.

The Friedländers lived in a lovely Brussels house, in which wealthy, elegant people came and went. Her parents did not have time to concern themselves with Magda's education. As Magda herself had been baptized a Catholic, since Dr Ritschel was a Catholic, and as it was customary in Catholic Belgium for well-to-do families to send their children to convent schools, the Protestant mother and Jewish free-thinking stepfather took the child one day to the Ursuline convent at Vilvorde.

The Ursuline convent of Sacré Coeur was one of the strictest girls' boarding schools in existence; mediaeval customs were still in practice there. The weekly bath was taken in a tub in which the young pupils sat covered up to their necks. Getting in and out, their chemises were so deftly changed by the nuns that no child ever caught sight of her own naked body.

The exciting life of the Belgian capital was as distant as the moon. A strong, deep faith and constant devotional exercises so dominated all activity and thinking that no ideas about the outside world could ever enter the girls' minds. The school admittedly imparted an extensive amount of knowledge, but complete submission of the whole being to the rule of the Church was demanded and resolutely enforced, breaking the weak and compressing the strong into its mould. It was no doubt during those formative years of harsh discipline that the young Magda acquired that self-control of which she would finally have such bitter need.

Magda remained for eight years in that austere, cloistered world. She was by no means unhappy, as life in obedience to faith came naturally to her. She was popular in the convent and gradually came to play a leading rôle. Pretty, angelic-looking even, with her pale gold silken hair, milk-white complexion and sparkling blue eyes, graceful, dainty and slim, she appeared to the pious nuns as something straight from heaven. With her lively mind, she gave them no trouble where her education was concerned; she was also kind-hearted and never presumptuous.

Holidays provided the only relief from this sheltered life. As soon as the gates were opened, both fathers were there, two socially active households awaiting her. The two men contended with each other in introducing her to the cultural life of old Europe, of the five neighbouring countries, Germany, France, Belgium, Holland and Luxemburg. In the course of blissful holidays Magda became familiar with all the well-known beauty spots. She was treated by her family as an adult rather than a child; at twelve years of age she was quite grown up.

Whilst convent schoolgirl Magda was kneeling in her white dress at the feet of the Virgin Mary, the lame, delicate young man in Rheydt was also kneeling before an altar, but in a tiny brick-built chapel in the suburb of Rheydt rather than in a magnificent old church in Belgium. His pious mother, the only person who bothered about him, the only one he himself really loved, took him with her to church almost daily. She prayed that he might be healed, although she knew, and the doctors had told her, that a shortened leg never grew any longer. Nevertheless it did seem to her that God heard her prayers. Of course the leg did not grow again – God would not change His natural law for her sake – but the young man was generously endowed mentally, as if to compensate him for his physical disability. The young cripple grew daily more intelligent; he was persevering, tirelessly diligent. His eagerness to learn practically amounted to an obsession, so fanatically did he devour every book that came into his hands.

He went of course to the grammar school, and as in those days school fees for higher education were relatively heavy, his father made the necessary sacrifice and even grew proud of his apparently deformed son. His Joseph would show the others what a young Goebbels had got in his head. The young Goebbels only left his narrow little room for school and mealtimes, never casting a glance through the window at the depressing smoke-blackened yard outside. He did his school work effortlessly. Joseph was the best in his class, though he was not a model pupil, often giving the masters disrespectful, even cheeky answers.

If his schoolfellows did not want him for a companion, and he could not impress them physically, he would dominate them mentally. The fifth-former read Caesar, Cicero, Virgil, even *The Iliad* in the classic original. But he was prevented by lack of opportunity from learning living foreign languages, an omission which he would one day regret bitterly. He read and studied voraciously; he read through the whole of Meyer's encyclopaedia, studied Mommsen's *Works on Roman History*, read every word Goethe had written.

His energy was boundless, but for lack of proper guidance he wasted valuable months, years even, on erudite works long since out-of-date, whose long-winded contents were more inclined to clog his mind that enlighten it. He amassed an immense fund of knowledge, but nevertheless remained basically ignorant. All the same, the amount of knowledge he managed to store up was quite astounding; nothing that the reservoir in his head laid hold of, did it ever let go. Of what use it was all going to be, Goebbels for a long time had no idea at all, but he was quite sure that his opportunity would come along one day.

The choice of their son's career was a matter of some concern to his parents. Being pious Catholics, they wanted him to study theology. When Joseph reached the upper sixth, his father made it his business through relatives and acquaintances to get the necessary introductions, as a result of which the Albertus-Magnus Society expressed their willingness to assist the foreman's son with his theological studies.

Joseph himself was not averse to the idea of becoming a priest; he was ready to seize any opportunity which would enable him to raise himself above the masses, to escape from his narrow existence. The priesthood offered him just such an opening. A shrewd and determined priest could gain influence over people, could lead them. Over the priest stood the bishop, and over him the archbishop and cardinal, princes among men, powers in the land. On the way to the top via the path of the Catholic Church, financial position and family background were not such decisive factors as with so many other, in fact nearly all, careers at that time. Many princes of the Church had come from the most humble of circumstances. Why should the pale, insignificant, lame youth with the passionately burning eyes not climb higher and higher among the branches of the Catholic hierarchy?

So Joseph Goebbels seized the opportunity and declared himself willing to enter the Church; he was then invited by the Albertus-Magnus Society to go for an interview with a priest. The sixteen-year-old youth rightly assumed that he would be put to the test, but he was not in the least nervous. Had he not, after all, read the whole of St Augustine, especially his *Confessions* and his major work, *The Kingdom of God,* and those of other fathers of the Church, and was he not fully versed in Catholic dialectic?

In fact, however, he was not questioned about anything of the kind. The priest merely conducted a conversation with him, enquired about his plans, his ideas about God, above all what he thought about the world in general. The test came to an end almost before it had actually begun. The talk, the casual conversation, was the test, and this the priest ended with the words, 'Young man, you don't believe in God.' Even at that extraordinarily early moment, the priest had seen through Joseph Goebbels.

The most astonishing thing, however, was that the Albertus-Magnus Society nevertheless granted the young man a two-year scholarship, by means of which he was free to study whatever subject he chose, with one exception – theology! So ironically, without intending to do so, a charitable organization facilitated the studies of the young man who was later to be one of the most dangerous opponents of the Church in Germany.

While Goebbels was still a sixth-former the First World War broke out. German youth hastened to join the colours with unparalleled enthusiasm, in a boundless spirit of self-sacrifice, to defend the beloved Fatherland under attack from wicked enemies. The diminutive sixth-former was infected with this spirit too.

Whether in those early days of August 1914 the urge for recognition or the prevailing intoxicating enthusiasm blinded Joseph Goebbels to his shortcomings is not known. Such an intelligent young man must in fact have realized that he would be useless as a soldier, but it may be that he only wished to demonstrate that he did not lack courage. He may also have thought that everyone, even the disabled, would be needed. In any case he limped along to the recruiting station, lined up in the endless queue and volunteered for active service. The doctor gave him a hasty glance and sent him back home.

Overcome by this rejection, he shut himself up in his room, threw himself on his bed and sobbed. He remained like this for thirty-six hours, refusing to see his mother – at least that is how the story went afterwards. In the momentous hour of decision, the Fatherland, his own people, had rejected him.

He avenged himself with the only means available to him – work. He worked like a tiger for the school and for his future. His exam results were the best in all Rheydt. While his healthy former school-fellows were fighting on the battlefields, gaining one victory after another, only to sink into a mass grave, Joseph Goebbels had won his first battle of the mind. At the prize-giving he was chosen to give the ceremonial address. When he finished the headmaster went up to him: 'Goebbels,' he said, genially shaking him by the hand, 'you made a first-class pupil, but you'll never make a good speaker.' He could not have been more mistaken.

In the first few days of August 1914 German civilians living in Brussels were forced to leave. The armed German invasion had taken the outraged Belgians by surprise. Protected by two ranks of soldiers, jeered at and stoned by the populace, the deportees, among whom were the Friedländers and Dr Ritschel, were driven back to the Fatherland, forced to leave house and home and all their goods and chattels behind.

In the small crocodile-skin case which Magda clutched tightly in her hand as she descended the steps of the Anhalt railway station in Berlin were all her worldly possessions. The few cases which Friedländer piled on to the taxi contained all that he still possessed. Nevertheless he started up again at once; he began by opening a shop as a cigar merchant, this led on to other things, and soon the worst privations were over. Before long Friedländer was once more in a good position and moved with his family into an imposing residence in the elegant surroundings of west Berlin.

The short period at the beginning of the war when the family needed to economize and curtail their expenditure depressed the teenaged Magda. Although she was not called upon to experience any real hardship, the very thought of poverty appalled her. Though she willingly endured the stark simplicity of convent life, she always took riches, luxury and beautiful surroundings for granted. It was as if the very stars in heaven paid tribute to such a demanding nature, for all her life Magda, whatever else she may have had to put up with, never again for a moment experienced material lack.

During the four years of war, she attended the Kolmorgen

Grammar School, a day school, and alternated between her parents' households, living a carefree, mentally stimulating, overcrowded life. The most decisive influence in her life came from her real father, Dr Ritschel. Unlike Dr Friedländer, who had had to start again, Ritschel had kept his family business in Godesberg and so had no financial worries. As she grew older Magda stayed with him more and more frequently.

It was here at her father's house that she first came into contact with Buddhism. Although a convinced Catholic, strong in the faith, Ritschel was deeply attracted by this mysterious Eastern doctrine, and just then, in wartime, amidst all the news and stories about the Battle of Verdun and the Chemin des Dames, the peaceful teaching of the great thinker Gautama held an even stronger appeal. Ritschel fired his precocious young daughter with his enthusiasm for Buddhism, giving her books to read and discussing them with her, until she too soon became an ardent, almost fanatical disciple of Gautama. From this time onwards, Buddhist literature was always to be found by her bedside. She did not speak of it to others: apart from her own narrow family circle, nobody knew of her interest, which deepened with time. Much of what she did in her life, and the way in which, in the end, she went to her death, is explained by the assumption that she believed in an earthly but purified rebirth, in the possibility that a life which had miscarried could begin afresh under other auspices.

While she was in Brussels Magda, in accordance with the Belgian custom whereby stepchildren when living in the stepfather's house bore the latter's name, had expressed the wish to change her name from Ritschel to Friedländer. Dr Ritschel, magnanimous and understanding as always, had granted her wish. Father Friedländer was to say later, shortly before his death, that this change of name by his stepdaughter was the nicest gift he had ever received.

But now in Berlin this change of name seemed to Magda almost like a bad joke, for hardly had all the formalities been completed, scarcely had she altered the name of Magda Ritschel in all her school books to Magda Friedländer, than she was told that her parents were about to be divorced. Why her mother dissolved what appeared to be an excellent and carefree marriage is not known; what is known is that the twice divorced 34-year-old woman now renounced married life for ever, and that Friedländer moved into a furnished room in Berlin, only concerning himself with his business affairs from then on.

In March 1919, in the weeks when Berlin Castle was the scene of fighting between the Spartacists and government troops, Magda took her final school examinations, unaffected by the political storms sweeping across Germany. Shortly afterwards she entered the finishing school at Holzhausen near Goslar, as a solution to the usual dilemma as to what a young girl on leaving school should do. She had hardly been at the school three days before becoming the dominant personality there, even where the teachers and the headmistress were concerned. In knowledge and culture far superior to most of the other girls, she also captivated everybody by her appearance; although only seventeen, she had the mature mentality and self-assurance of a young woman of twenty. She also knew how to get her own way.

In Holzhausen, it was chiefly with the older girls and teachers that she made friends, having long grown out of the foolish ways of her own age group. Even if she would have liked to, she could not bring herself to take part in the usual run of boarding school pranks. At home she was an only child and had never had friends of her own age; her two fathers had both treated her as an equal from childhood onwards. She consequently looked to every man to treat her as his intellectual equal and in no way as a 'little girl'. She herself, probably quite unconsciously, was most exacting throughout her life, and only acknowledged as real people those of a similar calibre to that of her two fathers.

One of her dancing partners at the boarding school, named Walter, could claim to be Magda's first boyfriend, but he was certainly not a person who came up to her expectations generally. A year older than she was and only just an upper sixth-former, by nature a likeable, romantic fool, he bewitched her with his smile, his white teeth and, his brown wavy hair. Magda being the most attractive and Walter having the pick of all the girls, he fell in love with her. Magda on her side did not try to impress him with her intellectual superiority; she generally won all hearts by never attempting to score off others. In fact, she really regarded the nice, big young man with a little tender sisterly or motherly feeling.

As she had had no experience at all of flirting and Walter behaved along the usual delightful lines of a middle-class sixth-former of his generation, their little love affair took a most romantic course. He covertly sent her a poem rhyming kiss with bliss, concealed in a little bunch of lilies-of-the-valley; she replied in verses hidden among forget-me-nots, also rhyming kiss with bliss. They met in secret, carved a heart with their initials intertwined in the bark of an oak tree and stuck little notes in its hollow, in a spot known only to themselves.

Although their conversation never touched on matters which seriously interested, stimulated or touched her, Walter was dear to her. His devotion made her feel enveloped in a mantle of warm, sensuous feeling. Her head stayed cool, the core of her being unmoved, but her heart was gladdened by him. This delightful episode came to an end after a few months, as Walter took his school-leaving examinations and went on to university. Although he had had no lasting effect on her development, Magda always cherished his memory.

Meanwhile Goebbels continued along his joyless way, a student of that age which, in times of peace, is said to be the best years of one's life, although in his case the saying did not hold good. The times were hard and he often went hungry. His grant was meagre and the cost of living so high that he could only afford one meal a day, and that of the cheapest kind. He possessed three shirts, two pairs of shoes and one suit of clothes.

In Heidelberg the happy days of the student fraternities were practically over. Goebbels lived in a stuffy little hole of a room looking out on to a small backyard. The other students were often weaklings like himself, unfit for active service.

Goebbels felt ashamed of his dragging foot and its unheroic origin. As nobody in Heidelberg knew him, he slid almost imperceptibly into a lie. It was not the first time he had lied, of course, but the first time he himself had actually begun to believe in the lie. Gradually he began to say that he had been wounded during an assault at Verdun. The name of Verdun, that hard-fought centre of a battle line that swallowed up men, was holy. Nobody questioned the matter; it gained him respect and increased his self-confidence, and he no longer felt himself to be an outsider. Many of his grey-coated fellow students treated him as a comrade, so that Joseph owed to his lie happy moments of warmth.

He now pursued his studies in the same random spirit as he had earlier amassed knowledge in Rheydt, studying nothing of a definite nature, always waiting upon impulse and an opportunity which would direct his mind and energy forward. 'What did I actually study?' he was to ask himself later, in 1928, in his autobiographical novel *Michael*, 'everything and nothing. I am too lazy and feel too stupid for science. I will be a man, establish myself, become a personality.'

But a way consonant with his boundless ambition and energy did not present itself as, expectant and restless, he cast around. The only thing left for him to do was to proceed on his random way further into the realms of learning. So he went on gathering up here a few teachings on philosophy, there a few centuries of history, and of creative art, and finally a handful of names from literature. As diverse as the subjects he studied were the places where they were undertaken. He changed universities in colourful succession – Bonn, Munich, Freiburg, Wurzburg, Cologne, Frankfurt and Berlin, all saw the young Goebbels come and go. The longest he stayed in any one place was at Heidelberg, which he attended no less than three times.

And it was at Heidelberg that an incident occurred which was of great importance for his future. Quite unexpectedly he became popular with girls, and with one girl in particular. Nothing could have been more surprising, seeing that he was desperately badly dressed, short, thin, half starving, lame, inhibited and shy. Could any man have been less likely to attract young women? But he must already at that time have possessed the mysterious aura which attracts women without their knowing why. Intellectual young women, particularly students, found Goebbels a good talker, in fact a gripping narrator. He had style and a certain charm. Looked at more closely, his sparkling eyes and dark brown hair were pleasing, as well as his unusual metallic-sounding voice which issued so unexpectedly from his sorry figure.

Thus, unbelievably, he found himself the boyfriend of one of the prettiest girls at Heidelberg, ousting all the other better-looking young men, the officers covered with glory, even the much-admired, one-armed riding master and holder of the *Pour le mérite*.

Each year in Heidelberg the prettiest girl student was chosen to be the 'Alma Mater'. Of all the students that year the Alma Mater, Anka by name, was Goebbels' girlfriend, a tall, slim blonde girl of good family. She was the first of the three women in his life whom he really loved, and she was above all the first woman with whom he ventured to sleep. This extraordinary triumph filled him with elation and gave him a self-assurance which he had hitherto not known. And his triumph persisted even when his happiness was shattered. When, after a summer of unclouded harmony, Anka turned to another student, he was not as upset as might have been expected. Goebbels was shrewd enough to see that an affair between two such sharply contrasted individuals could not outlast the summer session. It was enough for him to have won the heart of this young woman and to have bound her to himself for a few months. He remained grateful to her and never forgot her. She was to turn up later in his life.

Defeat and revolution were overwhelming Germany, but Goebbels continued to pursue his random studies, unmotivated, still uncertain of his course, vacillating in his attitude towards the radical changes then taking place in the country, which would inevitably drag every young man into political activity of some kind.

Not so Goebbels the student, who on the one hand was indignant when he saw the shoulder tabs of brave officers, even those of wounded fellow students, ripped off, while on the other it was bliss to see those so deeply humiliated who hitherto had towered over him. However, the wild mobs who noisily and jubilantly celebrated the ending of the war by quarrelling in the streets repelled him. Since politics can only be practised with the masses, who can never comprehend the mind of a truly great man, Goebbels found politics hateful and vulgar and turned away from them.

He applied himself instead, in this his last Heidelberg period, to one of the great European minds, the literary historian Friedrich Gundolf, one of the giants of the Stefan George school, and friend of the poet. Gundolf, whose real name was Gundelfinger, was surrounded in his private life by mystery and rumour. Joseph listened eagerly to the Gundolf lectures on the Romantic movement and took part in the Gundolf seminars. As a student Goebbels had nothing against the Jews whom later he persecuted to death, nor against Gundolf or Professor von Waldberg, both Jewish, under whose auspices he obtained his doctorate with a thesis on 'Wilhelm von Schütz – a contribution to the history of the drama of the Romantic School'.

Goebbels read the democratic *Berliner Tageblatt* each day, and venerated its chief editor, Theodor Wolff, also a Jew. He sent him more than fifty articles, all of which found their way back to him. In return for this, in 1933, Goebbels drove Theodor Wolff to emigrate and suppressed his paper. Moreover, his admiration for the Jewish writer Heinrich Heine was so great that he sent Heine's book of songs to Anka as a Christmas present, inscribed to the effect that Heine in his opinion was one of the greatest of German writers.

A grant from a Catholic foundation helped Joseph Goebbels with his studies; Jewish professors helped him to complete them successfully. Both foresaw a great future for one so intelligent and energetic, 'provided', remarked Gundolf when Goebbels took leave of him, that you seize with determination the first opportunity to do justice to your talents'.

The young Goebbels was to follow this advice.

2

Betrothal to Günther Quandt

While the awkward Heidelberg student had, to his own amazement, won a lovely girl's heart for the first time in his life, Magda was also to meet the first real man in her life. By chance, while travelling by rail from Berlin to Goslar at the end of the holidays, she stepped out into the corridor just as a gentleman in the next compartment, absorbed in documents, happened to raise his eyes. He was so struck by her appearance that he rose at once, went out to the window and stood beside her. His manoeuvre, he was pleased to think, had passed unobserved. It took a real lady, he reflected, to act in that way. A frivolous type would have smiled at him, a narrow-minded one would have edged away.

With a rapid glance he summed her up. Any men who liked blondes would naturally have considered Magda beautiful. Moreover, a connoisseur of women would immediately have perceived how innocent she was and that she came of a good family. She wore no make-up and used hardly any face powder, her clothes were discreetly elegant, styled very plainly from the best material. Her shoes were expensive, her white collar immaculate, her hat fashionably simple, and she wore no jewellery. Although still a young girl, she had a womanly air about her.

From experience and with a sure sense of the right approach, he avoided any attempt at striking up a banal acquaintanceship with a fellow traveller. He did not mention the weather, nor that the compartment was too hot or too cold; he merely bowed slightly saying, 'My name is Günther Quandt.' Magda betrayed neither surprise nor shock. She turned slowly towards him, in order to take a better look at him, and noticed that he was not particularly elegant or especially good looking. Nor could he pass for young any longer; she took him to be in his early forties, though he was actually only thirty-seven. He was nearly bald and inclined to corpulence. Nevertheless he cut a definitely impressive figure. If his appearance was only average, his face, forehead and manner were distinctive. Obviously he was a man who counted, who exercised power and was supreme in his own particular field.

Magda did not grasp all this straightaway, but intuition told her that a personality was standing next to her. So she allowed herself to be drawn into conversation.

Günther Quandt has himself described his first meeting with Magda in an autobiography written at a much later date and intended at the time only for relatives and friends.*

Meanwhile I discovered that an exceptionally beautiful young person stood beside me, with shining blue eyes, lovely thick fair hair, a face with well-cut regular features and a slim figure. We discussed the Berlin theatre, travel and other matters of interest to a young girl. Time simply flew. When she got out at Goslar, I helped her with her luggage and so had an opportunity of unobtrusively learning her address there.

On my arrival in Cassel, I sent off my first letter to her that same evening. 'I will take the liberty,' I wrote, 'on my return the day after tomorrow to break my journey in Goslar at 3.30, to call on your headmistress and introduce myself as a friend of your father (at the time I was thirty-seven years old). I would be most happy if you would let me know promptly by letter or telegram whether my visit would be agreeable to you.'

From Günther Quandt we learn how matters developed.

Postal connections – I really must say this today, looking back – were in those days surprisingly good. On the morning of my return journey I had her reply which, together with her friendly assent, also contained a few words from the headmistress as to the school regulations with regard to visitors.

On arriving in Goslar I found accommodation and purchased a bunch of Maréchal Nil roses – not for the young lady, but for the headmistress! Thus armed I went to pay my visit. I was given a very kind reception as a friend

*Published by his sons Herbert and Harold Quandt, July 1961, Mensch und Arbeit Verlag, Munich.

of her father, whom I naturally did not know. After chatting for half an hour, there came the question, 'And I suppose you would certainly like to see Magda?' 'Very much, dear lady,' and with the telephone already in her hand, she said, 'Magda, please come over at once. A friend of your father's is here, just passing through.'

And Magda came. Our greetings were accompanied by violently conflicting emotions. We confronted one another at once formally, as two who hardly knew each other, amicably, as two who were pleased to see each other, cordially, as a friend of her father. The conversation with the headmistress continued for a few moments longer, Magda replied only when spoken to. Finally the headmistress said, 'You would, I feel sure, like to go for a walk together, but you must bring the young lady back by seven o'clock.'

All the women in the house from the most senior teacher down to the youngest pupil were in raptures over the visitor. Magda would have been a very unusual seventeen-year-old had she been anything but flattered that a man like Günther Quandt had gone to such lengths on her behalf.

Quandt was in every respect the soul of propriety. He set out in the first place to win the confidence of the headmistress, who soon capitulated; he then invited the whole school to the best patisserie in Goslar, followed by a dinner to delight the heart of any epicure at the leading hotel. Nothing more was heard of him for a fortnight. The next time he came, he invited Magda and three friends for a day's excursion to Schierke in the Harz Mountains, to the very exclusive Fürst Stolberg Hotel, for lunch.

It was not until his third visit that he was able to have a serious talk alone with Magda. He learned that she did not wish to stay on much longer at the dull boarding school, but was going back to Berlin, whether her mother agreed or not. That would, however, only be possible at the end of term and there was still some time to go. Meanwhile Quandt's visits practically became the talk of the school; they envied Magda this wonderful uncle. That he was in fact her uncle was never questioned, it was so obvious from the fatherly way in which the generous visitor treated her. There was never a false note, not a single gesture which could have been misconstrued.

How did Magda herself react during these weeks? Was she unaware of his real intentions? Was he, as far as she was concerned, just another 'father' with whom she could confidently enjoy a tender, intimate friendship? In any case she seems to have been taken completely by surprise when, during a car ride through the

Harz, he suddenly asked her to become his wife. She kept her head and asked for three days to think it over. In view of the big difference in their ages, Quandt could hardly have expected any other reply; he agreed and ordered his chauffeur to turn back.

Magda did not make use of her three days' grace to seek the advice of her mother or two fathers, but instead turned the matter over in her own mind. The question of money did not count with her. She was well provided for by Dr Ritschel's allowance and what she could expect to inherit from him in due course. What attracted her in a life with Quandt was the demands that would be made on her. She would have social obligations to fulfil, the kind of thing with which, even as a young girl, she had long been familiar. She would have the company of an important man of wide experience. She was not calculating, did not seek social recognition for herself, but she was very ambitious. She imagined herself playing a part in his business life, having to run his large house for him, to which she would attract influential people, fostering his business connections and entertaining his friends. It all seemed to her attractive.

Finally, she would have children to bring up, his successors. Günther Quandt had explained to her that he had lost his wife a year previously and now had two sons, Hellmuth and Herbert, who needed a mother as much as he needed a companion.

So Magda decided to say yes. He was overjoyed, and embraced her for the first time. It was only after she had given her answer to Quandt that she told her mother and her two fathers that she was going to marry him. It had never occurred to her that, under the existing law at the time, her parents could, if they did not approve her decision, prevent the marriage for at least three years until she came of age. She knew, however, that they would not refuse her anything on which she had set her heart.

Dr Ritschel did not object to the marriage, but together with Friedländer warned her that she could be making a great mistake in marrying a widower twenty years older than herself, with two sons. Magda's mother was appalled and reacted with tears instead of arguments.

In fact Magda herself also began to waver, wondering whether perhaps she had given her word too hastily. The disapproval of her parents and their warnings, coming as they did from those whom she knew had only her well-being at heart, made her think. The fact that at eighteen she would be stepmother to two boys, only five and eight years younger than herself, particularly worried her.

Quandt exerted all his powers of persuasion, reinforced by his shrewdness and understanding of human nature. Meanwhile Dr Ritschel, as a conscientious businessman and father, made enquiries in commercial circles about his daughter's suitor, whose standing in the German economic sphere was extremely high. He received the most glowing reports. Günther Quandt was one of the wealthiest men in Germany and a leading industrialist. His extensive business enterprises and financial interests were recognized internationally, and had been built up not through clever speculation but through sound judgement, excellent quality and skilful administration, prudently fostered over three generations.

The engagement was announced. There was general amazement at the boarding school at the sudden promotion of the kindly uncle to fiancé. Magda's friends were consumed with envy at her good fortune. To them a multi-millionaire conjured up visions of luxury villas, large country houses, travel to Nice and Venice, expensive furs, magnificent jewellery and large cars.

Quandt, however, was not slow to make demands. First he asked that Magda should become a Protestant and reassume the name of Ritschel. He did so not from anti-semitic motives (although he later gave evidence to the contrary), or because he was an enemy of the Catholic Church, but because he was a man who felt bound to represent a conventional public image. He wanted his wife to share his faith and to bear the name of her true father. Magda was quite willing to meet her future husband's wishes. She was also shrewd enough to realize that every marriage, even the happiest, required constant concessions to be made by the woman, so she became a Protestant and changed her name for the second time.

The engagement was celebrated on 28 July 1920 in Berlin. The event, in spite of Dr Ritschel's reservations with regard to his prospective son-in-law, passed off in the most friendly atmosphere; her father and her fiancé were both well-mannered men of the world, and additionally Dr Ritschel had succeeded in obtaining the concession that twelve months should elapse before the marriage took place. As both parties were living in Berlin, this was felt to be quite a bearable waiting period.

In spite of the pressing demands of his many business trips and responsibilities, Quandt made ample time available for Magda, accompanying her to the theatre and on car drives through the surrounding countryside of the Brandenburg Mark, and inviting her and her mother for weekend excursions. Moreover, there were family visits to be made. The Quandts in Pritzwalk and Wittstock, provincial towns in the Mark, still firmly rooted in the last century, laid great store by time-honoured practice and were anxious to meet Quandt's eighteen-year-old fiancée.

Günther Quandt had been born in those parts. His father, his father's father and his father-in-law had created their fortune there, extending gradually from small beginnings. His relatives who had gone on living there, including Günther's brother Werner, revered tradition; for decades they had not modified their life style. The elegance and superficial brilliance of Berlin at the turn of the century was, for the reclusively inclined multi-millionaire, merely a sign of progressive decadence, perhaps even the harbinger of future disaster. The children in these circles were brought up very simply, but with benevolent firmness.

Thus when Magda came to visit these relations, as the wife-to-be of the forty-year-old Günther, pretty as a picture, very young, a good linguist, well-educated, they were unable with all the good will in the world to find any common ground, or scarcely anything to say to one another. Although Magda was unobtrusively elegant and at that time used no cosmetics, Günther's family found her too modern, too young and above all too self-confident. They also made her well aware that she was only the second wife of her husband. The memory of the first wife of Günther Quandt, the mother of his two sons, was still very much alive in the villas of these factory owners of Wittstock and Pritzwalk. Frau Toni Quandt too had come from this area and had been dead scarcely more than a twelvemonth.

The visit to her fiancé's brother, Werner Quandt, was for Magda a comforting surprise. Werner had recently married a young woman of Magda's age, Eleonore Quandt, known by the family as Ello. From the moment they first saw each other, Magda and Ello conceived a mutual liking which developed into a firm friendship lasting for decades, surviving Magda's divorce from Günther Quandt and standing the test of her marriage to Joseph Goebbels right up to the dreadful end.

Ello was eighteen, educated on similar lines to Magda, vivacious, pretty and supremely skilful in dealing with every conceivable social situation. Ello did not feel happy in the small provincial town, neither was she well-suited to Werner Quandt, her husband, who, unlike Günther, had not broken away from the narrow provincial life and had remained parochial, unable to make up his mind to free himself from his restricting family circle and strike out into the world.

Map of the central government area of Berlin. Most of the ministry gardens between Wilhelmstrasse and Friedrich-Ebert-Strasse can be identified

Gunther Quandt, Magda's first husband

Dr Goebbels during the 1926 elections

Goebbels (third from left, seated) aged sixteen, surrounded by fellow
pupils at the grammar school in Rheydt

Disappointed by her family-to-be, Magda returned to Berlin from her stay in the Mark. She was worried about her proposed marriage, which she had begun to realize was not going to be all rapture and intoxicating happiness.

Quandt, sure by now of Magda's hand, sought to train her to conform to his ways. His dominating, authoritative manner reacted against her all too precocious self-confidence. Big things were not involved, just little habits and tendencies of Magda's of which he disapproved – a hat that didn't please him, acquaintances whom he didn't like, a theatre play seen by each from a different angle. Quandt had hitherto never been contradicted by anybody or had the rightness of his judgment questioned; none of his contemporaries did so, let alone an inexperienced young girl. Magda found it incomprehensible that anybody should check her, should expect her to surrender her own opinion and submit to the views or taste of a partner. How differently her fathers behaved in this respect!

So the difficulties were there, even before the marriage. It is strange that Magda, knowing this, did not draw the obvious conclusions. But perhaps this too was implicit in her character. She always carried on to the bitter end, draining to the dregs the cup which she herself had poured, even when the first drops tasted bitter.

3

Wife of the Multi-millionaire

On 4 January 1921 Magda stood with Günther Quandt before the altar, wearing a lovely bridal gown of Brussels lace. The wedding took place in Godesberg, followed by a small party in the Hotel Godesberger Hof. The honeymoon trip was to Italy, at that time the country most favoured by the bourgeoisie. They travelled in a large Mercedes driven by a chauffeur, but had scarcely arrived in Italy before a telegram recalled the bridegroom to Berlin. The trip was abandoned and they were soon back home again.

But the short time in Italy had sufficed to disillusion Magda. She discovered that her husband did not appreciate the real Italy, the essence which cannot be found in Baedeker marked by a star; he merely went sight-seeing. She realized that fundamentally he was a man lacking all aesthetic sensibilities, a thorough-going pragmatist to whom art and beauty meant little. Nature, too, left him quite unmoved. As they travelled through Umbria, through a landscape of classical beauty and historical significance, passing Etruscan tombs and Hohenstaufen castles, with stately cypresses lining the roadside and the cupolas of Florence on the horizon, Quandt was explaining to his wife the geological structure of the soil and calculating its possibilities for industrial exploitation.

Back in the cool, practical, workaday atmosphere of Berlin, however, things promised to be easier. Magda took fresh heart and realized that her husband, on other planes than that of art, possessed outstanding qualities; she reconciled herself to having married a brilliant businessman and threw herself into her new tasks.

The Quandt villa was spacious, but for a man of his resources by no means luxurious. The ten rooms, apart from the domestic quarters, were furnished in good middle-class, at times homely, style, with a few *art nouveau* pieces alongside red plush armchairs eighty years old. Only the garden was really beautiful, well shaded, sloping gently down to the waters of the Havel, on whose shore stood a boat house with a luxuriously equipped motor boat.

But more important were the children to whom Magda was in future to act as mother. To begin with, because of her age, Magda dreaded this responsibility, but she soon established a frank and good relationship with the youngsters. Herbert, the younger of the two, nine years old, was fair and small, a shy, reserved child, far too short-sighted to be able to lead a normal child's life. He did not go to the local school, but was taught at home by a private tutor. He was inclined, no doubt because of his eye trouble, to have complexes and be suspicious. Doctors had told his father that Herbert would never be able to follow a career but only to have an occupation which largely excluded reading (they were grossly mistaken). So Quandt acquired a magnificent estate in Mecklenburg for his son to take over later on.

Hellmuth was the exact opposite of Herbert. He was twelve, with soft, dark hair, and large, dreamy brown eyes; unlike Herbert he was artistically sensitive, highly musical, vivacious and open, learning without effort. Everything came to him that he needed to know.

Magda turned instinctively to the older boy whose disposition corresponded so closely to her own. His real mother had perhaps shown more love to the ailing, difficult younger child than to the older, whom nature had so generously endowed. The young stepmother, however, found it difficult to care equally for Herbert and not to let him feel that she favoured his brother. But Herbert did feel it and suffered on that account.

For household staff, Magda was provided with housekeeper, cook, parlourmaid, gardener and chauffeur, and a tutor for the boys. For an upper middle-class household, by the standards prevailing at that time, this was too few rather than too many employees. There would usually have been a nurserymaid, a manservant and a lady's maid as well. The housekeeper had to be dismissed straightaway, because she was jealous of her young mistress, and her post was never filled again. All the same Magda had under her control seven people, including the two boys. Many young women would have tried to assert themselves so as to command respect, but it never occurred to Magda that her authority as mistress of the house would be challenged. She simply exercised her usual charm and soon all the staff were devoted to her, the boys loved her, and the tutor gazed at her with adoration.

She was shrewd enough to interfere as little as possible with the staff. Magda knew that she lacked domestic experience of any kind. Her education and training had been entirely intellectual and social. She was unable to cook and could only sew a little; housewifery held not the slightest appeal for her. Now and then her conscience would prick her and she would work from morning till night with her staff, cleaning the house from top to bottom. Once, when the cook was ill and Magda herself had to prepare the meal, she spent the whole morning in despair on the telephone to her mother, asking for instructions.

There was none of the convivial entertaining in Magda's house that she had imagined, no glittering social gatherings or noisy cocktail parties, nor even teas on the lawn. Quandt was not a gregarious man, and saw no point in leading a social life. He had no ambition to frequent exclusive salons and it was not his habit to do business elsewhere than from his office desk. He was a hard, persevering worker and only attended social gatherings or gave a party himself when he could not avoid doing so. Then he would don white tie and tails or dinner jacket and would again become the genial, charming talker he had first shown himself to be that day in the train between Berlin and Goslar. Whenever it was important to Quandt to win a person over, he could always do so. No lady whom he had ever taken into dinner was known to complain of boredom; only his own wife had reason occasionally to do so.

Magda was no pleasure-seeker but she did need distraction, and pressed her husband now and again to take her out to a theatre, a concert or a ball. He was an unwilling dancing partner but, not wishing to deprive his young wife of this pleasure, he invited a cousin of his, who was dependent upon him and deeply devoted to him, to accompany them. It was the young man's duty then to dance with Magda while her husband discussed everyday matters over a glass of wine with business friends.

Where theatres and concerts were concerned, the difficulties were not quite so easily overcome. Like so many creative, outgoing men, Quandt was a bad listener, and Magda often had to waken him cautiously before the curtain came down or the last drum roll died away. On one occasion, when Magda and her husband were at one of Charell's Revues at the Admiralty Palace, an incident occurred which aroused great amusement, though not on Magda's part. On the stage a group of lovely girls, each wearing nothing but a tiny muff, were dancing. At the end of the dance each one drew from her muff an evening dress and threw it over herself. They were not simple dresses, however, but proper model gowns with a long row of buttons at the back, which had to be done up. For this purpose the beauties descended from the stage and distributed themselves among the audience, each asking the nearest gentleman to do up her dress, an enticing request with which the men in the auditorium only too willingly complied – with the single exception of Günther Quandt. He, after a heavy day at the office, was fast asleep. As the spotlights followed the girls around, the dazzling light caught the sleeper full in its beam, focusing all eyes upon him. Confused and half-blinded, he could only rise slowly and unsteadily to his feet, while the girl, her dress unfastened, danced up and down nervously in front of him. Of course the audience in the Admiralty Palace enjoyed the contretemps enormously, laughing and applauding his fumbling efforts.

Magda soon learned how very jealous he could be and avoided giving him the slightest excuse. She had hoped before the marriage to support him socially in his business life, but to her great disappointment she met with no response on his part. The capabilities which she had brought to her marriage were not called upon at all -- her social graces, knowledge of languages, wide reading and self-confidence, all of which might have been of great help to Quandt, particularly as Berlin in those early postwar years was markedly lacking in centres of culture. But Quandt was a man whose whole being was concentrated on work, who seemed to have no time at all for social activities.

Magda was therefore thrown back on her own resources and able to devote herself all the more to her stepsons, who encouraged her to play the piano and sing to them. She had time for reflection, too, much perhaps, but this in itself was useful in as much as it helped her to realize quite early on that she was not going to be able to change the ways of a man more than twice her own age. His values, his abilities, his achievements lay beyond her reach.

Her husband's enormous wealth was no compensation for what she lacked. Günther Quandt's greatest, most disastrous mistake where his married happiness was concerned was his peculiarly erratic form of economy. Instructions could, for example, be issued in the offices of the Quandt enterprises that no more shorthand notebooks were to be purchased, that secretaries were to cut open and use old envelopes instead. On the other hand, Quandt paid his diligent workers well above the average and was generous in the provision he made for the sick. Magda was soon made to realize that she was not being kept in a gilded cage. The master of the house himself ordained what was to be cooked and eaten. He screwed the household budget down to such a level that even the chauffeur could boast that he ate better than his master; the ironical situation occurred of a liveried footman with white gloves serving, with much dignity, such dishes as *Königsberger Klops mit Kartoffelpüree* (meat balls with caper sauce and mashed potatoes).

At the beginning of the 1920s, Günther Quandt was thought to be worth some 10 million marks. By the end of the decade he owned taxed property to the value of 70 million, which at today's values would amount to some D.M. 50,000 million. His economic genius enabled him to preserve intact the substantial part of his fortune throughout economic crises, inflation and the Second World War, with its devastating consequences, right up to the subsequent German 'economic miracle', in which he was himself involved. Today the Quandts own the second largest family business empire in the Federal Republic.

In Germany as elsewhere, very few family business organizations or wealthy individuals were able to hold on to so much of their property throughout such turbulent times. Certainly where Quandt was concerned a rigid spirit of economy was one of the underlying factors. This Magda all unsuspectingly came up against. At first she was given a small sum as pocket money for her personal needs and had to account for every penny spent in the household. She wore a sable-dyed coney fur coat and owned less jewellery than the wife of any chief clerk in her husband's works. No outsider would ever have suspected that the mistress of the lovely villa in Babelsberg, the much-envied wife of the great Günther Quandt, had such a small amount of money to spend on herself.

Meanwhile the living conditions of Joseph Goebbels did not improve. If the young wife in the lordly villa almost for the first time in her life had to face financial restrictions, the young doctor from Rheydt was destitute. The grant from the Albertus-Magnus Society ceased when his studies finished and he was left with nothing.

The ultimate achievement of his irregular, unusually long years as a student was a doctorate, and this did not even enable him to get enough to eat for himself. He was one of thousands swelling the numbers of the academic proletariat, a monstrous superfluous supply of educated people who flooded the professions in those postwar years. If he had not been so restless he would perhaps have taken a teaching qualification and so earned his living, if only partially, as an assistant master, his doctorate degree not by itself qualifying him for a teaching career. In fact his doctorate proved a drawback. His father, a much-respected worker for decades in his firm, could have obtained a job of some kind for him, but in those days it would have been unthinkable for someone with a doctorate to do a manual worker's job. Even had he wished to do so, no employer would have agreed to take him on.

Instead he managed to scrape miserably along with casual work as a coach or temporary secretary. When he had exhausted all his money he would go home to Rheydt where at least a small room, bed, chair, table and meals awaited him – though the humiliation for Dr Goebbels in having to seek food and shelter in the house of his father, the Works foreman, burned like fire in his ambitious soul.

Goebbels' father could no longer understand the world. Through self-sacrifice and privation he had managed to provide an education for his clever son. After passing his school examinations brilliantly, and with the support of an ecclesiastical foundation, Joseph had been enabled to study for many years, hopefully ensuring that, as an educated man, he could obtain a good pensionable post. Instead of this a thin, shabby, starving son came back to the parental home, and not only had he not climbed up in the world, but he failed to belong anywhere. He was neither at home among the petty bourgeoisie like his parents, nor among the more superior established middle class. In those days, to belong to the middle class, one had to have a regular monthly income and a reputable post. But Joseph was neither a workman nor a middle-class citizen, he was just nothing. And his father began to be ashamed of him.

Even his loving mother found herself unable to console her son, who wandered about with an embittered, dejected look on his face, full of boundless loathing towards everything. Joseph was fully aware of the extent of his gifts, estimating his own potential highly, perhaps even more highly than was justified. He knew quite well that all he lacked was the right opportunity to prove himself, that all he needed was a start and a purpose. He simply could not understand why he was unable to find such an opening.

He was prepared, indeed more than prepared, to seize any opportunity, whatever it might be. He was not inhibited by any old-fashioned principles or ideas, which at that time prevented so many one-time active officers from adopting a new means of livelihood. Joseph Goebbels was not bound up with any student fraternity mentality, nor tied to any religious or political philosophy, nor encumbered by family tradition. For him the whole world lay open, but where was the door through which he could enter?

Menaced by constant under-nourishment, miserably clad, with burning eyes in a sallow face, thin, lame, ascetic-looking, he resembled a mediaeval monk in an old engraving. But Joseph Goebbels had neither religious nor political faith; he had practically nothing and believed in nothing; he was a nihilist. He had only one thing, and that to excess – time for reading. Later, when he came to write his autobiographical novel *Michael,* he described how, in those years, politics did not interest him in the slightest; he strove only to learn about men not as individuals but humanity in the mass.

There is a book by the French writer Le Bon, often named but little read, *On the Psychology of the Masses,* which Goebbels devoured time and time again, until he was able to repeat substantial parts of it from memory. Later he was to apply with success much of what he learnt from this book. With equal enthusiasm he read all the writings of Walther Rathenau, one of the most intelligent and highly cultured of all German Jews. This important man had just been appointed German Foreign Minister, and was shortly to conclude the Treaty of Rapallo, thus effecting the first breach in the so-called dictated Treaty of Versailles. In June 1922, however, Rathenau was murdered by young right-wing radicals. Goebbels was not concerned about the murder, but the doctrine of economic socialism propounded by the books of Walther Rathenau fascinated him.

Among the great writers of world literature who influenced him the most was Dostoyevsky, amongst whose evil geniuses he recognized a kindred spirit: Peter Stepanovitsch Verschovensky, a reluctant nihilist, an unbeliever, restlessly searching for an ideal – or for a man whom he could follow unconditionally. Where for Joseph Goebbels was this man to be found?

At the beginning of May 1922, continually suffering from hunger, Goebbels went to Munich, not for any particular reason but merely because he had to be somewhere. Instead of sitting around at home all the time, he hoped to find casual work in such a centre of intellectual activity.

What he found primarily in Munich was a group of men like himself, who were uprooted, seeking a purpose, some meaning in life. They were mostly young officers, students, mercenaries and refugees from occupied territories, men who, less through their own fault than as a result of six years of war and its aftermath, could no longer adjust to normal peacetime conditions. They were as poverty-stricken as Goebbels and equally embittered. They detested capitalists. As the majority of them had been in the Imperial army or came from good middle-class families, they hated the republic, and therefore the new government. Nevertheless since they, in spite of everything, still remained middle-class citizens, they abominated communists and socialists. The main political parties were therefore all targets for their biting criticism, and not only the German National Party which numbered capitalists and the big agriculturists among its ranks. These young people hated all who held property, in which they themselves had no share.

When Goebbels began to mix in these circles he was warmly welcomed. A doctorate still counted for something among the descendants of one-time middle-class families, and moreover he was a brilliant talker who could express in coruscating terms all that they themselves were so dimly thinking, wishing and feeling.

The salient weakness of Goebbels' new-found friends lay in their failure to unite. They quarrelled among themselves over ideas and objectives. As Goebbels himself did not believe in anything in particular, it seemed to him that it would be better for all these groups and cliques to find some common ground, whatever it might turn out to be. They could only achieve anything by concentrating their all too feeble powers.

But his efforts to get the young radicals to compromise miscarried completely. Joseph Goebbels was just on the point of seeking his fate elsewhere, possibly among the communists, when it was suggested to him that he should go that evening to the Zirkus Krone (Crown Circus). Smiling ruefully, he waved the suggestion aside: he had no money to waste on clowns and performing elephants. When it was explained to him that there was no question that evening of the usual circus performance, but that a national radical group had hired the circus hall for a political meeting and that a certain Adolf Hitler, chairman of the group, and known to be a rousing speaker, was going to address them, he allowed himself to be talked into going. He went, he listened and suspected, indeed hoped, that here could be the long-looked for opportunity for him and his talents.

At the close of the meeting he climbed on to the platform, walked up to the table and entered his name in a book lying open upon it – thus becoming member No. 8762 of the National Socialist German Workers' Party (N.S.D.A.P.).

When, after this evening in the Zirkus Krone, he walked back through the streets of Munich to his miserable lodgings, he was by no means sure that he had been wise to join this new party quite so hastily. How strange that this Adolf Hitler had so impressed him. He, always so cool-headed, had been swept off his feet, completely enraptured; he had hardly known what his fingers were doing as they signed the book containing hundreds of other names. No. 8762! What did that actually mean? What good was it to him to be one among 8762? No doubt this N.S.D.A.P. was the most important, already perhaps the largest, of the radical national groups. Equally, no doubt, Joseph Goebbels had come along too late to have any influence over the statutes, ideas and objectives of the Party. He deplored this and asked himself where he would actually stand among these people, since as far as he, Goebbels, was concerned, ideas did not exist either to be believed in or followed. For him ideas had only one purpose, to impress crowds and non-active members; ideas were only valuable as a medium of propaganda.

Just before the end of their first year of marriage, on 1 November 1921, Magda and Günther Quandt had a son, who was christened Harold. The pregnancy had caused Magda, who was a model of good health, no inconvenience at all. The father, delighted at the birth of his third son, sent Magda flowers, and, after some gentle prodding by a third party, a silver dressing-table set. Further than that the thrifty multi-millionaire was not prepared to go. All the same he did allow Magda to have a children's nurse. She made a quick recovery, meanwhile hoping that the child would help her to become more firmly established in the household and in her marriage.

Soon after Harold's birth, Magda acquired three more children to look after. They belonged neither to her nor to Günther Quandt, nor were they related to their new (foster) parents even through marriage. The father of the two boys and the little girl, a Principal Assistant Secretary to the Ministry for Trade and Industry, Schulze by name, one of Günther Quandt's best friends, had met with a fatal accident following the death of his wife shortly before. Scarcely had

Quandt heard about the double tragedy than he decided to take the orphaned children into his own home. Expense did not matter: it was inherent in Quandt's disposition to extend the hand of friendship beyond the grave. He was anxious to do the best for the children and made enquiries as to a first-class boarding school for the boys and an even better one for the girl.

When Magda realized what her husband wished to do, she protested strongly against the idea of an institutional upbringing for them. Nothing could replace the family home of which the children had been so grievously deprived so well as another family home. The children's spiritual development was the most important consideration. Magda pleaded earnestly and passionately in favour of the Schulze children growing up alongside her stepchildren and their own son. Günther Quandt, convinced by her arguments, gave his consent, though not without misgivings. It was naturally a personal sacrifice for him, the lone wolf, the ardent worker, suddenly to have a home teeming with children. Nevertheless he put up with them all. He did not bother himself too much about them, however, and contented himself largely with a report each evening from Magda as to the day's events.

Meanwhile the difficulties between husband and wife became increasingly manifest. Apart from minor exasperations over material things, which weighed only relatively lightly with her, Magda complained of her husband's cold behaviour towards her. Although in offering a home to the orphaned Schulze children he had shown himself to be extremely generous, she often doubted whether he really had any feelings. In any case he did not show them. If Magda made herself look particularly attractive for his sake, he criticized her thin legs, so from that time on, when he was at home, she would only wear long afternoon gowns. But even so she did not always find favour in his eyes. One evening, when they were both going to an official ball, Magda chose a bewitchingly lovely dress of black lace, thinking it suited her to perfection. 'That,' said her husband, 'looks like a nightdress. I won't go out with you like that. Please go and change.' Magda protested a little, but did as he ordered.

She did not always obey him, however, and after the birth of her son she began to resist more strongly, occasionally even managing to get her own way. From a quite early age she had been used to coming down to breakfast in a dressing gown or housecoat, particularly after a bath or when expecting the hairdresser. This did not suit her husband, who thought it unseemly, betraying an inner lack of principle. Nevertheless she refused to give way on this point and finally he became used to it.

The couple lived in two wholly different worlds which hardly impinged upon each other. Soon there were practically two households under one roof – one for Magda and the six children and the other centred entirely round the master of the house. Hers began to function only when Quandt, who went to his office at seven o'clock, had left the house.

Magda then had all the children to see to. She had to organize their breakfast and see them off to school punctually, all except Herbert who on account of his eye trouble, could not go to school and for whom they had, as already mentioned, engaged a tutor. For educational reasons Quandt sent the other children to a local school.

Quandt did not return home for lunch, as was the usual practice in Berlin. It was too far from the city centre to Babelsberg; moreover, as a leading executive he liked to settle some of his business affairs over lunch in town. Hence at home at the Quandt lunch table there were usually seven – Magda, the tutor and the five elder children. In addition the household included Magda's own small child and five employees. No less than fourteen people, including the head of the house, were living under the same roof, all under Magda's charge. At this time she was just twenty-one years old.

The estrangement between the two grew apace at this time. Both were conscious of it but neither had strength enough to do anything about it. In spite of much goodwill and honest effort, there was no happiness to be found in the marriage. If Magda had given way to tears or pleaded with him, trying to awaken tender feelings in him, things might still have been different. But she could not bring herself to do so; her pride prevented her from showing her feelings.

Magda had actually become a rather unusual type of woman, explained Ello Quandt, her sister-in-law, many years later. What to outsiders appeared to be a unique combination of gifts and intellectual capacity had brought her no personal happiness. Her mature personality from a quite early age was only fully appreciated by a few people, certainly not by Quandt or, later, by Goebbels. Magda herself, perhaps only subconsciously, needed a partner at whose side she could stand as an equal. Most people only saw in her what caught the eye, namely a lovely, slim, well-groomed, desirable woman, in other words a man's woman by the prevailing standards. The popular view that men do not like intelligent women, however much they deny it, was certainly proved right in Magda's case.

Quandt wanted to lead her, to model her after his fashion. This, however, in the long run proved impossible, in fact intolerable, for so cultivated a woman. She could have contributed so much to the standing of a man of Günther Quandt's calibre had he only been prepared to accept her on her own terms, even if she did not always share his opinions. Since he lacked the necessary insight, Magda was frustrated – although she herself would not have known this much-abused expression of today.

If anybody was fully aware on what terms the two were living with each other, it was Ello, who was closer to Magda than anybody else for twenty-five years, seeing her several times a week. It was only with Ello, and not even with her own mother, that Magda discussed her true thoughts and feelings.

When Ello Quandt, who had long since been divorced from Werner Quandt, told me one day at the end of August 1951, in the course of one of the many long talks we had in her house in Munich, that Magda was only nominally a Catholic, had later become a Protestant, but was in fact a devoted Buddhist, I thought it absolute nonsense. Where could Magda, who went to a Catholic convent up to the age of fifteen and was thereafter in the care of her father and stepfather, have come in contact with Buddhism? However, Ello insisted that it was so.

It was only many years later, long after Ello's death, that I had confirmation of what she had told me. Günther Quandt himself wrote in his personal memoirs: 'Magda was, as I have already mentioned, christened as a Protestant [sic], but brought up as a Catholic. Later she again took Protestant religious instruction. Nevertheless she claimed to be in close sympathy with Buddhist philosophy.'

Though moderately stated, this seems to prove the truth of Ello Quandt's assertion that Magda was a convinced Buddhist. This explains much about Magda, particularly her action in taking her six children with her when she committed suicide. Buddhists see death as but a door between this life and the next, so that innocent children, having incurred no burden of sin to expiate on rebirth, are certain to begin a new and better life. Of course Magda could hardly have expected a man like Günther Quandt, firmly rooted in Prussian Protestant tradition, to understand what he would have called fantasies. So in this respect again she was left to her own devices.

One day, quite by chance, Magda came upon some old letters carefully tied together, letters from women which her husband had received when a young man. These were obviously women to whom he had once been fleetingly attracted but had soon forgotten. The writers had been in need, as least so it seemed to Magda, though perhaps matters were not actually as bad as they appeared to her. In any case the writers lamented their misfortune and asked for help. How far Quandt had met these requests Magda was unable to judge, but she feared – which was partly confirmed by the number of letters – that the majority had remained unanswered.

The discovery made a deep impression on her. She lay awake at night trying to imagine what had gone on between her husband and these young women. She conjured up visions of idealized young girls, laughing and happy in the arms of the beloved. Then she pictured them distressed and abandoned like Gretchen in the last act of *Faust*. Magda imagined it all in dreadful detail and suffered through her fantasies. She felt sure he had behaved meanly to these unknown women. She never mentioned her sad discovery to her husband, but many years later these letters had quite an important rôle to play.

The more Quandt lost respect in her eyes the more her position in the household was strengthened. She freed herself inwardly from him. His reproaches, which had at first depressed her, no longer mattered. His anger, which had so frightened her earlier, now made her smile. She no longer automatically obeyed his orders, but often followed her own judgment. As time passed, she succeeded in assuming full control of the household, obtaining an adequate housekeeping allowance and even occasionally considerable sums for her own use. She was able to have clothes made by a good couturier and to buy a few beautiful pieces of furniture for the house.

Sadly, although after five years of marriage she was gradually gaining the freedom and authority which, as the wife of a multi-millionaire, were basically her due, Magda was no longer able to feel any gratitude towards her husband, who was making these concessions too late in the day. Nevertheless neither of them thought even then of dissolving the marriage.

At about this time Quandt learned by chance from a business friend that unless he was able to raise a certain sum of money within a few days he would face bankruptcy. Quandt offered his friend the money he needed against his making over to him the house he owned in the Frankenallee, not far from the Reichskanzlerplatz. It all had to be done very quickly, for his friend only had a few days, hours in fact, to save himself from complete disaster, and Quandt thereby acquired a spacious house on relatively favourable terms.

Magda was delighted at the prospect of furnishing the new house and immediately began to dream of spending happy hours in antique shops and with art dealers, selecting furniture, materials and pictures. But again she was to be disappointed. Not only was the house completely furnished, but all the equipment was already there down to the last tablecloth, spoon and broom. Not an egg cup, bedside rug or flower vase was lacking.

She did not let her husband know how deeply she felt about it, but when they looked at the new house together, she had to admit that it greatly exceeded their present house in New Babelsberg both in taste and in comfort. Though not antique the furniture was expensive. Carpets, curtains, pictures, lamps, even the ash trays and door handles – all was in perfect taste, obviously having been assembled by a family with great knowledge of art.

For reasons which even she herself could not have explained, Magda did not feel at home in the well-equipped new house. She felt as if she were merely a visitor there, as though the house still belonged to others, to the strangers who had lived there before whose presence continued to pervade the atmosphere so strongly, as if they lived on in the rooms they had so lovingly arranged.

Quandt, however, was proud of his new acquisition. 'See, dear,' he said to his wife, 'how wrong you were when you said that culture cannot be bought. I *have* bought it!'

4

Party Member No. 8762

After he became a member of the National Socialist German Workers' Party, Joseph Goebbels remained just as penniless and unable to find work as before. Adolf Hitler, who led the diminutive party in Munich, did not even know the new member by name. In fact his position actually deteriorated as a result of his hasty decision to become a Party member. Nobody was interested in him any longer: as Party member No. 8762 he was fully committed, so why should anybody still trouble to woo him? The Party was not concerned about him, only demanding membership subscriptions – if in vain. His earlier friends from the other right-wing radical groups left him alone, rather annoyed that the clever Goebbels had been disloyal to them.

There seemed to be no alternative but to return to Rheydt, since a room and a plate of soup at the family table always awaited him there. His mother and Maria, his young sister, were glad to see him – in fact they admired their learned son and brother – but his father and two brothers turned sullen faces towards him and spoke disparagingly about those who could not even earn their own living.

Goebbels swallowed all their scorn and suffered torment in silence. Day after day he walked the streets or slept, working unremittingly at night – though nobody seemed to know what he worked at. He was finally liberated from this hopeless situation by an event of great political significance – the occupation of the Ruhr by the French in

January 1923. The justification for this was that the German government had failed to comply fully with its obligations under the Treaty of Versailles.

A storm of patriotic indignation raged across the whole of Germany. Reich President Friedrich Ebert and the government under the leadership of Chancellor Cuno called for passive resistance. For the first time since the war the whole nation was united; confronted by this arbitrary action of the French, dormant national pride was aroused. Everybody from the Social Democratic Party to the German National Party stood staunchly behind the government.

In the Ruhr area itself, underground movements sprang up like mushrooms. The times were full of opportunity for young agitators, and Joseph Goebbels immediately perceived his chance. Borrowing a few marks from his mother, without his father's knowledge, he travelled to Elberfeld, the centre of the resistance movement. He thrust his way through until he found someone in authority and then announced that he was prepared to undertake any mission or act of sabotage, however dangerous.

At headquarters the limping patriot received a friendly if somewhat sceptical reception. His physical disabilities represented a great risk, if not for himself then for others. His club foot was a too conspicuous distinguishing feature in the event of an unsuccessful coup. Nevertheless, the group of activists under Leo Schlageter kept him at their side, but they considered that he would be more useful as an agitator recruiting and building cells.

The historic moment had arrived for Joseph Goebbels to make his first speech, before a handful of young people, students, workers and grammar school pupils. And since this first speech was successful, and Goebbels willingly agreed, they gladly permitted him to speak daily, almost hourly in fact. He spoke in small back rooms, schools, lofts, cellars and railway stations. He travelled incessantly here and there, always by rail, third class, speaking mostly in unoccupied parts of the Rhineland, occasionally also in occupied territory, calling upon the public to resist the tyranny of French bayonets. When addressing the workers he called the foreign troops 'slaves and hirelings of French heavy industry'; when addressing a middle-class gathering he called them 'apostles of internationalism'. Whatever he said at any time to any particular group, he said it with burning passion, using forecful and persuasive argument. In this way he easily won over his audiences.

It was Joseph Goebbels who made Leo Schlageter the hero of his movement, in the same way that he later made Horst Wessel, a murdered member of the Hitler Youth, General Rommel and the Attaché vom Rath into national heroes. Overnight he made Schlageter, the patriotic saboteur shot under martial law as a result of a French court martial, into the great martyr of a new political ideology, a symbolic figure for every National Socialist member willing to sacrifice himself – though Schlageter himself never belonged to the Party.

Goebbels was shrewd enough to appreciate that every word he spoke had at the same time to be propaganda for the Party whose service he had entered. The struggle for the Ruhr was only peripheral, providing a welcome opportunity to divert a few waves from the heavy seas of national indignation into the new National Socialist movement.

He exploited this opportunity in masterly fashion. People listened to him readily, their feelings were stirred by the power of his speech. With words that gripped, Goebbels described the dangerous but heroic struggle of the underground against the oppressor, the intrepid deeds being carried out. Brave Germans were still to be found: hourly, daily, particularly by night, things were happening, mad, audacious deeds, fantastic beyond imagination. And the young man who described it all so thrillingly had himself been there, in the forefront, always right in the very midst of the struggle.

The developments which were to be decisive for Goebbels' whole life had now begun. What he achieved during these weeks, showed him the path he was destined to tread. He had proved himself as a speaker, had been successful as a propagandist, had learned that he could win men over. Nevertheless there were still setbacks in store for him. Overnight the Reich government which had ordered the resistance resigned, and the new government gave instructions that the futile struggle in the Ruhr should be discontinued. The rest of the year brought the newly successful propagandist no further triumphs. Since he could not bear to return yet again to the family home in Rheydt as the prodigal son, he endeavoured to scrape along miserably with friends in Dusseldorf and elsewhere, fearing sadly that the political road he had begun to tread was not going to lead anywhere.

Relinquishing his hopes of a political career for the time being at any rate, he turned to writing, mostly verses and plays for the theatre, even one play about Jesus Christ, plays which no publisher would accept and which were never performed. His chief effort was the autobiographical novel *Michael*, published some six years later.

On 10 November 1923 he read in the press of the Munich revolt, and of the abortive march by Adolf Hitler on the Feldherrnhalle (the Hall of the Field Marshals). This was a further blow. He had so little contact with the National Socialist German Workers' Party that he had been completely unaware of their plans to seize power by force, and once again he reproached himself for having allowed a great opportunity to pass him by. In failing to participate in the historic march on the Feldherrnhalle*, he had lost a unique chance of distinguishing himself, or at least of becoming a martyr: he felt bitter envy for people like Göring and Hess whose names were on everybody's lips just then.

Although the collapse of the local Munich revolt scarcely affected him, since he had not been one of those involved, he was greatly inspired a few months later by Hitler's defiant attitude before his Munich judges. Earlier, at the Zirkus Krone (Crown Circus), as he listened to Hitler, he had only seen his own chances. Now Hitler won him over not so much by his political ideology as by his personality. Goebbels recognized in Hitler after his 'victory' in the court room in Munich an absolute master of propaganda, a genius in the art of publicity. Goebbels saw a new, still greater opportunity for this man whom he had given up after the foolishly planned revolt. And at the same time he also saw a chance for himself, if he were to stress his loyalty to Hitler. So he wrote a letter to the Führer in the Landsberg fortress prison, which in its spirit of refined calculation and cloying admiration left nothing to be desired. Right down to the quotation from Goethe's *Tasso*, by which he drew attention to his profound knowledge of literature, it deserved to be widely published:

You rose up like a meteor before our astonished eyes and performed miracles in clearing our minds and giving us back our faith in a world of doubt and despair. You towered above the masses full of faith, confident of the future, with the will to freedom on their behalf and with infinite love for all those who believe in the new Reich.

For the first time we saw with shining eyes a man who tore off the mask from the faces distorted by greed, the faces of mediocre parliamentary busybodies, a man who taught us how devoid of shame, rotten and vicious is the system in which the leader is chosen according to Party and speech. In the Munich court you grew before us into the full stature of the Führer.

---

*Hitler's conspiratorial attempt, in conjunction with General Ludendorff, to take over the city of Munich, and thereby overthrow the existing government. But the Nazis, meeting armed police resistance, were forced to flee. (Translator's note).

What you said there were the greatest words spoken in Germany since Bismarck.

You gave utterance then to more than your own pain and struggle; you described the hardship of a whole generation searching in confused longing for leaders and a mission. You preached struggle in place of cowardly slackness, you called for fanaticism instead of pacifism, taught love of the people, freedom and Fatherland with a passionate consuming fervour. What you said there is the catechism of a new political belief born out of the despair of a collapsing Godless world. You did not keep silent. God put our very sufferings into your mouth, you expressed our agony in liberating words, spoke with confidence of the miracle to be. For all of that we thank you. For all of that will Germany one day thank you.

But the recipient of this letter in his cell in the Landsberg jail did not reply to the unknown writer of the lyric prose. Hitler was wholly and exclusively occupied in writing his book, *Mein Kampf* (*My Struggle*). He passed all his correspondence to his friend and fellow prisoner Rudolf Hess, who did not feel that the wildly enthusiastic and all too fulsome letter of Party member Goebbels called for an answer. Just in case he failed to get a reply the writer of the letter had taken appropriate precautions. In no circumstances would the long letter be written in vain. He kept a copy of it and two years later published it himself.

While Hitler and Hess were in the Landsberg Jail, Göring flew to Sweden, Ludendorff went into hiding and the N.S.D.A.P. disintegrated. The inspired Reichsbank president, Dr Hjalmar Schacht, miraculously succeeded in halting the fall of the mark and the country made a rapid recovery. In 1924 the National Socialists held only nine seats in the Reichstag elections. It seemed now to be only a splinter party of no significance.

Joseph Goebbels' hopes sank to zero. At the same time the other right-wing radical groups and cliques saw their chances increase, since competition from the National Socialists had been eliminated by their foolish revolt. Each of these groups sought to win over as many as possible of Hitler's followers, all those who had lost faith in their Führer and his languishing movement.

One of these right-wing organizations was the People's Freedom Party, from whom Goebbels accepted a post at a salary of 100 marks a month, in return for which he had to persuade faithful followers of the Nazis to become equally faithful Freedom Party members. He was no doubt conscious of the unworthy nature of the rôle, but poverty and hunger forced him to sell himself. Goebbels was not acting contrary to his beliefs when throughout 1924, in speeches and at meetings, he attacked the N.S.D.A.P., and even Hitler himself. He had no beliefs. But he was acting against his own better judgment. However much the Hitler movement had been flattened, Goebbels knew it would rise again as soon as Adolf Hitler was released. In view of the leniency of the Munich judgment and the act of grace operating in Hitler's favour, this could be quite soon.

One day Gregor Strasser, Hitler's trustee and a deputy Party leader at the time, happened to be in the hall listening with a mocking smile as Goebbels, founder of so many National Socialist cells in the Rhineland, thundered against the Nazis. Strasser made enquiries and learned that the speaker was paid 100 marks a month by the People's Freedom Party, who were therefore getting him very cheaply. Strasser decided to offer him more, but not much more. After the meeting he sought Goebbels out and suggested he should come and work with him.

How much more Strasser offered is uncertain. In any case, Goebbels turned about straightaway and from that day was once more a National Socialist. At Christmas 1924 Hitler was pardoned and released from custody; that moment, as Goebbels had expected, a new and fresher wind began to blow through the ranks of the Nazis.

Gregor Strasser and his brother Otto founded the Kampfverlag (Campaign Publishers) in Berlin at about this time. As Gregor Strasser was no longer quite satisfied with his former private secretary, a certain Heinrich Himmler, he offered the post to Goebbels, whom during recent months he had found hard-working and a good propagandist. He knew, too, that Goebbels was open to bribery, and therefore offered him a monthly salary of 200 marks, twice as much as he had been getting from the People's Party, so as to rule out any possibility of his going back to them.

Strasser had not made a bad bargain. Goebbels was worth his money. Whatever he did, he did with all his heart and soul. While the Party was low in funds, those who served it had to take on more than one job at the same time. Goebbels very soon became not only Strasser's private secretary but also the National Socialist agent for the North Rhineland region.

That gave him precisely the scope he needed. The demagogue could once again demonstrate what his passionate speech, obsessive energy and grandiose imagination were capable of. He was tireless and thrived under his new assignment. With the confidence of a sleepwalker he accommodated himself to the public at any given time. He knew instinctively what kind of people he faced. A gifted speaker, he would address three, four and five meetings a day, and through each he painstakingly gained new members.

Finally, at Strasser's behest, he published a campaign news-sheet, 'Letters from a National Socialist'. In these he supported an alliance with the Soviet Union, praised Lenin, attacked capitalism and property and prophesied, with an astonishing degree of farsightedness at that time (1924), that when Russia awoke she would show the whole world a national miracle. In 1925 he also prophesied 'Germany's sons will bleed to death on the battlefields of Europe as mercenaries in the service of capitalism, more than likely in a holy war against Moscow. Could anything be more abominable than that?' In Munich this sort of talk made people feel uncomfortable. In any case the name of Strasser's private secretary became known.

When that same year the German left-wing parties demanded a plebiscite on the question of compensation to the deposed royal and princely families for the expropriation of their extensive estates and fortunes, open hostility broke out between Strasser-Goebbels and Hitler himself. Goebbels argued passionately for the plebiscite in opposition to Hitler, who had monarchist connections. 'I don't believe wholeheartedly in Hitler any more,' wrote Party member No. 8762 in his diary on 22 November 1926. But he did not only turn against Hitler in his private diary entries. At a meeting of twenty-four regional party leaders he demanded a change in the Party structure and shouted in the hall, 'I demand that the petty bourgeois Adolf Hitler be expelled from the Nazi Party!'

Is it to be wondered at that Hitler never forgot this incident? Nevertheless, he must have valued Goebbels' abilities very highly indeed to have been able to suppress the memory of this betrayal. This explains much in Hitler's attitude towards his later Reich Minister. He never fully trusted Goebbels again until, at the very last, Goebbels of his own free will remained behind with Hitler in the bunker, to die with him.

It says much for Hitler's skill in handling men that at his first meeting with Goebbels, shortly afterwards in Bamberg, he gave the impression that he was ignorant of what the excitable Goebbels had recently demanded. He greeted him in his most engaging manner. Goebbels melted at once in the face of the Führer's affability and kindness. Hitler then offered him something that was at that moment more important to Goebbels even than money, the opportunity to do something effective: Hitler offered to let him speak in Munich, at one of the mass rallies of the newly risen Party in the Bürgerbräu.

For ten days in Munich Goebbels was Hitler's guest. The practically penniless Party speaker was the guest of the powerful leader of the N.S.D.A.P., who already appeared to dispose of considerable funds and drove a Mercedes. He was also a most generous host. Ten days sufficed for Goebbels to fall wholeheartedly under Hitler's spell. He felt that Hitler appreciated him and needed him; finally he acknowledged the powerful man as his friend.

On 17 April, shortly after he left Munich, Goebbels wrote in his diary, 'Adolf Hitler I love you because you are a great and at the same time a simple man.' On 20 October 1926 Hitler appointed him *Gauleiter* (regional leader) of the N.S.D.A.P. in Berlin.

The title suggests that the post was a prestigious and powerful one. In fact a more thankless and dangerous task could hardly have been imagined than that which Hitler assigned to his new friend and one-time adversary. Berlin was preponderantly social democratic. One hundred thousand highly organized communists constituted the very active left wing. In contrast there were barely 1,000 National Socialist Party members, scarcely one of whom paid their subscriptions. The Party headquarters were located in a filthy, poky little cellar. Instead of files there were only loose sheets and exercise books; there were no training evenings, only occasional drinking sessions.

That was the state of affairs when Dr Goebbels arrived one grey November evening in 1926 in Berlin. His salary as Gauleiter amounted to 150 marks a month, provided it was covered by the receipt of subscriptions from members.

Berlin that evening was quite indifferent to the little man who had come to conquer it. Nobody in the city could have known that the activities of this man would, barely nineteen years later, help to bring about its total destruction.

5

Magda's Marriage Falls Apart

A blaze of lights streamed from the windows of the Quandt house into the surrounding darkness; at Magda's insistence one of their very few winter dinner parties was being held. The mistress of the house had taken on a new air of beauty. Although only twenty-five she was already a woman of the world. It was a matter of general regret in Berlin social circles that young Frau Quandt was so seldom to be seen, but her husband, as always, kept their social life to the absolute minimum.

Magda herself had other, more important things to concern herself with. Caring for the growing children absorbed all her time and energy. Harold, her own son, was now six years old; Herbert was fifteen, and Hellmuth, his gifted, handsome elder brother, almost eighteen, and already a young man; the three Schulze children were all at difficult ages. The young mother had no light task in bringing them all up. Her shrewdness and sure instinct nevertheless enabled her successfully to reconcile the opposing elements in the highly individualistic children and even to establish a surprising degree of harmony between them.

Herbert Quandt's extreme short sightedness had obliged his father to take him away from the Arndt Grammar School in Berlin-Dahlem, where he had been placed as a boarder, and to have him tutored once again by specialists in memorizing techniques, so that he was eventually able to take his school-leaving examinations as an external student quite successfully. In fact his eye troubles were to improve to such an extent that he was later fully equal to exercizing his responsibilities as a leading entrepreneur. He, whose health had once been the cause of such anxiety to his father, is the only one of the three Quandt sons still living today.

For Herbert, Quandt acquired the 1,000-acre Severin estate near Parchim in Mecklenburg. After much consultation with ophthalmologists, he decided that a farmer's life would probably be the best for a young man with such poor eyesight, since what little reading and writing was required could well be done by a good manager. Quandt invested a lot of money in the estate. The manor house was extended and furnished with pieces of antique furniture from the parental family home. The swampy meadows were drained, the soil improved and Severin developed into a model estate with a yield previously thought unobtainable. Günther Quandt entrusted his former wife's brother-in-law, Walter Granzow with the management of the Severin estate on a fifteen-year irrevocable contract.

Magda and Günther now saw each other much less frequently. When they did meet it was as if they were separated by a wall of glass. When he left the house in the morning, his wife was still asleep. On his return at night Magda soon withdrew. There were abundant opportunities for evading each other. When he acquired the house in the Frankenallee, Quandt did not sell the one in New Babelsberg; they now used it at weekends, and Magda would often stay on for several days with the children, especially during the summer.

The Severin estate, which lay in the heart of extensive forest land, was three hours by road from Berlin. The manor house was not large, but was solidly built, seeming almost to be a natural part of the landscape. Magda never really enjoyed being at Severin. She had never lived in the country until her marriage, and had nothing in common with the landed families of the eastern Elbe on the neighbouring estates. She only went there occasionally for the sake of the children for whom, as at Babelsberg, there was ideal riding country, and facilities for sailing and walking. Neither Magda nor her husband had any liking for sport. The one distraction which Günther Quandt allowed himself was travel. Though his trips were primarily for business purposes, for Magda they provided a welcome interlude in her everyday life. They visited London and Paris a few times together, and while Quandt went alone on his first extended visit to America, since it was entirely on business, Magda did accompany him on his next, even longer visit there.*

Quandt later realized that it had been a bad mistake on his part, as far as his wife was concerned, that they did not go by themselves on the long trip, but in company with another married couple, friends of theirs. They boarded the *Berengaria* in the middle of October 1927, a vessel which Quandt knew very well, always maintaining that it had formerly been the German ocean giant *Imperator,* requisitioned after the war. During the outward voyage Magda suffered an attack of suppurative tonsilitis so severe that she had to be taken straight from the vessel to a nursing home, but she made a quick recovery and was able to continue the journey to Philadelphia, Boston, Buffalo and Niagara.

It goes without saying that wherever they went industrial undertakings, car factories and so on had to be visited, and the ladies were expected to play their part. Quandt himself wrote: 'After we took our ladies with us to two dry battery works and in Chicago were conducted through the big slaughter houses of the Armour Meat Canning empire, the two ladies refused to make any more business visits.' Not so the two men.

They devoted themselves for several more weeks from early morning till late at night visiting factories of all kinds, then returned once more to their wives, travelling on to Florida, Cuba, the Caribbean and Mexico together. In Mexico City both Quandts fell ill from a painful form of colic, so severe that the worst was feared, particularly as no doctor seemed to know of a remedy. But the colic went as rapidly as it had come.

Magda, who not long before had had a miscarriage, failed to regain her health for some time, and on their return from America she went to Bad Nauheim for heart treatment, where her husband, deeply concerned, visited her several times. From Nauheim she went to Graubünden, accompanied by her stepson Hellmuth, for a further course of treatment.

'In the spring, I suggested to Magda,' wrote Günther Quandt, 'that she should go with me to Egypt or Palestine for five or six weeks. This time it was to be a trip for the two of us alone. Unfortunately she declined for no reason at all. I had to go alone and

---

*Günther Quandt wrote an account covering no less than six volumes of his experiences in America and with the Americans. However, in accordance with his wishes, only two volumes of this massive work appeared in print. Both were lost by the end of the war through fire and bombing.

wrote a few lines or a long letter to her every two or three days. The first and only reply reached me at Naples on my return via Brindisi.' Quandt's profound unhappiness can clearly be felt. Shortly afterwards the following appears in his memoirs: 'I wanted to go with Magda to the Riviera, but received a second refusal. She even arranged for me to make the trip with the two daughters of one of our close friends and neighbours in Babelsberg.'

Quandt blames himself for their estrangement: 'Between Magda and myself there was continual friction, the causes, as so often in these cases, being trivial. But for the first time I felt that I had made some bad mistakes where Magda was concerned. I should not have gone without her to Egypt and then again to the Riviera. Our earlier good and sympathetic understanding with each other suffered greatly.' She was highly strung and insisted on returning to Nauheim. There too she went alone, but he again visited her, and brought her back, and the two of them made a tour of England in their own chauffeur-driven car. In London they called on Hellmuth, who was taking a course of studies there.

Magda had always been a cool person, at times almost cold. She had learnt to be severe with herself and lacked a certain quality of gentleness in her make-up. She no longer had any feelings for Quandt: he had mastered her, had dominated her too long; in her imagination he had become her enemy. Now that she could so easily have won him over, it didn't seem to matter any more.

It is arguable whether she was really as cold as she seemed. Could it not have been that the romantic, emotional side of her nature remained unfulfilled and that deep inside her lurked a profound sense of dissatisfaction?

Meanwhile, right in the heart of the family, a dangerous situation was building up. Hellmuth, her stepson, was now eighteen years old, on the very threshold of manhood. He was highly gifted, tall, slender, delicate, almost girlish in appearance. Learning came easily to him; he had amassed a surprising fund of knowledge and combined intelligent thoughtfulness with a deep sensitivity. As a child he had adored his lovely young stepmother, and now he worshipped her more than ever, with all the ardour of a teenage heart. He could see that she was unhappy. When the parents quarrelled, he sided with her against his father; he was anxious to protect her and if necessary was prepared to sacrifice himself for her.

Magda was shrewd enough to appreciate the dangers which such a romantic youthful devotion could give rise to, and tried to behave towards him with a mixture of reserve and tact. On the other hand she could not remain unmoved by such selfless devotion on the part of her handsome stepson.

As soon as his final school examinations were over, she prudently arranged for him to go to London to improve his languages. He went reluctantly, able to remain there at first only by exercising a stern degree of self-discipline. His letters home were full of despondent appeal. On his eventual return to Berlin, he was older and more mature, but by no means less sensitive. His father was well aware of his son's attitude to his stepmother, but like all fathers considered Hellmuth, in spite of his eighteen years, to be still a child, not to be taken seriously. They therefore decided to send him to Paris to further his language studies. Paris, the city of love and women, it was thought, would live up to its age-old reputation where love was concerned and help him to channel his feelings in a more suitable direction. Paris would make it easier for him to forget his lovely young stepmother.

So Hellmuth went to Paris, where he was to remain for a full twelve months, not returning to Berlin until it was time for him to go to the university. Stepmother and stepson would not see one another for a whole year. However, he had scarcely been in Paris more than a few weeks when he was taken seriously ill with appendicitis, and had to undergo an operation. Magda and Günther were sent for from Berlin and sat next day at his bedside, but in view of the patient's age it was not considered that he was in any particular danger. The operation was successful, or so it appeared. The surgeon assured his parents that all was well and no complications were likely. They returned to their hotel, their anxieties relieved, and were drinking a glass of champagne to Hellmuth's recovery when a phone call summoned them back to the clinic. Complications had set in, a crisis was anticipated, and the worst was feared. They hastened back, and towards midnight Hellmuth died in Magda's arms.

Both parents were hard hit by this blow. Many years later Günther Quandt expressed the view that Hellmuth's unexpected death was due to a wrong diagnosis on the part of the surgeon and that the nurse, an ill-trained White Russian refugee, had not followed his instructions properly. Other misunderstandings were involved; a chain of unhappy circumstances had led to the death of the unusually promising young man. Hellmuth was fully conscious until the end, and told his father how sorry he was not to have been able to help him professionally, above all not to have been able to succeed him.

In order to find distraction for Magda and himself, Quandt decided to take his wife with him on a long business trip to America. Once again the Americans regarded the truly feminine yet intelligent Magda with a mixture of astonishment and admiration. Mr Hoover, nephew of the American President and one of the richest men in America, whose wealth exceeded even that of Günther Quandt many times over, was very struck with her – though she acknowledged his attention with nothing more than a smile. She was to hear more of him later.

The Quandts remained in New York for three months, followed by a similar period in South America, before returning to Berlin. Magda had proved her worth during this long journey. In both Americas, in the South even more than in the North, social connections played a more significant part in business than was customary in Germany at that time. Agreements which failed to come off round the conference table were often more easily concluded at the tea table or on the garden terrace, when the parties met as ordinary human beings. Magda had the rare quality of being able to captivate those whom she wished to win over.

Her personal success received recognition after her return. Quandt allowed her more independence than ever before. For the first time she was able to assume full control of the household, something to which she had aspired for many years; she was able to invite to her social gatherings those of her own kind and choice, and to exclude those whom she disliked. She also gained more scope in the personal domain. Her husband no longer enquired each morning as to her plans for the day; he ceased to criticize her clothes and showed himself more generous where money was concerned.

Magda could at this time have found more satisfaction in her marriage. Harold, her own child, idolized her. Quandt's remaining son loved her dearly, and the Schulze children willingly submitted to her authority. 'Why is it,' Hellmuth used to ask her, 'why is it that we all have so much respect for you? You are so young yourself, you never grumble at us and yet we all do just as you say.'

Nevertheless what Magda had now achieved, what Quandt had finally conceded to her, had come too late. Tragically the gulf between them was too wide by this time to be bridged by concessions. After seven or eight years of living coolly alongside each other in a state of daily skirmishing, after countless disappointments, Magda now interpreted her husband's concessions as an admission of weakness.

She had often thought of leaving her husband. It was Hellmuth who, as long as he was alive, had with growing despair dissuaded Magda from this. Time and again he had convinced her that she would make all the children most unhappy if she left them. But things had changed. Carola Schulze had married, her brothers were grown up; Herbert was well looked after by his tutor, Dr Koehler, and could do without his stepmother; Hellmuth was dead.

So Magda asked her husband to give her her freedom. She wished to take Harold with her, and expected Quandt to make her an allowance only until such time as she had acquired the necessary qualifications for a career and was in a position to earn a living for her son and herself. Günther Quandt refused even to discuss the matter, and though Magda reverted constantly to the subject, she always met with the same negative response. On her own initiative she was not able to pursue the matter further since, as the law stood at that time, she had no justified legal grounds for divorce.

She was given the usual, if somewhat uncongenial, advice, to have her husband watched by a private detective. It was hinted that Günther was not indifferent to certain types of women, and it could therefore be assumed that if he were subjected to observation by an expert a marital offence could be established, proof of which would enable her to obtain a divorce irrespective of his consent. Magda emphatically refused to avail herself of such unworthy means.

She was now nearly twenty-seven years old, and more beautiful than ever. Her clothes came from a leading Berlin couturier, she was one of the best-dressed women in Germany. It was her fervent wish to be divorced. She had never really been in love, but quite suddenly this came about. A young man, whom we shall call Ernest, made her acquaintance at a ball at a friend's house. She caught his eye as she came into the salon at her husband's side. Magda noticed him too. The interchange of this first glance affected them both as if they had together partaken of some rare philtre. It happened exactly as in any sentimental novel of the nineties. He went up to her, bowed and asked for a dance, during which he whispered, 'You are not happy. I love you . . .'.

When she did not turn immediately and leave him standing there but continued to dance, he knew his gamble had paid off. They arranged to meet next day. It seemed he was a student in Berlin and came from a cultured, wealthy Rhenish family. His father, a well-known legal expert, was a man of the world. It was Ernest's youthful zest and gaiety, his old-fashioned romantic nature, which made him so attractive in Magda's eyes. He was handsome, tall, slender, with light brown hair and grey eyes. He had an extensive wardrobe and wore his clothes with a natural elegance. His attitude towards Magda from the start was made up of that particular combination so beloved of women – the courtesy and discretion of a true gentleman together with the spirit and fervour of a lover, convinced that he is wooing the most wonderful woman in the world.

Magda was enraptured by him. He was an excellent conversationalist such as she had not met for years. He could discuss the theatre, music or the latest books; he described his travels, admired her clothes and listened attentively to her views, all things which since her marriage she had sorely missed.

Magda did not allow her conscience to trouble her. She had gone into her marriage with Günther Quandt imbued with the highest ideals and with the honest intention of giving herself wholly to him. Whichever of them was to blame, Quandt had failed to capture her heart. Now somebody had come along who knew how to take and how to give. After the many barren years, life suddenly blossomed. Deep within herself Magda felt liberated, felt she could do as she pleased. After all, she was still a young woman; she had often begged her husband to release her so that she could lead her own life independently, but he had consistently refused. So now she easily found the excuse that force of circumstances alone held her marriage together.

Ernest was an ideal lover. He could always find time for Magda, could always manage to forego his studies, was at her disposal at any time of the day or night. He was full of new ideas, fundamentally good-humoured, the most agreeable of companions. No better partner could possibly be imagined.

When Ello Quandt told me about him some twenty-five years later, the then fifty-year-old lady seemed to change into a young girl of fifteen as, with flushed cheeks, she enthused about Ernest and confessed that she, Magda's best friend, had envied her for having found such a perfect lover. When in 1950 we sat together in Ello's house, Ernest was still living in Cologne, happily married with three children. As he was three years younger than Magda and Ello, it could well be that he still finds himself in the best of health – a strong reason for not giving his true name.

It was the most perfect love affair. Romance and flowers, passionate love and good comradeship between two cultured and spirited people, both too well-bred to be indiscreet in front of third parties, both, however, too proud to behave furtively. And it was precisely in this respect that they were most unwise. They travelled together, even stayed together in the best hotels. Magda considered herself justified in doing so, since she was in love and did not wish to stay with her lover as Mr and Mrs Müller in quiet little inns. She looked upon this experience as something which Fate owed her. She had never before been able to give expression to the romantic side of her nature, and now at last was able to do so. Why they should have spent two or three days together in the Hotel Dreesen at Godesberg on the Rhine is quite incomprehensible, nevertheless. It was contrary to all good sense.

Günther Quandt naturally noticed the change taking place so surprisingly in Magda. She looked radiant, and left the house much more often than ever before. Quandt, a cool-headed, discerning man, did not share Magda's reluctance to have her partner watched. He employed a private detective to tail her and soon knew where and with whom Magda was keeping appointments, knew also about their visit to Godesberg together.

He waited until she returned and demanded an explanation. Magda was far too proud to deny anything and admitted everything straightaway, but blamed Quandt for the way things had developed. She had asked him often enough for a separation. Quandt, his whole world collapsing around him, turned her out of the house immediately, hardly allowing her the time to pack a couple of bags, and instructed the staff never to allow her to enter the house again. So after nine years of marriage with Günther Quandt Magda left with nothing more than a few suitcases. She took a taxi and went to her mother, who had long since expected something of this kind to happen. She did not reproach her daughter, express regret or give her sympathy.

A few days passed before Magda fully realized the practical consequences of what had taken place. Whatever the actual reasons for the break-up of the marriage, as the law stood at that time she was the guilty party, and there was no doubt that she would be divorced as such, thereby losing the most precious thing in her life, her son, with no claim for alimony against her husband.

Up till now the wife of one of the wealthiest German industrialists, overnight she had become penniless. She did not possess the type of jewellery whereby she could live on the proceeds, nor expensive furs, nor did she have her own bank account. Gifted and skilled as she may have been, she suffered nevertheless from the drawback of so

Press photograph of Goebbels as the newly-appointed Reich Minister for Information and Propaganda

The former Prince Leopold Palace on the Wilhelmsplatz in Berlin, which housed the Ministry of Propaganda (*Promi*) during the Nazi regime

In the final battle for Berlin, even the *Promi* was practically destroyed

many society women, who knew enough about most things to be regarded as well educated, but were not sufficiently good at anything to earn their own living.

Ernest was prepared to marry Magda straightaway, but she refused so firmly that he did not repeat the offer. The 'eternal' student lived on the monthly remittances made by his father; he was younger than Magda, and she, moreover, was determined not to marry again. Ernest was the ideal partner for a romantic affair, but not for a life companion. However much she loved him, Magda was not blind to his limitations.

Magda was now in no enviable situation. She would not live with her mother, and while her father had at once expressed his willingness to support her, she did not wish to be dependent on him again. She had to train for a career, but it might take years. Yielding to pressure from Ello, and on the urgent advice of her father, Magda went to a lawyer, one of the most respected legal men in Berlin. The lawyer clapped his hands to his head when he heard how irresponsibly she had behaved, and so losing her son and her future security. Sober, practical legal man that he was, he could regrettably see no way out of the situation for her.

But Magda could. She suddenly remembered the letters which, nine years earlier, as a young married woman, she had come across in an old writing table of her husband's in Babelsberg. From a legal point of view they were completely worthless, since the 'aberrations' which one might wish to prove from them lay far in the past, in her husband's bachelor days. By prevailing standards they were in any case trifling; few people were likely to get indignant about things which had happened so very long ago.

But Magda was aware that the Quandt family, particularly her husband's parents, their whole existence firmly rooted in the small provincial towns of the Brandenburg Mark, were no modern folk. They would have been profoundly shocked, indeed horrified to learn that their son had had love affairs in his youth.

Not long since, Magda had refused to have her husband's comings and goings kept under observation, so it is difficult to understand what she was now prepared to do, but circumstances had changed, and the custody of her son and her own livelihood were at stake. Although she knew that Quandt had ordered the staff not to allow her to enter the house, she went along to the Frankenallee, rang the bell and told the housemaid who answered the door that she had forgotten something which she now wished to collect. She had always been friendly and considerate to her staff, and she now reaped the benefits. They allowed her in, as the master was away in the city until much later in the day. Magda sought and found the key of the Babelsberg house and drove out there without delay.

It was a stroke of luck that she was still able, after nine years, to find the bundle of letters again in less than five minutes. She seized the yellowed papers and went back to her lawyer the very next day. Things then moved swiftly in her favour. The lawyer asked Quandt to call, but the letters were only mentioned casually in passing. It was a matter instead of joint responsibility for the failure of the marriage; a true marital relationship had long ceased to exist, and Magda had actually asked her husband more than once for a separation. Until Quandt's refusal to agree to a divorce Magda had undeniably been a model wife. So now Quandt, having meanwhile recovered his calm and found time for reflection, was pleased to say that he was prepared to agree to the divorce. The letters remained in the lawyer's safe; it is not known whether they played a significant part in the negotiations or not.

In his memoirs Quandt maintained a gentlemanly discretion on the subject of his divorce from Magda. Amid glowing reports of the developments of his multiple enterprises, he regretted that on account of his numerous obligations he had not been able to be as attentive to Magda as he should have been and as she undoubtedly deserved. He, who had often bitterly reproached himself because of this concluded however: 'But do we not all at times assume the blame, when in fact we are not in the wrong?'

It was only much later in the memoirs, when he came to mention the National Socialist menace, that he cast a short glance back at his frustrated marriage:

In the summer of 1929, I separated from Magda Ritschel. . . . We divorced on friendly terms, agreeing that our son Harold should live with his mother until he was fourteen and thereafter, and in any case in the event of his mother remarrying, that he should return to his father's house. Since then we have enjoyed a friendly relationship with each other, and I was often entertained in their house in the Reichskanzlerplatz.

Not a word about Magda's adultery; in fact there was no question of a guilty party since Günther Quandt had acknowledged his contributory responsibility.

The dissolution went through quite smoothly, the otherwise so thrifty husband behaving extraordinarily generously. As mentioned, he granted her custody of Harold, subject to his returning to his father's house if Magda remarried. Magda agreed to this condition all the more readily in that she had firmly made up her mind never to marry again. For Harold and herself she received a monthly income of nearly 4,000 marks, as well as the sum of 50,000 marks with which to purchase a new house. In addition Quandt put 20,000 marks on deposit in case of illness. Taking into consideration the value of the currency at that time, the settlement would be worth some three or four times as much today. And apart from everything else, Harold could in due course expect to inherit half of all his father's wealth, then one of the biggest fortunes in Germany.

Once the contract was signed, Günther Quandt, a gentleman of the old school, sent Magda a huge bunch of flowers and invited her to a meal at Horcher's, Berlin's most exclusive restaurant. From that time on her relationship with her former husband was friendly. They met frequently and got along together much better than ever before now that the marriage fetters had been removed. Harold often saw his father, who proved to be a firm but understanding parent.

6

Gauleiter Goebbels

In the meantime Dr Joseph Goebbels set about conquering the city of Berlin, capital of the German Reich, keeping his plans to himself for the time being. He started off by strengthening and reorganizing the small National Socialist groups in various parts of the city and throwing out half of their members. Of those that remained there were scarcely 500 in the whole of Berlin, a city of four and a half million, on whom he could thoroughly rely. He knew it was not worth trying to build up the membership by just making speeches or inserting notices in the press. He also knew instinctively that his miserable little group would disintegrate if something decisive didn't happen soon. In order to attract attention to make themselves noticed, they needed adversaries, opponents who had to be tackled seriously. Berlin was a noisy, lively city; they would have to provoke rioting before people really became aware of their existence.

Gauleiter Goebbels organized his first meetings in the working-class districts of the north and east. They were poorly attended, but he irritated the communists and social democrats with such ingenuity that before long fighting broke out in the hall. Meeting hall battles proved to be the right idea. Blood had seldom ever before been spilt at political meetings, but Goebbels soon brought violence to such a pitch that at a single meeting in the Pharus Assembly Rooms over ninety were injured, a record sensational enough to be reported in the Berlin press. Overnight the National Socialists earned banner headlines on the front pages of the newspapers and, more important, Dr Goebbels' name came to mean something in Berlin. On the day following the Pharus 'battle' three thousand members signed on. It was obvious that Goebbels really did understand how to manipulate men.

Like every other successful tribune of the people, Goebbels owed his influence over the masses to his contempt for them. He had long realized that it is a waste of effort for an intelligent man striving after power and prestige to seek recognition in intellectual circles. The masses give spontaneous expression to their feelings; they are more easily led by hunger, envy, hatred and love than by clear reflection. Crowds react as a body; it is easier to discern the wishes of a thousand or ten thousand people than of three who each have their own opinion, so that nobody can tell how they will react.

To tell the crowd what it wants to hear, hammering their own desires into their hearts and heads – that was the secret of his success. Alone among his contemporaries, Goebbels was master of the refined art of being consciously primitive, so belying his keen intellect and penetrating mind. The great deception succeeded. Until the late 1920s, the vituperative Goebbels presented himself to his followers, and above all to his opponents, as an impulsive, vehement man, lacking all self-control, who allowed himself to be carried away, giving vent to the wildest fulminations and hysterical outbursts. In fact everything that he did, said, planned and organized was the outcome of a particularly clever form of hypocrisy. He quite deliberately made himself out to be more stupid and boorish than he really was, thereby achieving exactly the effect he wished. He won over untold thousands of followers, because he was astute enough to mask his wisest measures as dilettantist.

'It is quite amazing,' he said later to Ello Quandt, 'what people will believe. Sometimes I think the masses are even more primitive than I supposed anyway.' Another time he said to her,

The intelligentsia are as different from the masses as a connoisseur of wine from the tippler. The epicure enjoys precious drops of liquid amber and the enigmatic taste of the wine, while the man who polishes off the hard stuff raves about its kick and intoxicating effect. There is no need therefore to argue with the masses, slogans are much more effective. Believe me, slogans are like strong drink to the people. Actually they should not be called people, because the crowd doesn't react like men but like women, who rely on their feelings, rather than their intelligence – if any!'

He was no less astute in his dealings with his deputy leaders. The danger here at first was that the riff-raff would reject him as an intellectual, but the sly old fox easily overcame this difficulty by allowing them all to think that they were each mentally superior to him, if only to a minor degree, just enough for them not to be jealous of him.

Thus before long he had made himself generally admired by his henchmen, yet while keeping his distance he managed to remain one of them. They did not take his knowledge amiss and willingly tolerated his ascendancy, especially as he always made a point of his working-class origin. They not only forgave him his doctorate but were proud of the fact that one of their own number had, through hard work and ability, achieved academic status which at that time was still highly regarded, and yet had sacrificed himself on their behalf. For the time being, at least, Goebbels had to keep away from his own kind, the Berlin intelligentsia. While the leaders of the left-wing parties were to be seen moving in Berlin society, attending big receptions, charity balls and first nights, Goebbels kept outside that world altogether. After much thought he had decided that his adoption of working-class speech, his offensive début and his outbreaks of violence precluded him from mixing in prominent circles. This attitude was in fact one of the most important factors in his strategy. He had no inhibitions, no scruples whatsoever, about making use of any means which were conceivable or useful.

'Propaganda does not need to be clever, but it must be successful. If it is ingenious or sophisticated, it must not be recognizably so.' Occasionally he would add, 'Propaganda is a great, a difficult and a noble art, therefore it calls for genius. The greatest, and by that I mean the most successful, propagandists in history were Christ, Mahommet, Buddha and Zarathustra.' Only modesty, presumably, prevented him from naming the fifth!

He was equally skilful in defence or attack, vindicating himself at first, then swiftly becoming hostile. The left-wing press occasionally referred to him as a super-gangster, so he signed his articles for a long time 'J.G. Oberbandit' (super-gangster). At one point his opponents drew up a list of all the penalties and indictments he had incurred as a result of his activities, such as defamation, breach of the peace, incitement, and similar offences. He immediately made use of the imposing record for his election propaganda, having it printed in huge letters on placards exhibited in their thousands on advertisement hoardings throughout Berlin and bearing underneath the comment 'and would you want to choose *me*?'.

Goebbels was elected, and on 20 May 1928 took his seat in the Berlin Reichstag as member for the National Socialist German

Workers' Party. He now had the enormous advantage of official immunity, which meant he could say what he liked without fear of punishment. Unless a member of the Reichstag goes so far as to steal the silver, he is invulnerable. In gratitude for this democratic discrimination common to all parliaments, he signed his articles 'I.d.I.' (*Inhaber der Immunität* – Holder of Immunity) instead of 'M.d.R.' (*Mitglied des Reichstags* – Member of Parliament).

The achievement of the National Socialist Gauleiter over the eighteen months since his arrival in Berlin was phenomenal. The Berlin party membership had increased a hundredfold within eight months. In the Berlin elections of 20 May 1928 the National Socialists gained no less than 500,000 votes. This success was the outcome of long years of hard work, years which for Joseph Goebbels had been full of pain but empty of fulfilment.

Standing supreme, however, was not the dwarfish, limping agitator but another, Adolf Hitler, calling himself Leader. Party member No. 8762 had not been involved in founding the Party, had had nothing to do with the formulation of the political programme, and was not present at the march on the Feldherrnhalle (and even the most skilful propaganda could not wipe out these facts). He was not at the Landsberg Prison, nor did he belong to Hitler's circle of intimates. Not being a founder member of National Socialism, he was not consulted on matters of policy. For Hitler's 'old guard', maybe for Hitler himself, Goebbels was only the booster, the maker of the ballyhoo, smart enough to deliver the goods that others manufactured. Indeed, Goebbels did not even count as a model henchman, having been disloyal on several occasions. He was not acknowledged by the old Nazis as one of their own. They instinctively felt that he could never become a truly convinced National Socialist.

Goebbels' inordinate ambition, his uninhibited craving for social recognition and his astounding vanity became known in the course of time. The old guard, particularly those around Strasser, soon grasped that this intellectual had only joined their movement because of the opportunity it offered him to develop his talents and so make his way ahead. What Goebbels really thought about National Socialism his adversaries around Hitler instinctively surmised better than they knew or could prove. Goebbels himself later often spoke about it to his family, including Ello Quandt. 'There was no National Socialist philosophy, no National Socialist world policy, nor a clearly defined political programme,' he would explain. 'But the people thought there was partly because they didn't really think about it seriously enough, and partly because we always maintained that all these things did exist.'

Many of his speeches and writings prove that the Berlin Gauleiter and later Reich Minister for Propaganda was never a true National Socialist. Not only did he, before his arrival in Berlin, stand firmly for an alliance with Soviet Russia and often speak favourably of Bolshevik Russia, but he did not by any means share the National Socialist racial theories, at least not during the so-called campaign years.

In 1926 he could still write: 'A good racial mixture quickens the circulation of the secretions.' Later, after he had long been Reich Minister and had vainly endeavoured to break the monotonous presentation of the State-controlled press, he exclaimed to his colleagues, 'What I need now is a dozen clever Jewish journalists.' Goebbels never glorified the blonde Nordic type as the ideal German. He whom his fellow Party members pejoratively nick-named 'Schrumpf-Germane' (wizened old German) was the one man who could not be expected to do so. It was precisely because he himself was the exact opposite of the National Socialist prototype that he attacked the Jews so fiercely – as propagandist for anti-semitism, as organizer of the Jewish boycott, as the person responsible for the suppression of Jewish literature, as ringleader of the German 'Crystal night'.*

Goebbels was one of those responsible for the gruesome final solution, for the unheard of atrocities later committed against millions of Jews. His guilt is all the greater in that he did not himself accept the doctrines of anti-semitism. Even during the war he would read to his family and friends from Naumann's book *In Borrowed Plumes* (*Mit fremden Federn*), which he knew almost by heart. He openly admitted that he owed much to the encouragement and stimulation of Jewish literature and science. Nevertheless, a few years later he allowed his own writings in praise of Jewish authors to be burnt in public. No doubt the intellectual versatility and satirical pungency of many Jewish authors was more akin to his mentality than the 'blood and soil' writings which his ministry had to promote in line with Nazi concepts. Among his friends he spoke of Rosenberg's *The Myth of the Twentieth Century* as being philosophic

---

*Ninth of November 1938, when all Jewish Synagogues were burnt and Jewish shops smashed up.

rubbish, as pertinent as it was contemptible.

Though Goebbels was by no means convinced of the necessity for persecuting the Jews, he put the full weight of his mighty propaganda machine behind it. Obedience to the Führer demanded this, but it was also in his own interests to allay the mistrust of his opponents in the Party, and if possible to dispel it altogether.

Even his enemies in his own ranks, of which he had more than enough, had to acknowledge the value of his achievements. He seemed to be consumed by a burning energy. His capacity for work was insatiable, his need for sleep negligible. His powers of persuasion were impressive; he was far more successful than any other Gauleiter. His membership numbers went soaring up. What especially recommended him was his complete lack of moral scruples. 'Conscience,' he said years later, 'is nothing more than a crutch for cowards', thinking no doubt of Hamlet. And when occasionally Hitler hesitated to make a particular decision: 'My Führer,' he prompted, 'you can perfectly well do that; nobody will know that you did it.'

The longer and the more prominently he was active in the Party, the more he held back his own personal views and convictions. He deliberately rejected any disturbing intrusion of his own judgment, ruthlessly promoting the line which Hitler laid down. His success as a propagandist was therefore all the more overwhelming in that he himself did not believe all that his eloquence and ingenuity hammered into the masses. As a reward for his outstanding services the Führer appointed him on 1 January 1929 '*Reichspropagandaleiter*' (Reich Propaganda Leader). His first act in this new post was to unleash a quite unnecessary, but from a propaganda point of view extraordinarily successful, agitation against the Young Plan.*

Goebbels' initiative against the ostensible enslavement of the German people for decades roused the mass of the people, unleashed controversy and brought the communists as well as the National

---

*According to this plan, named after Dr Owen Young (1874–1962), the American financial authority, (1) the amounts (not yet fixed) to be paid by the German Reich as reparations to the victor were limited, and (2) the system of payment was laid down. During the Paris Conference of 1929 a total sum of 21 milliard marks (the value of the mark at that time) was agreed, payable by 2 milliard instalments until 1988. Although two years later this proved to be quite impossible, nevertheless the Young Plan was a substantial improvement over the previous plan, which involved unlimited claims by the Allies.

In view of the heavy burdens on the German public at that time the government ordered a referendum, which the N.S.D.A.P., among others, opposed. However, the Plan was accepted, but by 1931 its execution had practically been brought to an end by the so-called Hoover moratorium.

Socialists new supporters. Although the agitation miscarried and the Young Plan was adopted, the Nazis obtained twenty per cent of all the seats in the Berlin local government elections of November 1929. The worthy middle class were so nervous of the 'Reds' that many overcame their distrust of the clamant, brutal, intemperate Goebbels and voted for the lists of candidates of the N.S.D.A.P.

The miserable little cripple from Rheydt no longer starved. Compared with former days, things were excellent. He was now living in Steglitz in a small but tasteful house. Though he himself still lived modestly, he had no more worries about paying the rent each month.

Where propaganda was concerned, he made the most of everything he could lay his hands on, but he gave no thought at all to his own appearance. It never occurred to him that a good tailor could make his unfortunate figure look better. He was equally indifferent to what he ate – in fact he often forgot to eat at all. Goebbels' opponents found him repulsive, but to his supporters it didn't matter what he looked like. They liked the skinny little man because of the fervour which he exuded; he seemed to be obsessed with the ideology for which he sacrificed himself.

The fact was that during those years Goebbels was truly inspired not so much by Hitler's grandiose conceptions as by what he was able to make out of them, by his own propaganda, by the very art of propaganda. He pursued it one might almost say, as an end in itself, and was amazed at its overwhelming power.

7

Suitors for Magda's Hand

When her friends and acquaintances discussed politics, which was not often, Magda hardly listened. To her it was the most boring of topics; she had too much else to think about, particularly with regard to reorganizing her own life.

At last she was free. She now had more money at her disposal for herself than ever before: nearly 4,000 marks a month, which allowed her to lead the sort of life she had never envisaged even in her wildest dreams. She made up her mind to enjoy herself and to make the most of her opportunities.

At first she leased a seven-room luxury flat at Reichskanzlerplatz 2 in New West Berlin, an elegant modern district. Furnishing and equipping it was an exhilarating experience and she took her time over it, spending weeks on end visiting and consulting with antique dealers and interior decorators. History of art had long been one of her favourite interests and was now her mainstay in making her choice. When the place was finally complete even the most critical and artistically knowledgeable of her visitors had to admit that there scarcely existed a more tasteful yet comfortable residence in all Berlin. Magda understood how to combine beauty and utility in one harmonious whole.

Apart from a reception room, music room and dining room, there was a bedroom for herself, one for her son Harold and one for guests. The household was run by a first-class elderly cook and a housemaid.

Magda did not own a car as she did not drive and would have needed a chauffeur. She worked out the relative cost and decided that taxis would be cheaper.

Her former robust health, which had suffered in recent years through the breakdown of her marriage, had now returned. Her nerves recovered, and the occasional heart spasms which she had attributed to nervous tension were things of the past. She had never been able to work off emotional upsets, disappointments or fits of depression by giving vent to her feelings, nor had she even wished to do so. She came to terms with everything on her own, deep down inside herself. But that was all over and done with. She went forward radiant, like a new woman, into her new life.

Moreover, she still loved Ernest. The young man had, during the divorce interval, proved himself to be a perfect gentleman. As previously mentioned he had been prepared to marry Magda straightaway, but on mature reflection there were two disadvantages, the chief one being financial. Magda's income would only be paid by Quandt as long as she remained single. She would also have to relinquish the custody of Harold if she married again. So whoever thought to marry Magda would take to himself a wife without means of her own. Ernest did not earn a penny; he was still a student, and a not very keen one at that.

In his impetuous infatuation Ernest was quite prepared to give up his studies and seek employment. But Magda realized fully that two people of their tastes and style of living could never be happy in reduced circumstances. Moreover, although she certainly loved Ernest, she could not envisage him as a husband. He was not a man of the same sort of calibre as her two fathers and Günther Quandt. In reaching this decision she revealed the basic dichotomy of her nature: the romantic side, the sensual longing for warmth and tenderness, Ernest could well satisfy, but the other side, her strong intellectual leanings and her need for sure, clear leadership, were beyond him.

So the situation remained as it was before the divorce. She travelled with him to Paris, watering places, Godesberg, the sea, accompanied him to balls and carnivals, went almost daily to the theatre, concerts and museums. Both enjoyed the immense variety of entertainment which cosmopolitan Berlin had to offer in the late 1920s.

Strangely enough she hardly availed herself at all of the social opportunities open to her as the former wife of Günther Quandt; she deliberately avoided contact with those who were still in touch with her former husband. Few close friends remained to her from former years, her one true confidante being, and ever remaining, Ello Quandt. Magda had no inclination to form new friendships. She regarded social life at the top, with its intricate rules of etiquette and good manners, as a curb on her freedom, reacting almost compulsively against the slightest suggestion of restrictions of any kind.

One day, quite out of the blue, she received a visit from Mr Hoover, nephew of the former President of the United States, whom she had come to know during her trip to America with Günther Quandt. Hearing of the divorce, he had come over to Berlin to ask her to marry him. He was good-looking, very much in love with her and immensely wealthy, his assets dwarfing by comparison even Günther Quandt's considerable resources, and was able to offer Magda all that she could ever wish for. Nevertheless she valued her new-found freedom even more, and told him, one day on the terrace of the Wannsee Golf Club, that she could not marry him, that in fact she would never marry again.

When he realized that her reply was really final, he sat silent and crestfallen, staring blankly out over the hilly landscape of the golf course. Magda rose to leave. He followed her to his car and drove at break-neck speed along the motorway in the direction of Berlin. Magda deliberately refrained from telling him to be careful. Just before turning off the motorway at the entrance to the main road, the car overturned. Hoover himself was uninjured, but Magda suffered a double fracture of the skull and other injuries and lay, surrounded by flowers, for several weeks in the West End hospital. The culprit was never seen again, but Günther Quandt did all he could to ensure her recovery.

It is not known whether she ever regretted her decision. She herself would never admit to wishing she had chosen otherwise – though Ello Quandt, on a number of occasions later in her life, pointed out to Magda how much more carefree an existence she could have enjoyed as Mrs Hoover than she ever had with Joseph Goebbels.

The long months in bed after the accident gave Magda plentiful time for reflection, and brought about a major change in her outlook. She now no longer wished to go back to her old way of living, devoted purely to pleasure. She realized that the life she had been living was superficial and meaningless, that something vital had been lacking, a sense of personal responsibility, above all a true purpose.

The beloved Ernest was as charming as always, concerned and devoted. But he was just a playmate, not a lifelong companion. And she no longer wanted to play, but to live. When he was on holiday with his parents she yielded to his wish and went to visit him there. His parents received her with much warmth, making it clear that they by no means disapproved of the friendship, and rather seeming to hope that the two would one day marry. Magda soon decided to return home, and Ernest accompanied her to the station. It had been arranged that he should remain with his parents until the end of his vacation, but as the train began to move he jumped on the footboard on the spur of the moment, without baggage, coat or hat, and travelled with her back to Berlin. Magda was moved and delighted. It was just this sort of thing which made him lovable in her eyes, although at the same time his impulsive, unreliable behaviour deterred her from marrying him. Being the elder of the two, she was conscious of her responsibility towards Ernest and insisted on his resuming his long-neglected studies. She reproached him when he absented himself from lectures, refused to receive him or go out with him if his written work was not submitted at the proper time. Finally the young man grasped the fact that he had to do some work; he dug into his studies, later emerging with astonishingly good results in his examinations.

His serious approach to his work, and in particular preparation for the examinations, meant that Magda was left more on her own than previously. She decided to undertake some training so that, in case of need, she would be able to earn her own living. She thought for a time of studying the history of art and qualifying to become curator of a museum. The law also attracted her. She had other ideas, too – of working with children, or of becoming an interior decorator, both occupations which appealed to her. She had the energy and the patience to carry out such plans, and the means for Harold's and her own subsistence meanwhile. As she was discussing these possibilities with friends, chance intervened, making overnight the choice of any career unnecessary.

It is not known who was 'guilty' of telling her that she should go occasionally to the Sportpalast, to one of the Brown Shirts' rowdy meetings. Such working-class pastimes as listening to election speeches and attending political gatherings had no attraction for Magda, who never went to boxing matches, six-day cycle races or women's wrestling. However, one day, when Ernest was at a seminar she caught sight of a garish placard advertising a massive Nazi meeting in the Sportpalast and went in, probably out of sheer boredom.

The blaring introductory march music tortured her ears, and the huge red swastika banners massed overhead somehow made her feel uneasy. She knew instinctively that red was the colour of the proletariat with whom, in view of her income of 50,000 marks a year, she could hardly be expected to find common ground. Nevertheless, the speaker of the evening drew her fascinated attention. For the first time she now saw Dr Goebbels as, short and puny, he limped down the long gangway through the ranks of the brown-shirted S.A. men, beneath hundreds of outstretched arms and a forest of banners. As he mounted the platform his physical handicap was clearly evident. Magda immediately perceived that he was also miserably clad, his hair badly cut, his shirt collar much too wide.

As he spoke, however, his eyes glowed with a remarkable fiery light, and sparks seemed to fly from the tips of his feverishly agitated hands. His dark, at times metallic-sounding voice, reinforced by loudspeakers, seemed amazingly powerful, as he thundered to the crowd of more than 5,000 listening to him below. His manner of speaking, raising and lowering his voice with a nerve-racking monotony, was as unusual as what he was actually saying. Finely calculated pauses were interspersed with the rolling phrases, each meticulously aimed to hit his unseen adversary at his most vulnerable spot. The longer he spoke the more biting grew his irony, the more scathing his sarcasm, until finally he wound up in a hurricane of curses and threats against the enemies of the N.S.D.A.P. and, in an astonishing anti-climax, with a hymn to the Führer.

Magda followed the speech with amazement, with mounting interest, and finally, unbelievable as it seemed to her later, with enthusiasm. She was fascinated by what she had heard, fascinated and enthralled. This speaker convinced her as no man had ever managed to convince her before. He succeeded, as so often with his women listeners, in working on her feelings alone, her intellect suspended. The speaker had almost put her into a state of trance.

Some days later Magda became a member of the N.S.D.A.P. Barely twenty-four hours previously she would have laughed in the face of anybody who had suggested that she should interest herself in politics, and would have been indignant had anybody hinted at involvement on her part with a lot of trouble-makers like the Nazis. Nevertheless she became a member of that very party, joining the National Socialist district group, Berlin-West End, which annoyed her friends as much as it delighted the Nazis.

The local N.S.D.A.P. group in this high-class residential area was limited in numbers, consisting principally of a few shop assistants and several caretakers of flats. With Magda Quandt they acquired for the first time the name of a woman of means on their list of members.

The Party warden hastened to call on her and welcome her, nervously but heartily, as a member of the Party. He may possibly have thought the whole thing was a misunderstanding and that she might wish to withdraw. But no such thing. Magda intended to remain a member. The warden thereupon, true to his Party's opportunistic ethos, offered her a minor appointment, as leader of the National Socialist Women's Organization of the local West End group. Without in the least knowing what duties were involved Magda accepted.

Of course the principal question of her choice of career was by no means solved, but she had been given a little responsibility and a few duties, and this to some extent held at bay the emptiness of her present existence. The work in the Women's Organization was not enough for her, however, and she soon found herself wanting to be more seriously involved in the movement to which she was now attached.

At a bookseller's on the Reichskanzlerplatz she purchased a copy of Hitler's *Mein Kampf* (*My Struggle*), and read the thickly bound volume from beginning to end. At the same time she bought Rosenberg's *Myth of the Twentieth Century*. She also obtained an N.S. news-sheet, studied training instructions and followed Hitler's speeches in the press. She even concerned herself with the Party programme given her by the warden.

Magda soon found the activity in the Women's Organization bitterly disappointing. Like most educated people, she was more in sympathy with simple, almost primitive types than with the partially educated, but it was the latter with whom she had to deal. There were few real workers in the West End district, so the local group consisted largely of the petite bourgeoisie, who from porters' lodges and small houses at the rear looked resentfully out on to the large front houses.

When Magda took over the leadership of the West End Women's Organization a wave of astonishment, envy and mistrust surged up against her. The women in it greeted the sudden if genuine idealism of the new leader of the local Women's Organization with scepticism. To them Magda Ritschel, formerly Quandt, was a mysterious person, a scented lady who was busying herself with politics out of boredom. When Magda gave a talk they sat dumbly on their seats eyeing her maliciously, calculating what she had paid for her suit and speculating whether the young man about whom they gossiped would be visiting her afterwards.

As far as the young man was concerned, Ernest was one of those who could not take politics anything but seriously. And he could not follow Magda on her new path. As a son of upper-class parents and as a realistic observer of contemporary events, he rejected the Nazis utterly. He considered them to be complete charlatans and did not believe a word they said, especially Goebbels.

Magda made no serious attempt to convince him but did not allow Ernest to stop her from doggedly following her new path; her relationship with him suffered its first deep rift in consequence. Quandt, who occasionally had a meal with his former wife, showed little enthusiasm either. He maintained that the Nazis had no understanding whatever of economic matters and prophesied that if they ever came to power it would be catastrophic for Germany. Even Magda herself did not think they would. It was sufficient for her to have found something to do which fulfilled her to some extent.

She soon penetrated too deeply into the National Socialist world to be able to bear her disappointment with the local group any longer. Drawing the logical conclusion she resigned from her post as leader of the Women's Organization West End, but she remained determined to continue her involvement with the Party and to seek some form of activity more suited to her capacities. Since she was, or had been, Frau Quandt, it seemed inappropriate to her that she should be satisfied with any hole-in-the-corner job, and she finally decided to go direct to the National Socialist *Gauleitung* headquarters in the Hedemannstrasse to offer them her services.

She was received with deferential politeness. Her name, address, knowledge of languages and special capabilities were noted, and she was asked to call again in three days' time, when she was given the post of secretary to the deputy Gauleiter. She attended the *Gauleitung* headquarters daily thereafter, finding the work a good deal more satisfying than that with the Women's Organization.

Shortly afterwards, as she was descending the stairs there, a short, dark man in a trench coat was coming up. It was Dr Goebbels who, although seemingly in a hurry, stopped and regarded for two whole seconds the lovely young woman passing him on her way down. Magda recognized him, and was aware of his interest, but carried straight on down and left the building without returning his look. The Gauleiter proceeded immediately to the secretary at the reception desk and enquired who the lady was and what she wanted. He was told that she was the divorced wife of the well-known industrialist Quandt, and that she had recently come to work on a voluntary basis as secretary to the deputy Gauleiter. Somewhat nervously the Gauleiter instructed that she should be asked to go and see him next morning.

Magda sat, deeply interested, opposite the man whose stirring words had won her over to the Party some three months earlier. Without exaggerating in the least she was able to assure him that it was entirely due to his speech that day in the Sportpalast that she had been prompted to join.

Goebbels was shrewd enough not to betray to the society lady how flattered he felt by such praise. He behaved objectively, almost sternly, enquired briefly as to her education and knowledge of languages, and appeared to reflect as to which post would be most suitable for her. He was of course doing no such thing. The Berlin Gauleiter of the N.S.D.A.P. had no need to reflect, having already made up his mind the previous day, directly after the meeting on the staircase. But for the sake of form he made a number of suggestions, only to dismiss them straightaway. Finally he enquired whether she would like to manage his private archives for him.

Magda naturally had not the faintest idea what private archives were like, but agreed without hesitation Goebbels thanked her briefly and promised to have a word with his deputy. She might then start her work in the private archives section at the beginning of the coming month. During the whole interview not one personal word passed between them. The great propagandist knew how surprising, how completely novel, it must be for a spoilt upper-class woman to be treated by a man in such an impersonal and objective way.

Magda described her new post in the Hedemannstrasse to Ernest, but received no encouragement, he realized that Magda's new interest would before long deprive him of her company. He now committed the understandable blunder of laughing at her. Not content with that, he made fun of the National Socialists in general and Goebbels, the so-called mudslinger, in particular. He then light-heartedly mocked Hitler's speech-making, his gestures and into-nation. Magda refused to stand for it and from then on their friendship suffered.

The private archives of the Berlin Gauleiter was a highly important set-up maintained under the strictest secrecy. It consisted primarily of a collection of overseas press cuttings and radio broadcast items about National Socialism generally and Dr Goebbels in particular. Magda soon came to understand the high degree of trust which the Gauleiter was conferring upon her in entrusting the control of his private archives to her. On becoming familiar with the work she was surprised to discover how well-informed the Hitler movement was about everything spoken and written about the Nazis all over the world.

She soon realized that it was not actually the N.S.D.A.P. which was so well-informed but Dr Joseph Goebbels himself. On the very first day her chief explained to her that she must never speak to anybody about her work, about the records or even their existence.

'But why do you keep it all,' she enquired, 'if you don't place such vital material at the disposal of the party as a whole? Of what use is the collection then?'

'You have a lot to learn, dear lady,' laughed Goebbels. 'In politics you can't perform miracles. Knowledge is power, but only for such people who, after weighing it up carefully, have their knowledge available when the right opportunity turns up, or if it doesn't, even then do not waste it.'

In fact the archives provided Dr Goebbels with decisive leverage. Throughout his early struggles and later as head of the Ministry for Propaganda, they enabled him to remain au fait with everything, even the murky patches in the lives and early histories of the other National Socialist leaders. He had on file criticisms from the London *Times* of the contents of his latest speech, what Mussolini did not like about the N.S.D.A.P., the appreciative words of the leading Japanese paper *Asahi Shimbun* about the Labour Services, and so on. The Reich Propaganda Leader knew which French papers complained about the excesses committed by the Hitler Youth; equally he had kept the comment in an Austrian paper to the effect that in his last speech he had spoken only of the dead Nazis of the Feldherrnhalle and not of the two million fallen of the Great War.

He was much too shrewd to quote foreign press commentaries in his own daily papers, to damn or to praise, to justify himself or to inculpate others. He kept to himself the fact that he had all these press extracts ready to hand. Then suddenly he would arrange, for example, for a group of Hitler Youth to cross the frontier somewhere in Alsace and help some poor French peasants to lift the harvest, or he would surprisingly give a speech in honour of the two million dead. Later, as Minister, Goebbels developed this practice further. He always regulated his official appearances, his demands, often too his behaviour, according to the secret information available from his private archives. He was able to defeat most offensives almost before they had begun, provided he recognized in time where they originated from.

So Magda was suddenly installed in this secret control centre from whence a political gambler steered events. She learned to her astonishment what a complicated mechanism behind the scenes moved the crowds, what precision work controlled the brown marching columns and enabled the outbreaks of fighting at the meeting halls to be won. Goebbels gladly explained to her why these tactics were unfortunately necessary. Such methods were forced upon the usually honest and straightforward Nazis by perfidious opponents; the brutal communists especially could only be confronted in this way.

Her chief, however two-faced and unscrupulous he may have been, nevertheless displayed great personal courage. He was never afraid of the fighting in the meeting halls. Smiling, his arms folded, he would remain standing on the platform while quart beer mugs and chair legs flew past him. Magda could not do other than admire him, he was so fundamentally different from all the other men she had ever met.

But when at dinner she described her interesting new chief to Ernest, he found nothing admirable in him whatever. He considered that Magda had fallen in with a comedian or charlatan. In any case he thought Goebbels no more than a political ranter of purely passing significance.

The bitterly hated 'evil-minded creature' and much admired Propaganda Leader was in the habit of demanding from his fellow workers whole-hearted commitment to their work. He was no less demanding of the guardian of his private archives, compelling Magda to work long hours and often far into the night. But neither did he spare himself.

There was nothing in this man, so most people thought, to attract a woman. On the short, thin, misshapen body rested the over-large head with its pointed nose and deep lines around the thin-lipped mouth. His suit betrayed his morbidly thin arms and indicated how his ribs stuck out from the thorax. Although Goebbels didn't go hungry any more and no longer lodged in a small back room, he still dressed lamentably. And yet he had considerable resources at his disposal from his various appointments as Gauleiter of Berlin, Reich Propaganda Leader, member of the Reichstag and chief editor of the

Angriff. He certainly had a very large income compared with his previous scanty earnings, and apart from all that his contributions to the press and his books brought him in a steady return. He obviously did not place the slightest value on improving his appearance.

Most pampered women would have found his appearance distasteful. Not so Magda. Even before she herself first became aware of it, she had developed an overwhelming feeling of solicitude towards him. Her ill-dressed chief seemed to her basically a man to be pitied, a man whom nobody, in any case no woman, cared about, in spite of his sore need. She said so to her friend Ello, who listened disapprovingly, but she paid no heed to Ello's well-meant warnings. At the same time as Magda became aware of her motherly feelings towards Dr Goebbels he, on his part, began to flirt with her, perceiving the honest admiration, almost respect, which she felt for him.

Goebbels soon grasped the fact that Magda had joined the Party out of a sense of inner dissatisfaction, and realized that she sought to find the fulfilment denied her in her marriage with the materialistic Quandt. He probably surmised that all she was looking for in the party was a fairly interesting, possibly merely temporary job. It was evident to him that it was only by chance that she had joined them. Had she instead met a gifted priest, she could equally well have thrown herself into the arms of the Church. She had been seeking inspiration of some kind. He knew therefore that if, as a man, he wished to win her, he must captivate her intellectually. All else would follow.

He began to invite her to accompany him to debating groups where, among cultured people, he spoke in a completely different manner from that which he used to the crowds. He appeared with her in the houses of some of his intellectual friends, whose arguments he tolerated because he knew how to dispose of them. He involved her in philosophical discussions with himself, which went on late into the night, and invited her to small social gatherings in his flat, where she could see him not as a polemicizing public speaker but as a genial host, astonishingly well-mannered.

There are pictures of Goebbels in existence which show him as a private man without the brown uniform, relaxed, with a charming smile, and conversing naturally. His intelligent conversation and ability to laugh at himself deceived many people, particularly women.

Times had indeed changed. The one-time starving Heidelberg

student had emerged a successful man who moved in formerly exclusive Berlin social circles. He could be found sitting at the fireside next to the Hohenzollern Prince August William, son of the last Kaiser, politely kissing the hand of Her Excellency Frau von Dirksen, or greeting some foreign ambassador, bank director or politician from overseas. The nephew of a reigning monarch, Prince Christian von Schaumburg-Lippe, was shortly to be his personal adjutant and accompany him everywhere. He was now a figure of considerable interest to attentive observers of German domestic developments. Overseas correspondents contacted him, highly distinguished agents pumped him and were cunningly lied to. Economic experts who tried to get him to clarify the real objectives of the N.S.D.A.P. got just enough from Gauleiter Goebbels to send them away satisfied.

Magda enjoyed herself immensely in this world, in which she felt essentially at home. Her well-groomed appearance and her cultured air found recognition in those around her. The focus was, however, Goebbels, that peculiar man towards whom she, without admitting it to herself, felt daily more drawn.

Magda saw that his small flat was tasteful, both rooms being well furnished with antiques, with beautiful rugs on the floor. The few pictures showed judgment and discernment. She realized that he was quite a different man from the one who addressed the crowds. In his own home there was nothing coarse, common or vulgar.

Magda's friends of the nine years of her marriage with Günther Quandt strongly disapproved of her connections with the Nazi Party, and above all with Dr Goebbels. As a Quandt, even though divorced, she was still expected to have some regard for the family, and they were ashamed on her behalf.

Günther Quandt maintained friendly relations with Magda, as far as was at all possible, avoiding all mention of anything of political consequence, in spite of the fact that she reverted constantly to the subject.

Some time in Spring 1930, (he wrote in his memoirs),

Magda told me that she had been to a National Socialist meeting and been so inspired by Hitler's message that she simply had to join the movement. It was the only alternative to communism, towards which Germany in her serious economic situation was surely heading. After the meeting the propaganda speaker from Berlin, Dr Goebbels, came up to her. She asked him where and how she could join the party, whereupon he gave her an appointment for the next morning at the Hedemannstrasse headquarters, where in his publicity office she now assembles and files all the press cuttings which appear about him in Germany.★

Quandt could hardly have been pleased by what Magda told him. Though obviously she was free to think and do as she liked, she should have known him well enough to have avoided such a controversial subject. Unfortunately she did just the opposite.

'On my next visit, it struck me,' wrote Günther Quandt, 'that Magda had become an even more enthusiastic propagandist for the new cause and that she was wholeheartedly in favour of it. At first I thought it was just a craze for the oratorical gift of Dr Goebbels. As, however, each time we met the conversation turned ever more frequently to the same subject and no argument could win her away from it, I began to cut my visits down.'

At Christmas 1930, when her former husband lay sick in Florence, she went out to Italy to see him, taking Harold with her. They both then accompanied Günther Quandt to St Moritz for his convalescence, 'But here too,' continued Quandt in his memoirs, 'Magda still kept up her proselytizing, and when later I was prompted to send her an invitation now and then I refrained, as I did not wish to be upset.'

Magda was so strongly impressed by Goebbels that she also overlooked the mounting jealousy of her friend Ernest. When he flared up one evening and declared that she was in danger of losing her head to the club-footed chatterbox, she said sharply, 'You're mad . . . I could never love Goebbels!' She probably thought at that moment that she was speaking the truth. However, in the weeks that followed, she could hardly spare a moment for Ernest. Daily she sat until late at night at the desk facing Goebbels; week after week they worked ever more closely together. Soon he took no important decision without reference to her. She found herself, contrary to what she had said to Ernest, daily, hourly, feeling more sympathetic towards him.

She made up her mind to bring her friendship with Ernest to an end without delay. She told him that she had decided to marry Goebbels and thanked him for his friendship, loyalty and warmth, promising in the usual way to remember him always. He was dumbfounded at this disclosure, quite unable to understand how anybody could so coldly end a long-standing relationship like theirs, with so many tender memories. He remained silent and left.

★The details given by Ello Quandt do not quite agree with Günther Quandt's account. It may be, however, that Magda gave her friend a clearer explanation than she did her former husband.

A few days later Ernest asked Magda for a final talk. She could not refuse, feeling that she owed him that at the very least. Ernest came into the sitting room, still silent, drew a revolver and fired at Magda. She stood stock still. The bullet struck the door frame close to her. 'Drop the play acting,' she commanded icily, 'if you had really aimed at me and hit me, I might have been impressed. But I find your behaviour ridiculous.' With that she left him standing and went into the next room; she shut the door behind her and phoned the police.

When the police appeared shortly afterwards they found an excitable young man in the act of shooting at, and smashing to pieces, a magnificent collection of porcelain. 'This young man,' declared Magda, 'is behaving stupidly. I suggest you keep him in custody overnight for his own good.' Ernest was marshalled out of the room between two policemen, down the stairs and, much against his will, into the police car.

Having arranged for the arrest of her former friend and close companion over many years, Magda put through a priority call to his father. When he rang back she, by now highly excited, said to him; 'I love another and have just told Ernest so. It would be as well if you were to go and look after him, otherwise he might do something stupid.' Whereupon the father took the night train to Berlin, arranged for his son's release the next morning and took him back home to recover his balance.

Magda had obviously no sense of the heartlessness of her conduct towards the man of whom she had once been so fond. She was enthralled by Joseph Goebbels and nothing else mattered any more.

8

Sweetheart and Wife

It was in the late summer of 1930 that Magda's friends learned of her engagement to Dr Joseph Goebbels. She took to wearing what was obviously an engagement ring, although no announcements, at that time still customary, were sent out. The betrothal naturally created a sensation in National Socialist circles as well as in Berlin society, and the news of this at first hardly credible event soon spread at lightning speed.

Günther Quandt was one of the first to be told, and by Magda herself. He wrote as follows:

In July 1931 I received an invitation from Magda. However the next day the invitation was promptly cancelled. Instead she requested me to meet her the following day at 2 p.m. in the foyer of the Kaiserhof Hotel. I arrived punctually. Magda excused herself for the previous day's cancellation on the grounds that Dr Goebbels had suddenly announced that he would be coming to see her for a most important purpose.

He had come to ask for her hand in marriage and she had accepted him. I was to be the first to be told. Now, following on the divorce, I had to face her remarriage. I foresaw complications without being able to discern exactly wherein they might lie.

Of course I could well imagine that Dr Goebbels would learn of my negative attitude towards the Party. But that didn't seem to me all important; nobody at that time thought that the National Socialists would come to power in Germany. I only learned later that he objected to my friendly relationship with Magda. In any case Magda's invitations to me ceased from that time.

I visited her again, on 11 November 1931, to congratulate her on her thirtieth birthday. Then I saw Dr Goebbels for the first time and instinctively felt that we didn't like each other.

Those who had Magda's welfare at heart gave her serious warnings. Her mother entreated her not to commit herself to such a man. Dr Ritschel wrote her such a highly indignant letter that Magda broke off all communication with him. All this, coming as it did on top of Günther Quandt's grave cautioning about her involvement in the political movement, proved futile. Magda loved Joseph Goebbels and she took as a personal insult every word uttered against him.

Up till now, Magda, for reasons which even she herself was unable to fathom, had avoided introducing Ello Quandt, her best friend, to Joseph Goebbels. All that Ello had so far heard about him from Magda were superlative accounts of his brilliant mind, his peculiar charm and his wide range of knowledge. She had neither seen nor spoken to him. But it had to happen eventually, and the meeting took place at Severin, the estate of Magda's former husband.

Ello was fully prepared to share her friend's high opinion of Dr Goebbels. Her disappointment when he was finally introduced to her was therefore all the greater. Beside her charming, well-groomed sister-in-law this man looked like a caricature; to imagine the two of them as lovers bordered, according to Ello, on the grotesque. She told Magda quite frankly what she thought of him. But where Magda was concerned it was already much too late. Magda only smiled, more firmly convinced than ever that she loved her fiancé with all her heart.

Goebbels, who behind his back was known even by faithful National Socialists, as 'Schrumpf-Germane' (wizened old German), scarcely tried to hide his feelings of triumph at his conquest. Magda never realized how largely she contributed to his political advancement, but she represented a decisive gain for the Nazis. At last a woman of international prestige, until recently the wife of one of the wealthiest industrial magnates in Germany, had by her choice of husband demonstrated, particularly where foreign opinion was concerned, that the Hitler movement was not made up of a band of strong-arm rough-necks. Magda Ritschel, divorced wife of Günther Quandt, and fiancée of Dr Goebbels, together with the venerable Frau Bruckmann in Munich, Frau von Dirksen, stepmother of Ambassador Dr Herbert von Dirksen in Berlin, and Winifred Wagner in

Bayreuth, was to make the Nazis socially acceptable.

Dr Goebbels' wish to introduce his fiancée to Adolf Hitler as soon as possible was therefore understandable. This first encounter took place in the Kaiserhof Hotel, Berlin, where Hitler set up his headquarters from time to time. From the outset Magda treated the Führer with the greatest respect, experiencing in his presence a sense of tingling excitement. He drew her straightaway into a political discussion, thus allowing her to give her knowledge and mental ability full play. She had often wanted to ask him personally what he really meant by certain passages in *Mein Kampf*, or by a particular statement in one of his recent speeches.

With true instinct, Magda struck exactly the right note with Hitler. He answered her questions animatedly. As she had read all that there was to read about the National Socialist movement, this first discussion in the Kaiserhof was a lively and stimulating one. The Führer was delighted with her intelligence, her charm and the interest she showed in his affairs.

In spite of her engagement to Goebbels, Magda's meetings with Günther Quandt did not at first suffer any interruption. The couple had to keep in touch with each other on account of their young son Harold, whose upbringing and education were conducted between them in a most cordial atmosphere. If Magda now began to accept Quandt's invitations to a meal more frequently or herself proposed meetings, there was a particular reason. She was anxious to interest him in the Hitler movement in a practical way, hoping to get a donation from the wealthy Quandt towards the ever-dwindling propaganda funds of the N.S.D.A.P. Goebbels naturally had no scruples about trying to get money from the former husband of his future wife. And Magda herself had become so subservient to the movement that she no longer had any inhibitions with regard to the delicate nature of her mission.

But whereas Günther Quandt had, since the divorce, been prepared to make many concessions, in this respect he was quite inflexible. Not only did he regard Magda's proposed marriage to Goebbels as disastrous, but he categorically rejected National Socialism. Nor was his attitude influenced by jealousy of Goebbels; it was based on a thorough study of the Party and its objectives, particularly where the economic sector was concerned.

The standard authority at that time were the books and policy of Gottfried Feder, one of the Nazi old guard whom Hitler himself later dropped because bitter experience proved the absolute folly of his theories. Meanwhile the whole Party leadership still believed in Feder's fantasies of a completely new economic world. Even Magda allowed herself to be inspired by his Utopian outpourings. She brought Günther Quandt the books that she had read in the confident hope that he too would be convinced by them. But the books only convinced him of the economic madness which such a programme represented.

'No reasonable man could expect me to support anything like that,' he said to Magda, at the table they were sharing in the Hotel Bristol. 'It is absolute nonsense, naïve dilettantism; as a practical economist, I know that such plans are not possible. When people like that with absolutely no conception of economic realities come to power, we shall all be driven to destruction.'

Magda was furious with him. She could not forgive him for being unwilling to show any understanding for Hitler and his movement. When Magda informed Goebbels that her approach had failed, he gnashed his teeth and growled, 'Pig-headed capitalist. Men like him are incapable of grasping big ideals.'

It was later rumoured, but without any justification, that Magda, from her own resources or from those of her former husband, had donated 1 million marks to the N.S.D.A.P. Quandt never gave the Party a penny, and Magda, who would willingly have given millions, was, through her marriage to Goebbels, left entirely without means of her own.

Quandt's financial responsibilities towards his divorced wife ceased on her marriage to Goebbels. Harold had to move into his father's house. All that remained to Magda was the furniture in her flat and what she had managed to save during the few good years. The rent of the flat alone came to 450 marks per month and could not be kept on for very long unless Goebbels achieved a financial miracle So her marriage meant giving up a comfortable life and sacrificing a large income, which had called for no effort on her part at all.

But she did not take the step without carefully weighing everything up. Shortly before the wedding her mother reminded her once more of the enviable position she was forsaking in return for a highly uncertain future. 'I am convinced,' Magda explained to her 'that there are only two possibilities for the political development of Germany. Either we shall be swallowed up by the communists, or we must become National Socialists. If the red flag should ever fly over Berlin, there would be no more capitalism and so my income from Quandt would disappear. If, however, Hitler's movement comes to power, I would then become one of the first ladies in Germany.'

It is impossible to judge whether Magda gave such a realistic justification for her decision to marry Goebbels merely to counteract her mother's concern and reproaches. Such considerations may possibly have played a part, but they were not decisive factors. She told Ello Quandt round about this time that she would go to the ends of the earth with Goebbels, that she was in fact prepared to die with him if the Party met with disaster, since it would in any case be the end of him.

However excessive this might appear, it is undeniable that at that time Magda was obsessed by Goebbels to the extent of complete self-surrender. His egocentricity, his inordinate vanity and cult of self-promotion, his erotic drive, all that and much more Magda, completely beguiled, had yet to experience. For her he was the standardbearer of a great new movement, a man of fire and spirit, a loyal follower of the Führer obsessed with National Socialist ideals. It took ten years of living with him before she saw through him completely.

The interval between betrothal and marriage lasted only a few months. It was a period of carefree personal happiness for them both and of intoxicating success for the Party. Goebbels overwhelmed his devoted fiancée with attention; every hour that he spent with her was sheer joy for him.

His successful conquest had a catalysing effect on him. He chased around from city to city, from meeting to meeting, often speaking in three or four cities on the same day. He spurred his followers on, continually impelling them to ever more strenuous efforts. He himself canvassed by day and night, hardly allowing himself any rest at all, for the Reichstag elections of 14 September 1930 were approaching.

The National Socialists planned to strike in this election with unprecedented force, backed by a superbly functioning organization, the work of Joseph Goebbels. He had built up a staff of skilful speakers, covering the Reich with an ingenious network of strong points manned by trusted followers. No less than six thousand electoral meetings were held, causing the non-socialist parties to reel under the dynamic thrust of the N.S.D.A.P., whose potential they still failed to appreciate. Goebbels generated such a flood of propaganda that the fragmented centre parties were almost drowned.

93

Through the fateful election of 14 September 1930, a most portentous event in German history, the National Socialist party became overnight a power factor of world political significance. Never before or since has a political movement developed in such a short space of time from a small splinter group into the second strongest Party in the country. In Berlin alone, Dr Goebbels' own region, 550,000 people voted for the N.S.D.A.P. Since that November evening, scarcely four years earlier, when Dr Goebbels arrived at the Anhalt railway station, he had succeeded in swelling the numbers of National Socialist members by many thousands.

It was his greatest triumph so far, his finest hour, as, in the evening following election Sunday of 14 September, he sat alone with Adolf Hitler and Magda listening to radio announcements from the various cities and electoral wards. Goebbels himself had predicted that they might get some forty seats in the Reichstag. His opponents had derisively referred to this forecast as delusions of grandeur, and the government press had bluntly sneered at such an absurd notion. Even his own Party members were convinced of the impossibility of sending forty delegates to the Reichstag.

As was customary at that time, only partial results were broadcast during the night. Dawn broke before all the figures were available. Throughout the night the situation had fluctuated according to which part of the country the latest result had emanated from. Towards five o'clock in the morning Dr Goebbels rose, stepped in front of Adolf Hitler, stood to attention and, in a voice trembling with emotion, said: 'My Führer, I must announce that the total number of members of your Party elected to the Reichstag is 107.'

Magda clasped her face in her hands and burst into tears. The Führer, drops of perspiration glistening on his forehead, gripped the hands of his Propaganda Leader convulsively three times. From that moment Hitler was recognized as a man of power in Europe. From the small back room of German party politics to which it had been thought he could be safely relegated, Adolf Hitler had stepped out on to the world stage.

And with him one other, Joseph Goebbels, whose talents and obsessive unremitting diligence had helped facilitate the rise of the N.S.D.A.P. With Goebbels at their head, the National Socialists had admirably exploited the country's crisis situation. Unfettered by the responsibilities of those in government, it was an easy matter for them to promise every class, group and profession, in fact almost every discontented voter, exactly what he wanted. He promised farmers higher prices for their produce, promised industry bigger profit margins, promised workers higher wages and lower food prices. Scruples about the economic impossibility of carrying out all these steps at one and the same time did not hamper Goebbels.

Once the excitement had begun to subside, he allowed himself for the first time a few days' relaxation with Magda. They were spent surprisingly enough at the Mecklenburg estate of Günther Quandt. When the divorce had successfully gone through, on the friendliest of terms, Magda had been granted the right to reside at Severin and invite guests there. Until now she had hardly availed herself of this facility, except occasionally at weekends accompanied by Harold. As country life appealed to Magda so little, Quandt had scarcely felt it necessary to modify the concession to stay there, feeling that he could safely rely on his former wife's discretion in the matter.

Now this was no longer the case. Magda's association with the unscrupulous Goebbels had wiped out all feelings of delicacy in her. So for some time it had become the practice not only for Goebbels and his adjutant Graf Schimmelmann, but also for Hitler himself and other leading Nazis, to spend their weekends at Severin, in the mansion belonging to Günther Quandt, industrial magnate, multi-millionaire and opponent of the Nazis. Quandt asked Magda not to turn his property into a sort of headquarters for the Nazi leadership, but she no longer listened to him. She had ears only for Goebbels, who knew how to make good use of such exclusive alternative accommodation for himself and the Führer.

There were other factors, too. Granzow, the estate bailiff, was one of Hitler's earliest supporters, and to be able to receive leading functionaries of the N.S.D.A.P. opened up attractive prospects for his own future. The estate owner could not dismiss his bailiff, because of the long-term irrevocable service contract he held, nor would he have wished to, since he happened to be the brother-in-law of his (Quandt's) first wife. So, very much against Quandt's will, the most secret discussions of the National Socialist leadership took place on his property.

The wedding on 12 December 1931 was from start to finish unequalled for its lack of taste. Magda and Joseph chose to be married at Severin: so that Magda married her second husband in her first husband's house. Günther Quandt was neither consulted beforehand about the event to take place under his roof, nor informed later. His former wife's brother-in-law Walter Granzow, who arranged everything, was responsible for that. As Günther Quandt noted in his memoirs, he could well have turned up at Severin, to his own astonishment and that of all the wedding guests, right in the middle of the wedding of his former wife.

The civil ceremony was followed by one in the church, at Magda's wish, Joseph Goebbels being pleased to accede to her whim; Ritter von Epp was the first witness and Adolph Hitler the second. The altar was decorated with the Nazi swastika flag, draped around a crucifix.

The procession wound its way in ceremonial fashion from the Quandt mansion to the little church and back. Altogether there were eighteen guests. The newlywed Frau Goebbels was careful to guard her beautiful black silk dress with the brussels lace shawl, worn at her first wedding, from trailing in the dust of the village street. Behind her walked Hitler in civilian clothes, with Frau Behrend, Magda's mother, on his arm. Dr Ritschel, the bride's father, was not there; he was absolutely opposed to the marriage, and did not see his daughter again for twelve years. Nine-year-old Harold, in the brown uniform of the Hitler Youth, was also in front. Hitler's adjutant, Brückner, Hanke, Goebbels' loyal aide, and Granzow the bailiff and his wife were all in the procession, as well as Ello Quandt and Julius Schaub, Hitler's personal aide for more than twenty-five years. The wedding breakfast was held at Günther Quandt's table and the happy couple's health toasted from his glasses.

Twenty years later Ello Quandt could remember every detail and made no secret of her disapproval of Magda's behaviour, above all in the choice of Severin. She reproached her in no uncertain terms, but only received the reply that Goebbels had insisted because of the isolated nature of the place, which meant that the public could be kept at bay. Moreover, Walter Granzow had acted as though it was well within his purview to place Severin at their disposal: there is no doubt that he was later well rewarded for his pains. Soon after the seizure of power by Hitler he was appointed *Minister-präsident* (Lord Lieutenant of the County) of the Province of Mecklenburg.

The newly married couple set up house in the Reichskanzlerplatz, in Magda's expensive flat. One of the reception rooms became Goebbels' study; he in the meantime had given up his own small flat in Steglitz, and brought some of his furniture with him. Harold went back, as ordained in the divorce decree, to live in his father's house in the Frankenallee. Magda's flat was only a few minutes' walk away from the Quandt house, so the lad went frequently between the two, spending the greater part of his time with his mother..

The wedding of Magda Quandt and Joseph Goebbels, which took place on Günther Quandt's Severin estate near Parchim on 12 December 1931. Next to the bridegroom stands Harold, Magda's son by her first marriage, and behind him is Adolf Hitler, who acted as one of the witnesses at the wedding

Press photograph of the newly-married couple

Quandt tactfully avoided influencing him. Harold was, of course, impressed by the exciting atmosphere which encompassed his stepfather, the banners, the stirring torchlight ceremonies, the fanfares and the drums. Occasionally Goebbels allowed him to accompany him to the gatherings, the lad naturally wearing his Hitler Youth uniform. Harold stood on the platform, near Uncle Joseph's – the speaker's – desk. He could see the thousands of arms raised simultaneously in greeting, hear the rapturous cries of 'Heil Goebbels', amid the lowering of the banners and the thunder of the drums.

The grey poverty of Goebbels' early life was now forgotten. Even before the decisive 14 September he was receiving about 1,000 marks a month from various appointments (roughly D.M. 3,500 at today's values). This income Hitler now raised by a further 1,000 marks. This was for Goebbels a fabulous figure, though for Magda it was barely half of her former income.

Not only did the two of them have to live on this, but their many guests also. Magda's flat became the private headquarters of the Party leadership. There it was possible to meet without constraint, to speak without being overheard. Outwardly the impression conveyed by the Party leaders was one of strict military efficiency; the Nazi leaders had themselves to demonstrate what they demanded of their followers. The manner in which they walked, stood, comported themselves generally, was always a soldierly one.

In the long run this was very exhausting, so Hitler and his entourage welcomed the use of Magda's roomy flat, finding there an oasis where they could relax unobtrusively, often spending an evening listening to music. Magda's was a comfortable, well-run household in which they felt at home, where no watchful eyes, respectful or inimical, registered their every word or gesture, where no camera lay in wait, where no shorthand notebook might suddenly be produced. In the Goebbels' house everybody could be himself. No autograph hunter pestered the leading figures of the N.S.D.A.P., no hysterical women sought, sobbing with emotion, to kiss the Führer's hand. Whenever Hitler arrived in Berlin he came as a guest to the house, bringing his adjutants with him. Göring and Dietrich, chief of the S.S., used to come, as well as Röhm, Heinrich Himmler, Putzi Hanfstaengl, Leni Riefenstahl and countless others.

After his marriage to Magda, Goebbels' standing with Hitler rose steadily. For the Berlin Gauleiter and Reich-Propaganda Leader everything hinged on his maintaining and consolidating his favoured position. It was perfectly clear to him that without Hitler's patronage he would very quickly lose whatever influence he possessed. Goebbels had no backing other than that of Hitler personally. Göring still had his former flying colleagues and later the Luftwaffe (air force) as his personal bulwark; Röhm disposed of a private army in the shape of the S.A. (*Sturm-abteilung* – Assault Detachment); Himmler could rely on the support of the S.S. (*Schutzstaffel* – the Guards); Ley on the Labour Front*; Franck** on the National Socialist Lawyers. But Goebbels had nothing. He only had his region, the Berlin capital, and that could be taken from him by another Gauleiter overnight.

With regard to his activities, although the value of propaganda was fully appreciated by Hitler, this was not true of all the members of the Nazi hierarchy. As is so often the case with matters which are not properly understood, they all considered themselves just as capable as the *Schrumpf-Germane* of making propaganda. Political propaganda is not in any case taken very seriously, and particularly not when bolstered by ignoble means. Only Hitler himself realized how much the fabulous success of the Nazi movement owed to the richly inventive, cunning brain of Goebbels. The future of the N.S.D.A.P. also depended on him. It was a matter of particular satisfaction to Hitler that his Propaganda Leader always obeyed him unquestioningly, without any scruples whatsoever. It suited him for Goebbels to stand apart from the rest of the Party leadership; he could be all the more sure of his absolute loyalty and allegiance.

During the four years in which Magda and Joseph lived in the Reichskanzlerplatz, Magda immersed herself in the running of the household. Now for the first time in her life she could be the perfect housewife. She managed with a minimum of domestic staff, and never complained about the extensive demands made on her; on the contrary she felt fulfilled by the very scope of her new responsibilities. She often stayed up until the early hours of the morning waiting for her husband to return, when she would greet him effusively. He was frequently accompanied by guests, for whom Magda would provide coffee and sandwiches. She nearly always had

*The trade unions were dissolved by Hitler in May 1933, their funds confiscated, and Robert Ley was assigned to take over and to establish instead the Labour Front. (Translator's note)

**Carl Franck was a young Nazi lawyer, one of the judicial triumvirate set up as a court by Hitler to settle internal disputes of the Party in the early days. (Translator's note)

six to eight present at mealtimes. Whenever Hitler was in Berlin he would turn up without any notice. Since an attempt to poison him he had eaten all his meals at Magda's. This attempt, hushed up at the time, took place at the Kaiserhof Hotel in Berlin in January 1933, where he and his entourage regularly stayed.

One day about an hour after lunch all who had partaken of the meal were taken ill; they had stomach pains, vomited and were unable to stand. Doctors were hastily summoned. Adjutant Brückner suffered most, and for a long time there were fears for his life. Hitler was least affected, being a light eater and moreover a vegetarian. Poison was found to be present in the food, although in too small a quantity to cause death. From then on Hitler moved into the Reich Chancellor's palace and Magda herself, together with her old and trusted cook, prepared all his meals. Two sets of dishes were necessary because Hitler would not give up his diet, and the others all preferred a hearty meal.

It cost money always to be entertaining on such a scale, and Magda was unable to cope with the means at her disposal. Hitler would occasionally press an envelope into her hand with a contribution towards expenses; later he forgot, and Magda never liked to remind him. No doubt he assumed that Goebbels defrayed this portion of his household expenses from Party funds; he would certainly have been entitled to do so, but in any case nobody credited him with having any scruples. Joseph Goebbels, however, to whom the life of a man meant so little, was very correct where money was concerned. So long as the Party had not got power in their hands, he never allowed himself to benefit from a single penny towards the cost of entertaining the many guests who came to his house. Party funds were sacred to him.

In spite of the heavy demands that Goebbels made on his wife, they lived happily together. The intimate relationship of the 'turtle doves' struck many visitors as quite funny. Her pet name for Goebbels was 'Engelchen' – cherub. That spiteful character assassinator, Putzi Hanfstaengl, at that time one of Hitler's most trusted confidantes, used to comment: 'Magda calls 'Engelchen', but look who comes round the corner – the old black devil himself, club foot and all!' As a result of such remarks, Goebbels nourished a fierce hatred of Putzi, which manifested itself later when Hanfstaengl, fearing for his life, fled to Switzerland and England.

In the early days of their married life, Magda and Joseph behaved like two playful children. If she were called away to the telephone during a meal, he would shake salt into her coffee, hide her keys under a cushion or stick a clothes brush beneath the sheet. She went to great lengths always to appear at her best in his presence, went out of her way to distract him with pleasantries when he came back home cross or worried.

When they entertained in the evenings, the party usually went on into the early hours. Hitler came into his own at night; Goebbels only needed very little sleep. When Hanfstaengl, a gifted pianist, was one of the guests, there would be music. Magda and he would play by turns. Mostly, however, the evenings dragged away under the weight of one of Hitler's interminable monologues. He loved to speak his thoughts, to develop his ideas at the expense of his listeners. Without any serious intention behind them, these endless self-communings tended later to give rise to the most grotesque misunderstandings. When he became absolute ruler of the Greater German Reich, and even for a time overlord of Europe, his listeners regarded every word he uttered as a command. They would hasten back to their offices and make notes for their files, always beginning with the words: 'The Führer expects ... .', or 'The Führer yesterday decided that . . .'.

But in fact he had neither ordered nor decided anything, only spoken his thoughts aloud. He was sometimes appalled later at many of the instructions issued in his name, but mostly he did not hear anything about them. There is no doubt that this was a contributory factor, only later understood, in precipitating the subsequent disastrous course of events.

On one occasion, through the good offices of the Führer's adjutant Schaub, I was fortunate enough to receive the rarely given summons to the Führer's large round table in the winter garden of the Reich Chancellor's palace. There I was able to hear one of Hitler's endless diatribes. About a dozen of the prominent personalities at that time, among them Magda and Joseph Goebbels, were listening too, all seemingly deeply interested. It hardly bears thinking about what might have happened if some of the things that Hitler said in the course of these soliloquies had found their way into the press, either at home or abroad. I can remember now quite distinctly how Hitler, after enquiring about my impressions of Japan (from which I had just returned), particularly about the South Sea Islands formerly belonging to Germany but then owned by Japan, declared amongst other things that he had never forgiven the annexation of the German islands, that is the Caroline Islands and the Mariana Islands, by the Japanese at the beginning of the 1914 war. They would all be

German again one day – when the time came!

That same year he concluded the anti-Comintern Pact with Italy and Japan, equivalent to a military alliance. The three states guaranteed to maintain steadfast friendship with each other and to provide support in time of need or danger. It can hardly therefore have been the Führer's true intention to risk nullifying an agreement with the then mighty empire of the Rising Sun for the sake of a few worthless islands.

Dr Goebbels used to listen very carefully to such utterances, not allowing a single word to escape him. When Hitler let fall anything that Goebbels could use for his own purposes, he would issue it straight away next morning in the form of an order from the Führer.

9

Years of Struggle and Married Bliss

On 1 September 1932, ten months after the wedding, their first daughter, Helga, was born. Joseph was pleased, although he had hoped for a son. Magda was happy, because her husband had stipulated before the marriage that they should have a large family. As a young girl she had often declared that she would like to have a dozen children. In her marriage to Quandt this wish had remained unfulfilled because of a series of miscarriages. Goebbels had insisted on her consulting a specialist, who had successfully treated her.

During her pregnancy, which Magda got through without difficulty, Goebbels, like all egocentric men, paid little regard to her condition. It never occurred to him that she needed to be treated with special consideration; she herself never mentioned the matter. Until shortly before her confinement she stayed up late with guests, attending to their needs and putting up with the stale, smoke-filled atmosphere of the room. Even on the rare evenings when they were alone together, she did not go to bed until he was ready to do so, though it was often long past midnight. '*Engelchen*' could neither go to sleep at normal hours nor spend his evenings alone. He liked to spend several hours in conversation with his wife, recounting everything which had happened during the day and discussing plans for the morrow. Like every true wife, she was prepared to take as deep an interest as possible in his life. When Helga was born and the affairs of the household became more complicated, Magda did not burden her husband with her own small daily problems. She settled them by herself, just as she had done in her marriage with Quandt.

Goebbels was proud of his child. Although it was invariably late when he returned from the office, he would always go straight to the nursery, take his little daughter out of her cot and balance her carefully on his knee, while surrounded by his guests. Helga was a lovely baby; she never cried, was never impatient, but lay still, her blue eyes sparkling, listening completely uncomprehendingly to what the Nazi bigwigs were saying to each other.

Hitler, too, liked to show his affection for children, and would nurse Helga on his lap while continuing by the hour to weave his political dreams. Magda would sit happily by, but anxious at the same time for a break in the conversation which would enable her to seize the baby and take her back to bed.

Through her marriage, Magda's circle of friends changed completely for the third time; the only one of her old friends with whom she kept in touch was Ello Quandt. Frau Behrend, Magda's mother, could not come to terms with Goebbels as a son-in-law, particularly as he had induced her to drop the name of Friedländer and assume her maiden name of Behrend once more. It was an embarrassment for the Reich Propaganda Leader of the N.S.D.A.P. to have for a mother-in-law a lady with an unmistakably Jewish name. The old lady yielded to his wish, it is true, but she never forgot that she had been made to do so. She would gladly have stayed away from her daughter's house altogether, but kept in touch purely out of love for Magda and her grandchildren. As far as possible she tried to leave before Goebbels returned; if they chanced to meet, they were coolly polite to one another. Goebbels' vanity was wounded by the fact that he failed to win acceptance from his mother-in-law.

Although Goebbels' two brothers joined the National Socialists, Joseph did not maintain contact with them. Maria, his younger sister, formed a close friendship with Magda, however. Maria Goebbels was a lovely young girl; in spite of her simple origin, she was well educated and quite a lady both in appearance and manner. She was devoted to her famous brother. Until her marriage Maria came often to the house and helped Magda in a variety of ways.

By and large Goebbels' attitude to his family was very similar to that of Hitler. Although he did not turn his back on them altogether, he never lifted a finger on their behalf, never gave them any support either with their careers or with money, never recommended them to anybody or gave them work. It often seemed as if he had forgotten his early friends, together with his early life. In the long run this turned out to have been all for the best, for when the Thousand Year Reich came to its disastrous end the neglected family remained happily in oblivion.

Magda confronted each day's events as they arose and never attempted to plan her time. She therefore admired her husband's ability to plan his day so skilfully that, in spite of the colossal amount of work he had to get through, he never appeared to be in a hurry and could always manage to enjoy a quiet half-hour at tea time, without giving a thought to the mass meeting he had to address immediately afterwards.

His work schedule was, as might be expected, a rational one. He knew exactly when his energy would begin to flag, the moment when he needed to rest. He tackled energetically, rapidly and with concentration only those particular matters which required to be dealt with at that moment. No demands of his family life were allowed to interfere with any of his duties. Thus he spent the first Christmas of his marriage, a few weeks after the wedding, in a cellar among the S.A., only returning after midnight. Magda welcomed him smilingly, as if there was nothing at all amiss.

In the second year of their marriage they rented a small weekend house in Gatow on the Havel. It was situated on the shores of the lake, and there the family spent nearly every weekend. Goebbels was permitted, on Hitler's special instructions, to use his official car, a Mercedes limousine, for private purposes. It was a welcome facility and enabled them to enjoy the Gatow home much more than they otherwise could have done.

In September 1932 it seemed as if Hitler's triumphant progress had reached its climax and the trend to success was being reversed. When General Field Marshal von Hindenburg's seven-year period of office as president expired, the old man agreed, under pressure from the centre parties, to stand for re-election. Hitler was fully aware that, as opposition candidate to such a well-known, much-loved figure as the Victor of Tannenberg, he could never obtain a majority. He would have liked to reserve his position, and even pondered whether to support Hindenburg's re-election as Head of State. Goebbels insisted on his standing as opposition candidate, however. He too realized that Hitler could never overcome the massive popularity of the eighty-year-old who had acquired legendary fame in his own lifetime. But, as an arch-propagandist, Goebbels knew equally well that Hitler had no choice but to stand, if only to keep himself in the public eye. Even if he lost to the hoary old figurehead, at least there would be an increase in the number of votes to show for the effort. Hitler stood and was defeated, a result that had been obvious from the start.* But what had not been so obvious, even to Goebbels, was the state of despondency which would settle on all the members of the Party. They had believed firmly in Hitler's success, and having been confident of their Führer being elected Reich President, they took his defeat much more seriously than it deserved.

Hindenburg did not, as it happened, obtain an absolute majority of votes, and a second election was called. Goebbels redoubled his efforts. This time he arranged for Hitler to go everywhere by plane, thus increasing his mobility. Goebbels' own propaganda machine functioned at peak efficiency, his numerous Party news-sheets rolling daily off the printing presses. Although Hitler lost a second time it was not in vain, for thirteen million votes were cast in his favour.

In the autumn of 1932 it had looked as if the N.S.D.A.P. was in decline. The Reichstag elections in November had resulted in losses. The Führer was gloomy and silent; a movement such as his depended for its existence on a rapid succession of winning coups. All their speakers, Goebbels in particular, had harped continuously on the theme that victory lay just ahead, that power was almost within their grasp and the National Socialists were about to become the new rulers of Germany. Whether the Nazis themselves actually believed it all or not, at any rate their followers had done so, and disappointment was bound to follow.

Heated discussions were taking place in Magda's flat that autumn. For the first time an atmosphere of the greatest secrecy prevailed. Nobody, not even Magda herself, was allowed to enter the conference room, or even the adjacent room. In the past such discussions had been followed by convivial social gatherings, but now there was only a gloomy silence, broken occasionally by a curt remark. Hitler, Goebbels and other leading Party functionaries

---

*As there were four elections in 1932, confusion often arises about the results. These are the polling figures for the Nazis in the elections of that year:

	Nazis polled	
March	11,339,446	30.1% of total and an increase over 1930 of nearly 5 million
April	13,418,547	36.8% of total
July	13,745,000	38% and 230 seats in the new Reichstag
November	11,000,000 (approx)	

(Translator's note)

openly admitted that there was now only a very slight possibility of their coming to power. The Party was suffering severely from a lack of funds, debts were mounting daily. Ten thousand Party members had stopped paying their subscriptions. Worse still, it looked as if the Party was about to split into factions.

The radical wing under Goebbels' leadership was for either taking drastic action or, if that was not feasible, biding their time until full political authority was within their grasp. Gregor Strasser and his moderate groups, on the other hand, advocated participating in a coalition government even if only in a subordinate rôle.

Strasser, at that time Chief Party Organizer, asked for a personal interview with Hitler in Berlin. Hitler could not refuse him, since a large proportion of the founding Party members supported Strasser, as well as the group around von Papen and Schleicher, who kept in touch with Strasser because he was a moderate and a man of integrity. In order that nobody should steal a march on him and influence Hitler, Strasser betook himself to the Anhalt railway station, there to await Hitler and intercept him as he alighted from the sleeping car. He knew that Hitler had left Munich by the night train. But Hitler did not arrive.

Later everything became clear. First Goebbels, then Göring, had got wind of Strasser's intentions and had gone to meet the Führer. Goebbels managed to persuade the Führer to dodge the interview with Strasser. So he left the train at Jena, and Strasser's plan of talking the Führer into joining Reich Chancellor Schleicher's government fell apart. If Strasser's plan had succeeded, the N.S.D.A.P. might have merged with a normal government and so been neutralized.

The Thuringian elections shortly afterwards resulted in a catastrophic loss to the N.S.D.A.P. of forty per cent of their votes. The other parties, and particularly the government, congratulated themselves on this significant victory. The danger from the N.S.D.A.P. appeared to have been overcome. With the ever-improving economic situation, it was confidently expected that large sections of voters would withdraw their support from the radical parties and be won over to the moderate policy of gradual reconstruction.

Hitler now had to ask himself seriously whether it would not be wiser to participate in the Schleicher government than to continue to hold out for supreme power, when the National Socialists were losing so much ground. His chances were lessened with each refusal. Goebbels was the one who was being blamed at this time. If he had not frustrated the meeting between Hitler and Strasser, the National Socialists would by now have had a couple of seats in the Cabinet. Goebbels was aware that through this wrong decision not only was his standing with Hitler seriously threatened, but worse still his influence in the Party. His only hope now was to bring off a very big coup, and so save the movement which he had so fanatically served for ten years from foundering. In fact the coup which he thought up did succeed.

Lippe Detmold was not only a beautiful city but a diminutive state with barely 150,000 inhabitants, known by name to every German, the toy principality having been the subject of jokes for decades. Although so small it possessed its own parliament. This was only of minor interest to quiet Lippe Detmold itself, and outside Lippe nobody at all was in the least interested in it – except Joseph Goebbels.

On 18 January 1933 Lippe was due to elect its new parliament. Hitler's demon propagandist brought to bear on the miniature state all the concentrated art and cunning of which his fertile brain was capable. The full force of the Party's propaganda machine, backed by its remaining funds, together with other monies hastily scraped up, was hurled on to this tiny patch of country. All the prominent Party heads, Hitler, Göring, Hess, Frick and Goebbels, used to delivering orations over loudspeakers to delirious crowds, now canvassed in tiny wayside inns, in market squares and on village greens. Party propagandists called on every householder. Nazi leaflets were pushed through every letter box; swastika placards covered every wall.★

The other parties realized too late what was happening; Goebbels had been too clever for them. None of their speakers could get a word in edgeways; their sparse placards were torn down from the walls. The voters neither heard nor read anything but what Goebbels intended them to.

The impact of this massive campaign on such a small area was overwhelming. The National Socialists gained an absolute majority in Lippe Detmold. Winning an election in the pygmy state was not of course going to bring about the conversion of the 50 million voters in the rest of the country. Nevertheless, the Party trumpeter made it his business to see that their success there had the effect of a beacon on the mass of the population.

★More about this episode can be found in my book *30 January 1933, The Seizure of Power*, Bechtle Verlag, Munich.

The weeks preceding the election had proved a very worrying time for Goebbels. While he was desperately struggling to collect every single vote, Magda was at home fighting for her life. She was seriously ill, and the doctors had given her up. Goebbels was not told of this; he needed all his strength for the election. For the Party to lose Lippe Detmold would be to lose Germany. But both Joseph in Lippe and Magda in Berlin won their battles: by election day Magda was out of danger.

Hitler's victory in the diminutive state of Lippe Detmold, seen in retrospect a quite modest affair, nevertheless acted as a catalyst on the by now apathetic followers of the N.S.D.A.P. During the subsequent twelve January days, events precipitated themselves. Right-wing Party leaders, a few prominent bankers and industrialists, Dr Hjalmar Schacht and Herr von Papen conducted negotiations, partly in Berlin, partly in the house of the Cologne Banker Kurt von Schroeder, with Göring and Oskar von Hindenburg (son of the Reich President).

After prolonged discussions it was eventually agreed in principle that Hitler should become Reich Chancellor, von Papen his permanent deputy and Commissioner for Prussia. Other ministerial posts would be filled by specialists from the conservative and non-socialist parties. The final discussions between Hitler, von Papen and others about the definitive list of ministers was held in the house of Joaquim von Ribbentrop in Berlin-Dahlem; Ribbentrop was well-known as the son-in-law of Henkell, the champagne producer.

In the end, on 30 January 1933 at eleven o'clock in the morning, Paul von Hindenburg, the Reich President elected by the parties of the centre and the left, nominated Adolf Hitler German Reich Chancellor. He had no alternative; to have done otherwise would have been unconstitutional. Together with their confederates from the conservative camp, Hitler's party had the majority in the Reichstag.

On that gloomy day Magda, though not fully recovered, had left the clinic and was at home in bed. Her sister-in-law Ello Quandt was with her. Magda was of course aware that for days past vital negotiations had been taking place between the Reich Chancellery and the Kaiserhof, Hitler's headquarters. But that had often happened before, leading nowhere, so she did not attribute any particular significance to them. Joseph had after all told her only a few weeks previously that the N.S.D.A.P. had very little chance of ever coming to power. She was therefore greatly surprised, a few minutes after eleven, to receive a telephone call from her husband in the Kaiserhof. 'Magda what *do* you think? Just imagine, the Führer has just been elected Reich Chancellor. Now what do you say?' Magda was overjoyed and flung her arms around Ello.

Shortly afterwards Goebbels arrived home, in great haste, elated, triumphant, resolute. Rubbing his hands together he turned to Ello, 'What have you got to say?' Ello congratulated him on his success and added firmly, 'Now Doctor, this a serious matter. You must start to govern in a proper manner and really show what you and your friends are capable of.' Goebbels' reaction was startling. His face darkened, changing completely. Every trace of pleasure vanished. His mouth took on such an ugly leer that both his wife and sister-in-law were aghast. Never before had they seen him without the mask.

'We are the masters now,' he said in a menacing tone. 'Power is in our hands, whatever you say. Nobody is going to take it away from us again. *We* know all the tricks.' He said it with such biting cynicism that Ello's blood ran cold; a feeling that something frightful and irrevocable was happening overwhelmed her. She somehow knew that it was not a question of Germany's prosperity and well-being that was at stake, but Goebbels' personal exercise of power.

He turned on his heel and left the room. He was in a hurry to get ready for the gigantic torchlight procession to mark the triumph of the N.S.D.A.P. which only he could effectively stage and, what was even more important, to enter for the first time in his life the imposing doors of the Reich Chancellery.

Magda had to go back to the clinic for out-patient treatment, while Ello went on to the Brandenburg Gate to mingle with the crowds. In the midst of an immense throng of jubilant Berliners, she watched the endless columns of brown-shirted marchers, bearing 100,000 flaming torches, filing along the Unter den Linden and turning into the Wilhelmstrasse, the 'Whitehall' of the German Reich, created by the Kings of Prussia.

Adolf Hitler, the new chancellor, with Göring at his side stood on a balcony of the Chancellery, greeting with upraised arm his brown-shirted followers and the cheering crowds. Behind him the Party chiefs, the group of men who for years had striven for this hour, were exultant, waving their hands and laughing. Goebbels alone remained unmoved, staring ahead, pondering whether perhaps he might not have reached the peak of his achievements, now that his incontrovertible gifts had spurred the Führer and his party on to the great breakthrough. A success for the moment certainly . . . but what lay ahead for him?

The objective had been reached. Could they now dispense with bluster? Work still had to be done, but work in the first place that produced practical, visible results. The promises made over the years to the German people now called for fulfilment. Goebbels knew that only too well; knew too that much which had been promised could never be accomplished.

Behind them through another closed window, the white head of the aged president, Paul von Hindenburg, seated on a chair raised up by several layers of carpet, was clearly visible. The cheering crowds acknowledged him too, stretching their arms towards him in the fascist salute, their cries of 'Heil Hindenburg' echoing like a tocsin. The old man waved back half-heartedly. He realized that a new era had dawned. He didn't trust this 'Bohemian corporal', but von Papen and other right-wingers had advocated the appointment of Hitler to the chancellorship as the only solution, indeed as the salvation of the Fatherland.

My father, standing behind Hindenburg, clearly heard him mutter more than once: 'That's enough for now, children, that's enough. God only knows how all this is going to end.'

10

Wife of the Reich Minister

A few days after that historic Monday when Hitler was appointed Chancellor of the Reich, the new government was complete. Apart from Hitler only two other prominent leaders of the N.S.D.A.P. became ministers; Frick and Göring. Goebbels was left out. Presumably he had foreseen this; he may even have been warned by Hitler himself. But what he could by no means have anticipated was that there would be no opening at all for him. Day after day went by without a word from Hitler. Goebbels became increasingly restive. He began to fear that the spoils would be shared out and he be forgotten. While his rivals Frick and Göring were propped up in ministerial armchairs, he was pacing up and down at home in despair. After all, what was he? Gauleiter of Berlin.

And what was the good of being Gauleiter of Berlin if Hitler could appoint anyone he liked to be Lord Mayor of the capital? What was the good of being Propaganda Leader of the N.S.D.A.P. now that the great, decisive objective of the seizure of power had been achieved? He had hoped at the very least – and Hitler had indeed promised him at one time – that he would become Minister of Education and Cultural Affairs. Nobody could deny that of all the National Socialist leaders he was the most cultured.

In this respect, too, Goebbels was to be bitterly disappointed. The utterly insignificant, colourless, pedantic and, as it turned out later, relatively harmless Bernhard Rust, a former teacher, was given the appointment of Prussian Minister of Education and Cultural Affairs. When Goebbels learned this, he became even more despondent. 'The Führer,' he said to Magda, pale with anger, 'is most ungrateful.'

Magda proved herself during those difficult days once more to be an excellent wife. She stood by him, begged him to be patient, pointed out how overburdened Hitler must be with all that he had to cope with, and that he was undoubtedly keeping something very special for him. It would be unthinkable for her 'Engelchen' to be given a subordinate position. Prussian Minister of Education and Cultural Affairs was really not good enough. While Goebbels was tormenting himself with the thought that Hitler was now getting his revenge because Goebbels had on one occasion betrayed him, Magda insisted that her husband was, as previously, quite indispensable. While the disappointed Goebbels recollected with a deep sense of shame how at the meeting of Gauleiters in 1926 he had loudly demanded that 'that petty bourgeois Adolf Hitler should be expelled from the N.S.D.A.P.', his wife was quite sure that Hitler simply could not afford to drop him.

Finally, on the fourth or fifth day after the seizure of power, came the summons from the Reich Chancellery. Hitler sent word that he was ready to see Goebbels, who hurried as fast as he could over to the Wilhelmstrasse. 'My dear Goebbels,' began Hitler, 'I have some special plans for your future, but it is still too early to talk about them. Much more importantly for the moment there's something I want you to do first. Prepare an election for me for 5 March.'

Goebbels was comforted to some extent for the time being. At least he had a big new assignment with which to occupy himself, and to alleviate his disappointment at not having been made a minister. So he turned his thoughts towards preparations for the election.

It was not such an easy task as it might have seemed. Hitler had explained to him that this time it was imperative that he should have an absolute majority, at least fifty-one per cent of the votes. Goebbels therefore set out, whatever happened, to fulfil this wish on the part of his master. But caution was necessary. Now that Hitler was Reich Chancellor all promises would definitely have to be capable of being fulfilled. Mere promises were no longer enough. The credibility of the N.S.D.A.P., above all that of the new chancellor, was at stake.

The one thing about which something could safely be done was, in Goebbels opinion, the danger from communism. Whether he himself really believed in it or not was beside the point. Danger from the Reds could easily be used to frighten the voters. As already mentioned, the election was to be held on Sunday 5 March. On Monday 27 February, late in the evening, the Reichstag went up in flames. It was clearly a case of arson. Nobody questioned that. But who was responsible? The communists of course.

Goebbels, once more firmly in his own peculiar element, set out to prove that the communists were guilty of the treacherous deed. In fact it seemed so obvious that, to start with, proof was not called for. All the foreign press, except the communist-controlled, printed the allegation in banner headlines . . . even if only for the first few days. The burning of the Reichstag was to have been the beacon for widespread turmoil, the signal for a Red revolution.

That same night thousands of communists were arrested in Germany, their party suppressed, their newspapers banned, their offices closed. Many Berliners thought at the time that Göring, not the communists, was responsible for the fire. Later disclosures, and the contents of innumerable documents which became available after the collapse, gave rise to the suspicion that the man behind the burning down of the Reichstag was not the bombastic, unimaginative Hermann Göring but the highly gifted Goebbels, together with Ernst, leader of the Berlin Storm Troopers (who was shot on 30 June 1934), and Count Helldorff, the new Berlin chief of police (who was liquidated after 20 July).   This is not the place to describe this first major crime of the new regime. There is little doubt as to who, in the circumstances, was the chief culprit: the inordinately cunning Goebbels, with his profound understanding of human weakness, unsurpassed in his skill at conspiratorial intrigue – though sceptics about this theory have written thoroughly worthwhile books on the subject. But exactly how it was done is, in spite of prolonged and intensive investigation, still a mystery.

But if anybody among the hierarchy of the N.S.D.A.P. had expected that a decisive victory would be brought about by this great fire, he was doomed to disappointment. Whilst the ruins of the German parliament still smouldered, and in spite of relentless outright intimidation of the Opposition, and total prohibition of the K.P.D. (Communist Party) in the last relatively free contested election of the Weimar Republic, only forty-four per cent of the votes polled were for the National Socialists. Hitler did not get his desired absolute majority.

Hitler, Goebbels and Magda deliberately spent the evening of election Sunday in the public eye at a performance of *The Valkyrie* at the State Opera House. It would seem that they wished to evince a certain nonchalance as to the result of the election. The opera over, they drove to the Reich Chancellery to listen throughout the night to the election returns. 'A glorious day,' wrote Goebbels in his diary, but both he and Magda knew that the N.S.D.A.P., and the Propaganda Leader in particular, had to accept defeat. With only forty-four per cent of the votes Hitler was once more dependent on the centre parties. But these same centre parties, apparently blind to what they were doing, as a result of increased ruthless intimidation and violence on Goebbels' part, dissolved themselves and recommended to their electors that they support Hitler. On 23 March 1933 Hitler was deviously able to get the Reichstag to pass the so-called Enabling Act by a large majority. This empowered the cabinet to legislate by decree during a four-year period, but in fact gave Hitler full dictatorial power.

From this moment onwards Adolf Hitler was dictator of the German Reich. The seizure of power did not date from 30 January 1933, as so often said, but from 30 March 1933, when the parties of the still to a certain extent freely elected parliament, with one praiseworthy exception, the S.P.D. (German Social Democratic Party), laid total power at the feet of Adolf Hitler.

Hitler was satisfied at last. Goebbels had acquitted himself well in the most difficult circumstances. The Führer ordered the setting up of a *Reichsministerium für Volksaufklärung und Propaganda* (Ministry for Information and Propaganda), appointed Goebbels minister, and allowed him to set up his ministry in the palace of the former Prince Leopold in the Wilhelmsplatz, exactly opposite the Reich Chancellery. It was one of the great Schinkel's handsome, stately buildings on classic lines. But what was still more important was that Hitler assured his new minister that he, Goebbels, was his right-hand man, the most indispensable of all his satellites.

Though Goebbels at last had the long hoped for ministry, he and Magda still lacked a suitable private residence for themselves. The Leopold Palace was too small to allow for private apartments to be set aside for the Minister and his growing family in addition to the official offices.

In central Berlin there were to be found seven extensive gardens of which even many native-born Berliners were quite unaware. They had existed since the days of the first Prussian king and his son Friedrich Wilhelm I, who had laid out the elegant Wilhelmstrasse with its beautiful, tasteful, imposing buildings. Looking at the façades stretching from the then Reich Chancellery to the British

Embassy in the east, which was all that was visible from the street, nobody would have believed that huge gardens lay behind them, with clumps of age-old trees, silent pools, pavilions more than a century old, fountains, disused tennis courts and hothouses. In the garden of the Reich Chancellery Bismarck's famous pet dog was buried, as well as his favourite horse.

This garden was bounded at its far end, along the now renamed Friedrich Ebertstrasse, by the Zoological Gardens. The secluding wall followed the same path as the old Berlin city wall in former times. Most of the heavily built watch towers still continued to exist until after the end of the Second World War, linked by gentle slopes formed by earthing up the core of the old walls. Right up to the time of Kaiser Wilhelm II the hollow spaces inside these towers were used as ice cellars.*

Next to this, behind the Ministry for Agriculture, was another, very gloomy garden which had been allowed to run completely wild, as the Ministry was unoccupied except for the caretaker. The one-time water lily pond had become a swamp, the pavilions had fallen into ruins, the grass was overgrown and the hothouses were now only rusty skeletons. Wild flowers grew in profusion and rabbits, martens, squirrels and even owls lived there, in the heart of Berlin, quite undisturbed.

At the far end of this forgotten paradise stood a large whitewashed mansion, more than a century old, which had been built for a former Prussian court official. In the early days of the Weimar Republic it had been occupied for a short period by the family of the Secretary of State, but as it lacked all modern comforts it soon fell empty again. How Goebbels came upon this property is not known. In any case, without even casting a single glance at it, the Führer gave his minister immediate permission to acquire it.

It was taken for granted that money should come from public funds to provide appropriate accommodation for the heads of the Nazi Party, so the old building was transformed with lightning speed into a magnificent white palace. A team of gardeners from the State parks authority restored the natural beauty of the long-neglected garden, bringing back the well-kept paths, colourful flower borders

---

*These gardens are familiar to me in every detail because I spent a great part of my youth – a good twelve years – there. My parents occupied the right wing of the Presidential Palace, otherwise Wilhelmstrasse 73. Friedrich Ebert, the first President of the Reich, allowed us to share the use of the lovely garden behind his palace with his family.

and heated greenhouses. Only one thing had to go: the small gold crown from the head of the Prussian eagle which looked down from the top of the high wall upon the traffic in the newly named Hermann Göringstrasse.

The Führer's master propagandist now had exactly the type of residence that he wanted. His wife was even more pleased. Her finest hour had come. She was free to furnish, change things around, redecorate to her heart's content. Magda gave up the flat in the Reichskanzlerplatz, moved the furniture out, and bought some more. A further storey was added to the palace and a large private cinema built on. As the available furniture was insufficient, Goebbels supplemented it with carpets, Gobelin tapestries and paintings from museums and art collections. In his own sitting room he had a chest which had once belonged to Frederick the Great.

Magda had scruples about all this. She was not used to having other people's furniture in her house, even if by other people was meant one of the fathers of the State. She would have preferred to buy what she needed herself. But Goebbels reassured her. 'It is an official residence,' he said, 'and official residences are entitled to be furnished among other things with furniture and objets d'art from museums.' Moreover, he had permission from Hitler himself. And what the Führer permitted could never be wrong.

When Goebbels became Reich Minister, almost the first thing he did was to pay a visit to Rheydt, to see his aged mother. He wanted to show himself off to his family, and above all to let the people there see what he had now become. He called on the old lady, his brothers and his former headmaster. All Rheydt was delirious with enthusiasm. The visit itself was brilliantly staged – why should Goebbels, who always set the scene for the public appearances of others, not have done the same for himself for once?

The burghers of Rheydt lined the roadside in their thousands. Their city's most famous son toured the streets in an open car to the sound of cheering crowds and the whirring of film cameras. The presence of the triumphant propagandist generated a kind of mass psychosis. It does seem incredible today that such a thing was possible. Total euphoria gripped the population; the banners waved, music filled the air. Joseph Goebbels' birthplace was bedecked with garlands. In the evening long columns with flaming torches marched past that same window from which the crippled young man had once gazed despairingly into the future.

Utterly satisfied with himself, Joseph Goebbels looked down at the people. He despised the masses, knowing full well that these same people, who had formerly persecuted him and now so exuberantly fêted him, would reject him once again if Hitler and his movement were to fail. (As indeed turned out to be the case, twelve years later, when American troops moved into the city. White flags were everywhere to be seen, even on Goebbels' birthplace. Many of the citizens of Rheydt, if not perhaps the majority, greeted the American troops as liberators and waved in welcome to them. All this Goebbels had to experience while still living with his wife and six children in the concrete bunker under the Reich Chancellery. In his diaries recovered later, it can be seen how profound was his disappointment and his helpless rage with the 'traitors' of Rheydt.)

But now, with a feeling of relief, indeed almost of liberation, he returned to Berlin. Those haunting recollections of his poverty-stricken youth had been exorcized and replaced by the memory of his triumphal progress through the city. At last, it would seem, for him the past was really dead.

Goebbels was delighted with his new home. Magda had created a tasteful, cultured background; his was the most elegant of all the residences of those paladins of Hitler who had achieved importance overnight. Magda was well aware of the deadening result of vulgar ostentation and highly studied effects. She had nothing even outwardly in common with the other wives of the Nazi leaders, whose chief ambition was to rig up extravagantly the expropriated castles of now impoverished princelings.

Goebbels himself was at first less inclined to show off than most of his colleagues. He did not allow himself to be addressed as '*Herr Reichsminister*', but merely as Dr Goebbels as hitherto. Hitler had chosen the designation 'Reich Ministry for Information and Propaganda'. Goebbels tried to make him change his mind, on the grounds that even the best propaganda would to some extent be counter-productive if clearly identifiable as such. The art of his job, he explained to the Führer, was to woo the ordinary man or woman so subtly that motive and objective were imperceptible. He therefore suggested a less grandiose title, but Hitler insisted on his own original choice.

Goebbels now moved into the Leopold Palace on the Wilhelmsplatz. Its frontage on the Wilhelmstrasse faced the Reich Chancellery, right next to the Führer's official quarters. On the other side, its main façade confronted the old, highly reputable Hotel

Kaiserhof, long favoured by diplomats, leading government officials and visiting foreign statesmen. In the middle of the Wilhelmsplatz was the Kaiserhof underground station. At a time when few officials ran their own cars, the speedy central connection by underground was an important advantage for all those who had business with the Reich Ministry for Information and Propaganda, whose cumbersome style was soon abbreviated to 'the Promi'.

The Minister quickly established the fact that the affairs of his department were not liable to supervision. He had come last in the pecking order when the 'loot' was being shared out, and Hitler had left the function and scope of his ministry unrelated to those of the rest of the government. Right from the start, and during the whole of the ensuing twelve years, Goebbels fought a continuous energy-consuming battle to maintain his proper sphere of activity.

He appointed as Secretary of State his old comrade-in-arms Karl Hanke, an unusually energetic man and a deeply convinced National Socialist. He did not at first seek to give a consistent stamp to his subordinates, whose members gradually swelled to more than a thousand, or even to select them primarily for their standing in the Party. He shut his eyes to a lot of high-handed action in his department and allowed his departmental heads a lot of initiative.

The chief of the Promi was only too conscious of the difficulties attending his new appointment. He found himself rather in the position of the publicity agent who has to boost goods which have already been sold. For ten long years Goebbels had menacingly attacked the government and the State. Now he himself was a member of the government, and the N.S.D.A.P. was the power in the State, with Adolf Hitler at the helm. He dared not attack most of its deficiencies, let alone comment on the Führer's mistakes. Neither did he dare criticize officials or state installations. From now on he could only hurl his verbal missiles against a dwindling number of opponents. But this frightened handful was not a sufficiently rewarding target for the powerful propaganda machine which had been developed by Goebbels during the years of struggle.

In fact it was precisely the total success of his propaganda which threatened Goebbels with the possibility that his inspired gifts might no longer be required. There are aptitudes which can only be fully used in attack, in destructive criticism, in negative action. The victory of the N.S.D.A.P. condemned Goebbels largely to administrative duties, at best as overlord of the press, films, radio, literature and so on. As a result he acquired something which for ten years had been denied him: energy running idle and free time.

On becoming a minister he changed his appearance; he had his hair tended by a barber, his suits made by the best tailor in Berlin; a specialist in orthopaedic footwear successfully minimized the effect of his lameness. So the youngest minister in the world, as he liked to say of himself, appeared to the astonished élite of Berlin society in quite a different light from what they had imagined. Instead of the foul-mouthed, rampaging tub-thumper, there was a well-groomed gentleman with winning manners, who knew how to converse with charm and intelligence. Onlookers would scarcely notice that Goebbels, accustomed to speaking to multitudes, seemed on social occasions to be inhibited. Only members of his family knew what an effort it cost him to mix with people whom he either did not know at all or knew only slightly. Like most of those who come swiftly to power, he had an inferiority complex vis à vis members of the old established society, and as usual in such cases he over-reacted and behaved arrogantly.

In the course of the next few years, Goebbels acquired his own circle of friends, preferring where possible the company of those who were dependent on himself, such as adjutants and officials from the Ministry, as well as stage and screen artistes.

I witnessed for myself one example of Goebbels' social diffidence. He was present at a New Year's Eve ball (1933–4) in the exclusive Feldberger Hof Hotel in the Black Forest – though why the crippled Goebbels, who practised no form of sport whatsoever, should have chosen of all places to spend New Year's Eve in a hotel patronized by ski enthusiasts, is a mystery. With Magda and two married couples, the Reich Minister made his appearance relatively unobtrusively; he took possession of a reserved table in the background, and ate, drank and chatted with his guests without paying any special attention to others in the crowded room. While their guests danced together, Magda and Joseph remained seated, conversing animatedly with each other.

When the New Year was greeted with a lot of excitement and toasts, one or two pompous people pushed through to the Minister's table with ingratiating smiles on their faces, to wish him good luck for 1934 and to shake his hand. Goebbels seemed puzzled by what was happening. He stood up, held out his hand and said, 'Thank you – very kind' or 'thank you – the same to you'. There was no hint of a smile on his face, only a look of slight confusion, followed by one of utter helplessness, as one after the other most of the guests in the room, about 200 in all, formed themselves into a queue and moved slowly forward to shake his hand, following the example of the first couple.

Magda seemed to find the whole affair rather painful. She remained seated and went on ostentatiously chatting with her guests. When at last the awkward business came to an end, Goebbels sank back into his chair with an audible sigh of relief, mopped his forehead and reached for his glass.

Goebbels did not mix socially with the other members of the Nazi hierarchy. There were a number of reasons for this, not least his compulsive urge for recognition and social approbation. Wherever he was he had to be the focus of attention; he could not tolerate other gods in his vicinity. Intellectually he was vastly superior to all the other gauleiters and members of the Nazi leadership. He despised most of them and did not hesitate to ridicule them. The only real friends the Goebbels had were Philip Bouhler, *Reichsleiter* (member of the Party directorate) and head of the Führer's Chancellery, and his beautiful wife Heli. Goebbels had no competition to fear from Bouhler, who willingly subordinated himself, recognizing Goebbels' superiority. He and his young wife came from a respectable family background; they were versatile, reasonably well educated, and charming, but otherwise insignificant.

With other members of the German leadership he shrewdly maintained seemingly friendly relations. With Göring this was the most difficult. Goebbels had long been jealous of popular, 'big fat' Hermann. Among intimate friends he ridiculed the impudent, blatant way in which Göring ingratiated himself with the masses. The nimble-tongued Goebbels made malicious fun of Göring's many weaknesses, especially his obsession with uniforms. As Göring continued to indulge in his increasingly flamboyant way of living, he became more vulnerable than ever to the attacks of his rivals. He squandered many millions on his residence, his hunting lodges, his sumptuously built 'Karinhall'.* He spent enormous sums from State funds on lavish personal adornment, which included diamonds as big as hazel nuts. Nobody could quite understand how the relatively modest Hitler tolerated it.**

---

*Göring's fabulous estate near Berlin, named after his first wife. (Translator's note)

**Even his political opponents found it hard to believe in the tame lions with heavy manes which Hermann Göring kept as decorative domestic pets. Nevertheless it was quite true. I myself with some trepidation, came face to face with 'Leo' in Göring's palace in the Leipziger Platz in Berlin. One of my colleagues in the Foreign Office was distantly related to

Of course Goebbels was filled with moral indignation over the notorious relationship which Göring, Prussian Minister of the Interior and Reich Marshal, flauntingly maintained with the actress Emmy Sonnemann – though strangely enough he did not reproach Göring with the relationship itself, but only with the frankness 'with which he shamelessly acknowledged it'. Goebbels continued to ignore Emmy even after she became Göring's wife. He could not stand her straightforward, empathetic manner. And since Goebbels could not get on with the Führer's favourite henchman, he restricted his and Magda's contacts with the Görings to the absolute minimum. Magda willingly fell in with his wishes because she herself did not know where to begin with Emmy. They were so different that they could find nothing to say to one another.

Rudolf Hess was the second most important man in the Reich and Hitler's deputy. With him, too, Goebbels had an ambivalent relationship. He regarded Hitler's first standard bearer as warped and clumsy. He accused him of always play-acting, even among his own friends.

But it was Heinrich Himmler, the gullible, cranky, disdainful but nevertheless powerful 'éminence grise', whom Goebbels feared most. Goebbels believed the leader of the S.S. was capable of presenting a greater danger to himself than any other member of the old guard. He made a point of only coming into contact with him when circumstances forced him to do so. Himmler lived a very modest private life, in an atmosphere of lower middle-class comfort. Those who knew him socially and professionally before the outbreak of war could never even begin to understand the infamous deeds for which this one-time school teacher became responsible. Frau Himmler was scarcely ever seen in public; indeed very little was known about her.

Goebbels reserved his deepest repugnance and contempt for Herr von Ribbentrop, however. Anybody who had been so poverty-stricken in his early days as Goebbels, and had had to work so hard and so long for so little, could be forgiven for bearing a grudge against a man like Ribbentrop. The aristocratic puppet, in Goebbels' view, had never done anything except marry an enormously

---

Göring, and when the master of the house was absent on one occasion one of the adjutants showed us round the huge, magnificently furnished salons. Suddenly there appeared, to our no small alarm and astonishment, Leo, with his mane in all its glory. The beautiful, obviously well-fed animal meandered peaceably about over the silken rugs just as he liked, without so much as a fleeting glance at the visitors standing there stock still.

wealthy wife, joint heiress of the world-famous champagne firm of Henkell. Ribbentrop's blasé appearance and frequently stupid behaviour were abhorrent to Goebbels. The blundering, self-satisfied champagne merchant would, in the eyes of the Promi chief, severely damage the political reputation of the movement and most certainly the prestige of the Reich government. Goebbels warned Hitler, both directly and indirectly, about Ribbentrop. Hitler listened to everything without saying a word and soon changed the subject. Ribbentrop remained in the Foreign Office until the bitter end – which for him meant the gallows at Nuremberg.

Before the seizure of power and even for some time after, Ernest Röhm, head of the S.A., was a frequent visitor to the Goebbels' house. At that time he was a powerful, somewhat dangerous man with an army of a million uniformed National Socialist men behind him. Magda did not like him. Her feminine intuition detected the homosexual bias of this politically influential man. One day Magda and her sister-in-law Ello chanced to see how Sepp Dietrich,* Colonel-General, commander of Hitler's S.S. bodyguard, thrust Röhm away from himself with a curse when the latter had apparently come too close to him. After that Magda always felt an overwhelming dislike for Röhm and withdrew whenever he came into the house.

As Goebbels only drank when he was with Magda, and never became intoxicated, he was appalled by such habitual hard drinkers as Ley, Streicher and others. He considered it undignified, betraying a lack of self-discipline, to drink more alcohol than the nervous system could tolerate. Neither did Goebbels like the Minister of the Interior, Wilhelm Frick, whose pedantic, bureaucratic ways and devotion to red tape were so opposed to his own methods. The Minister of the Interior was utterly different from the type of enthusiastic revolutionary National Socialist such as Goebbels had been characterizing for years in his propaganda. Frick was far too correct by Goebbels' standards, relying more on the old officials in his ministry than on the new National Socialists who had been brought in. Goebbels also disliked the fact that Frick and his wife chose their friends from among members of the higher echelons of the civil service and the educated middle class. He referred to Frau Frick's popular house concerts as 'oases of boredom'.

*Said to have been Röhm's murderer.

So the Reich Propaganda Minister could count none of the powerful National Socialist leaders among his close friends, apart from the harmless Bouhler and the sick Minister for Church affairs Dr Hans Kerrl. Goebbels' appointment and status rested solely on his personal relationship with Hitler or, more precisely, on the fact that he was indispensable to Hitler. Goebbels seriously believed that if Hitler were to die, he himself would shortly afterwards be liquidated in one way or another. He frequently expressed this view to his family, especially during the war.

His relationship with the Officers' Corps was noteworthy. Goebbels sought to make contact with General Werner von Blomberg, at that time Minister of Defence in charge of the Reichswehr, drawn by a sort of love-hate relationship with the military and particularly with the Officer Corps. However, when General von Blomberg strongly advised against military intervention in Czechoslovakia, Goebbels lost all sympathy for him. 'The old fool', he said, 'has missed his one opportunity to cover himself with glory.'

Goebbels regarded with profound mistrust the remaining representatives of the previous administration, such as Vice-Chancellor von Papen, the Reich Transport Minister Dr Dorpmüller, Reich Minister Graf Schwerin von Krosigk, or the Minister for Postal Services Graf Eltz von Rübenach, and above all Dr Hjalmar Schacht, and the chief of the Presidential Chancellery for the past fifteen years, Dr Otto Meissner. They remained for him alien elements in the Third Reich. Their expertise was at first indispensable, but they would have to be replaced by loyal National Socialists at the earliest possible moment. And that is exactly what happened in the ensuing twelve years. Only three of the long-serving permanent officials remained to the end in their posts as Ministers of the Reich – Graf Schwerin von Krosigk, Dr Dorpmüller and Dr Meissner.

During the eighteen months after the setting up of the Third Reich, in which Hindenburg was still alive, Dr Joseph Goebbels felt himself too insecure in his appointment to direct his sarcasm at the hoary old man who had been projected from the distant past into the new age. Before Hindenburg even Goebbels himself was dumb, knowing as he did the authority still attaching to Hindenburg's name.

Today it is widely believed that Hindenburg was senile. Those who were daily in touch with Hindenburg in his latter years knew better. Apart from an attack of influenza in the last years of his life, when he lost his customary vitality for about three weeks, and during the days shortly before his death, Paul von Hindenburg was always mentally alert and receptive.

Goebbels' intimate circle therefore consisted only of a few on whom he felt he could unequivocally rely. Apart from his sister Maria, who lived in the house for several years before her marriage, they were principally Magda's sister-in-law Ello Quandt, who had meanwhile been divorced, and Secretary of State Hanke, Goebbels' loyal colleague, who was always in and out of the house.

Hitler was the focal point of Goebbels' private life. Up to the outbreak of war Hitler more or less lived as one of the Goebbels' family. Whenever Hitler entered the house of any other minister or Gauleiter, he was received with fulsome flattery and extravagant protestations of loyalty. It didn't matter what their lives were really like or what they actually thought; when the Führer called he was always faced with a perfect example of model family life. The host would hastily don his uniform, the boys their Hitler Youth outfit and the girls their League of German Maidens garb. The domestics greeted him with the Nazi salutation and nobody dared to smoke. Only vegetarian dishes were served.

But with Goebbels it was quite different. Goebbels understood Hitler better. He appreciated that Hitler had only set up guidelines for the masses to train them in accordance with his ideas. Even if the Führer was frantically obsessed with his ideology (unlike Goebbels, who secretly was not), he did not feel it incumbent upon himself always to be setting an example to others. He was very ready in the company of his friends to get out of his self-imposed brown strait-jacket. He always looked infinitely better in his well-cut dinner jacket than in the brown Party uniform.

Hitler found in Goebbels' house exactly the type of cultured atmosphere to which he aspired. There, at least during the early years after the seizure of power, he could still meet people who fostered his own ideas. The old-fashioned, exaggeratedly formal social manner-isms had been officially set aside, for example kissing a lady's hand and addressing her as 'gracious lady'. Hitler, however, an Austrian by birth, always gallantly kissed a lady's hand and called her '*gnädige Frau*'.

Goebbels succeeded in arranging for Magda's son by her first marriage, from whom she could not bear to be parted, to remain with her, though according to the divorce decree he should have gone to live with his father. This had clearly been achieved by blackmail. Summoning Günther Quandt one day to the Ministry of Propaganda, Goebbels charged him in brief and forceful terms with bringing up the youngster to be critical of the National Socialist state. Without giving Quandt time to refute the charges, Goebbels went on, 'Because of your negative influence over the lad it is much better if Harold goes on living with us. Only in that way will he get an upbringing of the kind we wish.'

Quandt calmly replied that he had concluded a legal agreement with his former wife, according to which he was entitled to sole guardianship of Harold. Goebbels then went further. It had been agreed with the Führer, he insisted, that the boy should be returned to his mother. It was therefore a command on the Führer's part. Quandt could not see what the Reich Chancellor had to do with his son, who was still a minor, and declared that he would establish his rights through the Court of Protection for Wards. 'You are quite at liberty to do that,' countered Goebbels with a wry laugh, 'but you would be a ruined man. We are not yet through with capitalist swine like yourself!' Hitherto Quandt had not realized just how arbitrary, unlawful and blatantly cynical the actions of the new regime were likely to be. 'I yield to authority,' he said as he rose. 'No,' said Goebbels also getting to his feet, 'you yield to your own good sense.' In silence Quandt departed.

In his memoirs Günther Quandt records that he was arrested on 3 May 1933, shortly after Hitler was made Reich Chancellor, and kept in detention for three months. His arrest was obviously not connected with Goebbels' intimidation over Harold. Quandt had no idea why he was imprisoned at that time, neither did he learn it on his release. No charge was made and no trial took place. Such wild arrests were frequent, especially in the early days of the Third Reich; they presumably served as a form of threat or intimidation, though they could also have been the result of personal spite on the part of somebody or other newly risen to power. Hitler may well have known almost nothing about such goings on. On the other hand, he might have considered it most unwise to reveal his intentions for the future quite so soon.

Magda repeatedly intervened with Goebbels on behalf of relatives and former friends, as well as for her first husband. She tried to persuade Goebbels that it would not do for anybody closely associated with her, and certainly not for the father of her son, to be persecuted, arrested or even harassed by National Socialist officials. Though Magda's influence over Goebbels was by no means as strong as that of Emmy Göring over Hermann, nevertheless he did occasionally give way to her. So it could be that Günther Quandt was released at her instigation.

On 13 April 1934 Goebbels became a father for the second time. His daughter Hilda was born. He had again hoped for a son, and could scarcely conceal his disappointment. 'I've now got enough women around me,' he grumbled, though not in Magda's hearing. When the Führer came to congratulate him, Goebbels suggested that condolences might be more appropriate. But Hitler found a suitable consoling thought: 'Just think, my dear Goebbels, how unhappy your sons would one day be always finding themselves overshadowed by a great father. Geniuses should only have daughters.'

Since Goebbels' appointment as minister, the relationship between husband and wife had imperceptibly changed. While a radiant Magda had assured Ello on the first anniversary of their wedding that it was just as if they were still on honeymoon, a honeymoon that was going to last for a decade, a mere three years later the picture had changed. There were many reasons for this. Goebbels no longer had to work at such a pitch as previously. He missed the massive opposition and the exhilaration born of struggle. Anybody else would probably have found himself fully extended by the duties which still remained to him, but for Goebbels they were by no means enough.

In the depths of his being he was a nihilist; a man void of all belief himself, he was continually at pains to convince others, never himself. When he collaborated so strenuously to bring Hitler to power he himself felled the tree with the axe which up till then had been his *raison d'être*. This Germany which he had helped to conquer for the National Socialists might well be a very fertile field for others; he could neither sow nor reap therein.

Though so gifted, Goebbels was not the man for a programme of reconstruction; his forte was negation and destruction. Often referred to as 'Mephistopheles' the name suited him admirably. He denied everything in spirit even while making promises of the most positive kind. 'The time has come,' said Hitler, 'to reconstruct.' What should he then rebuild? He could not set up new armament factories, create an S.S. or Luftwaffe, build new motorways, organize 'Strength through Joy' package tours, or conjure up new housing estates. All these things were for his colleagues, Göring, Himmler, Todt and Speer, to accomplish.

What scope therefore did Goebbels still possess? Promises were no longer called for. It would have been stupid to attack others, since all opposition had been suppressed. His news-sheet was still called *Der Angriff* (*Attack*), but the editor now felt himself to be forced over on to the defensive, not against his former enemies, now powerless, but against his mighty, headstrong fellow leaders in the Führer Corps.

The Minister for Propaganda now had to curb his own sharp tongue, in fact to silence it altogether. It was his duty to be loyal and true to the government, to stick to the Party line and defend the State. For the nihilistic Goebbels this was bitterly frustrating; he would have loved to ridicule the dilettantish ways of the new rulers.

Now that Germany, within her own frontiers, enjoyed general political conformity, opponents were totally lacking – except the Jews. But they were already so harassed that it was difficult to find any further suitable point of attack. Nevertheless the Promi chief set about persecuting the Jews yet more violently than hitherto. He did so without any scruples whatsoever, delighted to have a target at which he could aim.

During the period of struggle, the opposition press had not hesitated to exploit the fact that Magda's stepfather, with the name of Friedländer, was presumably Jewish. This had naturally done some harm to Goebbels, but between him and Magda no word had passed on the matter. Joseph knew very well that Magda only cherished the happiest memories of her stepfather. When, at the beginning of the campaign of hate against the Jews, Ello Quandt asked her friend what she thought about her husband's anti-semitism, Magda became very thoughtful and hesitatingly answered – that Goebbels had explained that it was based on the rationale of the regime. The Third Reich was opposed to Jews, and as Propaganda Minister it was his duty through press and radio to proceed against them. 'That's what the Führer wishes and Joseph must obey.'

Just at this time the woman with whom Joseph had fallen in love during the summer days in Heidelberg, his one true 'Alma Mater', turned up again. They had not met for fifteen years. Anka was married, had several children and was now divorced. Financially things were not going well for her – obviously the reason why she had come. Goebbels, seated at his enormous desk in the palace, was reserved, but found her a job as journalist in Berlin. When the publishing house for which she worked closed down he found another job for her.

By way of thanks, Anka showed everybody the volume of

Heinrich Heine's poems given her by Joseph Goebbels fifteen years earlier, with its very personal inscription, from which it emerged that Goebbels considered Heinrich Heine one of Germany's greatest poets. But Heine was of Jewish extraction and his books had been taken out of the libraries and burned in public. Magda naturally learned of the book and its inscription. Her husband's apostasy from being a devotee of Heine to being the one responsible for burning his books seemed to her quite sinister.

It was naturally to be expected that the widespread anti-semitism in Germany would arouse fierce hostility to the new regime throughout the world. Numerous acts of intimidation, infringement of rights and sheer downright tyranny gave the foreign press plentiful material for attack. Hitler, whose political standing outside Germany was by no means established, disliked such concentrated attacks and pondered as to how he could silence his enemies abroad. He felt confronted by an insuperable obstacle.

Once more the helpful Joseph Goebbels was at hand. The Propaganda Minister succeeded in stifling the attacks for the time being and halting the very crisis which he himself had so vehemently promoted. In March 1933 he announced a general boycott of all Jewish businesses, firms and undertakings, a measure which if enforced would have economically destroyed the greater part of German Jewry within a very short space of time.

The boycott began on 1 April, and was initiated in the most calculated and ruthless manner. Every Jewish firm or undertaking was glaringly placarded; before every shop stood an S.A. man who politely or, if need be, threateningly pointed out to callers that it was a Jewish firm. It can well be imagined what a cataclysmic effect this would have had in small townships or in the countryside. Goebbels, who had never seriously intended to let the boycott run for very long, since it would have disorganized the whole structure of the German economy, ordered it to be halted at the end of the first day or two thereby, as he said, giving world Jewry time for reflection. This coup also appeared to be successful. Jewish circles in the free world did indeed – at least at the beginning – try to help their co-religionists by withholding their attacks against the new rulers in Germany.

On the grandstand of the Avus Arena, Berlin. Left to right: (standing) Margarethe von Hindenburg (daughter-in-law of the Reich President), Crown Prince Wilhelm; (sitting) Magda Goebbels, and (with back to the camera) Ello Quandt

Dr Goebbels on board his motor yacht, *Baldur*. To his right is his wife, and to his left, Ello Quandt

Goebbels in a favourite pose, at the helm of his motor yacht *Baldur*.
Unable to navigate himself, he depended on a crew of two on call from
Berlin

Magda with Countess Edda Ciano, daughter of the Duce, Benito
Mussolini, in the Berlin City Palace

11

Early Shadows

Before marrying Magda, Goebbels had exacted a promise from her that he should have the right to indulge in extra-marital affaires, undertaking at the same time to love no one but her, always to return to his beloved wife and frankly to admit to his misdemeanours. In his cunning way Joseph succeeded in convincing her that such behaviour was necessary for a man of his virility now and again, and could not in any way impair his close relationship with his wife.

Magda did actually agree to this. When passing this on to Ello Quandt, to whom she confided everything, she added: 'Such a brilliant man, who lives three times as intensively as others, cannot be judged by the usual yardstick of the middle-class moral code.' Ello was quite beside herself with indignation when she was told.

A small incident, for which nothing more than a little wind in the night was to blame, now gave Magda her first inkling that Joseph was actually indulging in such affaires. In the new villa in the park behind the Wilhelmstrasse the couple occupied separate bedrooms. Between the two rooms were a dressing room and a bathroom. One autumn night in 1934 a storm swept across Berlin and wakened Magda, who became aware of a door banging to and fro, preventing her from going to sleep again. Thinking it must be the door between the dressing room and bathroom which had been inadvertently left open, and worrying lest the noise should disturb her husband, who was sensitive to things like that, she got up to shut it. To her astonishment, however, she found that the door from her own room to the bathroom was locked from the other side. This discovery shook her profoundly.

She made no attempt to go into her husband's room, but lay awake for the rest of the night. Towards morning she heard him creep to her door and cautiously turn the key, so that the door could be opened. Magda now knew that he was deceiving her under her own roof with a woman guest of the family. For him just a casual affaire, a small misdemeanour, but in the eyes of his wife a serious breach of confidence.

Magda did not say a word; she made no scene, demanded no explanation. When next morning he cautiously asked why she was not looking well, she explained that she had a headache. As she was pregnant, he accepted the explanation without comment, got in his car and drove to the Ministry. At the breakfast table Magda sat opposite her guest. The two women were alone, and Magda forced herself to be more than usually agreeable. As they rose from the table she turned to her guest: 'My car,' she said calmly, 'will take you to the station. You haven't much time left to pack.'

During that same week the Minister for Propaganda began to invite well-known actresses to the house. Apart from control of the press, he was also responsible for theatres and cinemas, to direct or supervise in whatever way he pleased. The actresses he invited came eagerly to his house not least because they rightly thought that personal contact with the Minister could enhance their market value, while he for his part was delighted to meet rare creatures face to face.

A strange medley of names and personalities used to come and go in the Goebbels' house on the Reichkanzlerplatz. Leni Riefenstahl, Renate Müller, Willy Fritsch, Lil Dagover, Jenny Jugo, Lida Baarova, Gretl Sleczack, Maria Andergast and many others were invited by Goebbels. The hospitality offered to these prominent guests was simple, mostly a cold buffet or plain evening meal. In the Goebbels' house alcohol was not freely in supply. There were no orgies or feasting, and even less true conviviality. Sometimes there was music; amongst their more intimate friends Goebbels himself woud play the piano and sing, talents of which the general public were hardly aware. He had a really good voice, and sang folksongs and sometimes National Socialist campaign songs. His particular favourite was the song, '*Siehst Du im Osten das Morgenrot*' (Dearest, look to the east, where dawn is breaking).

More frequently films were shown. Scarcely an evening passed without one or two films being shown, usually foreign ones or those banned for general showing in Germany. In any case most of their guests were already familiar with the films being shown in the public cinemas. On one occasion the Propaganda Minister screened the American film *I was a Nazi Spy* for his guests, in which he was depicted as a conspirator and misanthrope, seated at a huge desk surrounded by enormous banners, busts of Hitler and swastikas. He grumbled later at being credited with such bad taste, protesting 'In my office there are no banners or busts of Hitler.'

Whether there were guests or not, the food served in the Goebbels' house was not particularly good; at times it was actually spartan. Magda was no gourmet, and Goebbels himself hardly noticed what he ate. Nor was he any connoisseur of wine; he delegated the choice to his adjutants, who were usually men of aristocratic birth, of whom for many years Prince Christian of Schaumburg-Lippe, married to a Princess of Prussia, was one.

In money matters, Goebbels was generous. He gave his wife the greater part of his salary, but unfortunately it was never enough. As we have seen, the egocentric, amoral Goebbels was in all matters involving money almost fanatically correct. He only allowed his salary as minister and Gauleiter to be paid to him, plus what his books and articles brought in, and claimed expenses only in respect of official receptions and not for private entertaining to which he, as well as other ministers, was fully entitled. He was particularly careful to see that the running costs of Magda's car were not covered from official funds. So although his income was large, it was never quite adequate. As the wife of a multi-millionaire Magda had often had to grapple with money problems; as the wife of a powerful minister she was still no better off.

During the first few years Maria Goebbels, Joseph's young sister, who was some ten years younger than her brother, was a faithful friend to Magda. She was in her early twenties, of striking if somewhat melancholy beauty. She dressed with simple elegance, was intelligent yet reserved, and kept very much in the background. Although Joseph had every reason to be proud of his sister, he seemed scarcely to notice her, only speaking to her occasionally and at times forgetting she was there. Magda's friendship with her quiet sister-in-law was therefore all the more warm-hearted. She enjoyed her company and was concerned for her future. The somewhat shy young girl, while living in her brother's house, had scarcely any opportunity of meeting the sort of men whom she would be likely to marry. Any unmarried men who might occasionally appear were of a too subordinate status to dare pay court to the sister of their exalted host. Magda therefore went out of her way to invite guests who might be suitable for Maria. As soon as she noticed any interest being shown, she would encourage and foster the liking. Maria finally married the film producer Kimmich. The marriage was a happy one, and survived the collapse and all its consequences.

The Minister increasingly surrounded himself with devoted admirers. Apart from his old friend Hanke, who occasionally dared to criticize, they were mostly sycophants. Those who didn't tell him just what he wanted to hear, or dared to contradict him, would be given a piercing look. Usually they would not be invited a second time. Goebbels did not conceal his inordinately high opinion of himself from Magda either, although in his heart of hearts he must have recognized, envied and perhaps even distrusted her compassionate nature and moral superiority. From time to time his streak of brutality, normally well under control, would erupt.

When the second rebuilding of their official residence had been completed, Magda, once again pregnant, with the help of her sister-in-law, was busily putting the empty rooms in order. Both women were themselves hanging the curtains and Magda was hammering nails into the wall, while the domestics were moving armchairs and other pieces of furniture back into their places. After a great deal of effort on everyone's part the whole place was once more beautifully and tastefully arranged. When Goebbels arrived home from the office Magda proudly showed him the completed effect. '*Engelchen*,' she coaxed him, 'isn't it lovely?'

'Yes, splendid,' he snapped. 'How lucky you are to have me for a husband. But be careful. If you don't behave yourself properly, I shall throw you out!'

At an official dinner in 1937, Goebbels happened to be my mother's table partner. She was known in Berlin society for her sharp tongue on occasion, as well as for her rather surprising ideas. She was, moreover, well aware of the Minister's vanity. 'I have long wanted to tell you, Dr Goebbels,' she began, in a tone as though to pay him a small compliment, 'how very much I admire you, indeed increasingly so each day.'

Smiling, the Minister bowed. 'Many people do likewise dear lady, but your admiration gives me special pleasure.'

'My admiration is chiefly for your financial genius,' explained my mother. Goebbels was visibly nonplussed.

'How is that? I have always refrained from any interference in the province of the Minister of Finance.'

'Yes, of course, Minister. But I am not thinking in milliards either.

I still remember your rousing speeches before the seizure of power. I was deeply impressed. We ourselves were, however, dismayed when you declared that there *should* be and that there *would* be no official, especially government official, earning more than 1,000 marks per month. You see, Dr Goebbels, that's just why I admire you so.'

Goebbels' smile drooped somewhat. 'Please explain a little more clearly?'

'With pleasure, Dr Goebbels, it's really quite simple. You live in a lovely palace in the park behind the Wilhelmstrasse. You own two villas on the Schwanenwerder peninsula and you have your wonderful motor yacht on the Havel, not forgetting the Lanke Castle estate on the Bogensee [see below]. So one must admire your financial genius – I mean, to keep all that up on only 1,000 marks a month!'

What could Goebbels, master of subterfuge that he was, reply to that? He laughed condescendingly, raising his glass and bowing slightly as he turned towards my mother. 'But my dear lady,' he said, 'I would have thought you too intelligent ever to have believed in any such stupid hot air on my part – that was not meant for people like you.'

She was silent at first in the car on the way home. 'He certainly knows,' she remarked thoughtfully to my father, 'how to bewitch his enemies. It is only when you have got away from him that you feel like choking with rage.'

It is impossible to understand, today more than ever, what effect the negative genius of Dr Goebbels had on his contemporaries, who all had reason to hate or fear him. 'A villain with charm,' said a Jewish actor a few days before he left his native Germany. 'As with so many of my colleagues, he has robbed me of any possibility of work and forced me to emigrate. But the way he casts a spell over people, the way he play-acts among small groups and large, that is really masterly. He gives himself out to be so charming while secretly planning the worst – that is skill indeed.'

What part Joseph Goebbels played on 30 June 1934, in the historic purge of Röhm and his S.A. lieutenants, or whether he in fact played any part at all, remains a mystery. He himself went in fear during those days, when so many of the old campaigners were being shot. It is impossible to judge whether Goebbels seriously feared Röhm, Himmler, Göring or any of the other dominant figures in the Nazi hierarchy. In any case, he hastened to Hitler's side immediately the latter's counter-blow was set in train. He obviously only felt really safe when in the Führer's company, and during those critical days remained close to him all the time. It was not until Röhm and his clique, as well as a few hundred others, some allegedly guilty and some innocent, had been liquidated without trial, that Goebbels breathed freely again.

Hitler, it was claimed, was extremely depressed throughout the entire period of the Röhm revolt. If the reports of those who were with Röhm shortly afterwards are to be believed, it seems likely that Röhm and his accomplices really were bent on overthrowing the government – at least it seems quite certain that Hitler thought so. 'I must always keep in mind,' declared Hitler to his cronies a few days after the catastrophe, 'how many proofs, in fact admissions, I had from the guilty ones, to reassure myself that what I did had to be.'

The Führer's nerves suffered badly at that time. Those who saw him then say that he aged visibly. In order to recover he went away on holiday with the Goebbels' family to Heiligendamm, but he did not find on the shores of the Baltic the peace he sought. Was it his guilty conscience about the mass shootings which gnawed at him? Was it fear at the thought of fresh crises or even assassination attempts? He could no longer stand being stared at by the people on the beach, by those who thronged the hotel, by the hotel guests who crowded the terrace where he ate at noon.

So Hitler and the Goebbels' family soon departed, in the bitter knowledge that they could never again enjoy privacy. In future they would have to seclude themselves within their own houses, set apart, protected by gardens and parks. Hitler and Goebbels had become their own prisoners.

The experiences of Heiligendamm led Goebbels to seek an extensive property in a beautiful natural setting. So he purchased Schwanenwerder. Where money was concerned, he must have changed much. Personal erosion of Treasury funds did not seem to matter any more.

The property was situated on a peninsula far out into the Havel, on a well-wooded hillside sloping gently down to a lake bordered by rushes. The large garden had run wild in a romantic fashion. The main structure, which was in English country house style, was not excessively large. At ground floor level there were a dining room, two living rooms, an entrance hall with cloakrooms, kitchen and pantry. On the first floor were bedrooms and a sitting room for the Goebbels, two nurseries for the children, a room for Harold and another for the two girls Helga and Hilda. On the second floor there were a few small guest rooms and rooms for the domestic staff. To accommodate guests other than the family there was an annexe, which had a fine entrance hall and fireplace, with four guest rooms and bathroom upstairs. The property also comprised a very large farm building with stables and garage, a house for gardeners and store rooms. The ponies and the little carriage in which the younger children used to ride round the large garden were also kept there.

The purchase of this imposing property was much criticized, since Goebbels had forsaken his earlier caution and allowed film newsreel in the cinemas to show shots of his family life at Schwanenwerder. He had reached the conclusion that ordinary people expect to see their rulers surround themselves with a certain amount of glamour. With ironic modesty he explained that Louis XIV had shared his view and that the English liked nothing better than to see their royal family drive through the streets in a golden carriage.

As Schwanenwerder was situated on the shores of a lake, a boat was of course a necessity, so a motor yacht was acquired. To crew the yacht it became necessary to employ two men, who had to be brought over from Berlin each time the yacht was to be used. 'You too must have a yacht, Führer,' said Goebbels proudly to Hitler, as one day they were skimming over the Wannsee. 'Would like to,' grunted the latter drily, 'but haven't got the money for things like that.'

Two years later, in 1936, Goebbels purchased the neighbouring property in Schwanenwerder, tore down the intervening fence and had the newly acquired *art nouveau* building transformed by clever architects into his so-called citadel. The former stables became a private cinema, without which Goebbels could hardly exist. Here he could be quite alone, free from disturbance. Even Magda had to telephone first before being allowed to go there, and she soon began to have doubts as to whether he really was on his own in his hermitage.

In making these purchases Goebbels had once more over-extended himself. He used the income from his book *From the Kaiserhof to the Reich Chancellery*, published in 1934 as well as advances kindly placed by the publishers at his disposal, but in the end not a mark remained in hand and his current income was insufficient to maintain the extensive properties properly. From the beginning there were never enough staff.

The lovely estate therefore caused Magda as much worry as it gave her pleasure. The fussy master of the house demanded that

Schwanenwerder and the Berlin household should function at all
times silently and smoothly. How Magda, as mistress of the house,
achieved this was no concern of his. He would, for example, warn
her by telephone towards noon that in half an hour he would be
bringing Czar Boris of Bulgaria and his entourage back for a meal.
When he invited the Duke and Duchess of Windsor to tea at
Schwanenwerder, the first thing that Magda knew about it was
when they arrived. The gardener was hastily despatched to the
village bakery for patisserie whereupon Magda had to put up with
bitter reproaches from Goebbels afterwards because things had not
passed off as well as he would have liked. Such distinguished guests
should never have been fobbed off with the ordinary sort of cakes
which a village baker sells. This illustrates once again his complex
attitude towards members of the old aristocracy.

The atmosphere of Schwanenwerder, the large park, the distant
view over the Havel, more than made up for any deficiency in
hospitality, however. Many a political discussion held there took on
a lighter, more relaxed note. Even the Czar of Bulgaria, one of the
shrewdest and most respected monarchs in Europe at that time,
burdened and sorrowful as he was, laughed happily as he strolled
through the park. The Duke and Duchess of Windsor felt at ease and
appeared to enjoy themselves. Lord Vansittart, Secretary of State at
the British Foreign Office and one of Germany's most bitter
adversaries, accompanied by his wife, a distinguished elderly woman
who spoke German well, relaxed noticeably at Schwanenwerder.

One of the catch words in current use at the time which Goebbels
had picked up was 'plutocrat'. His propaganda machine had just
made it popular. According to the head of the Promi, it was the
most pejorative term that could be applied to anybody. A plutocrat,
preferably of Anglo-Saxon origin, was an enemy of the people.
Plutocrats usually owned a seignorial estate and castle, most
frequently in England. Nevertheless scarcely two or three years after
his own meteoric rise, he too aspired to a seignorial estate and
castle. 'L'appétit vient en mangeant' (appetite comes with eating), as
the old proverb has it. Soon the villa in town and the two residences
at Schwanenwerder no longer sufficed. As Goebbels had no more
money and was in debt for advances, he had to find other ways and
means. Fortunately for him, these were ready to hand. One day the
City of Berlin placed at the disposal of the Reich Minister for
Propaganda the well-wooded estate of Lanke am Bogensee, about an
hour's drive from Berlin. Lanke was to be the official residence of the

Propaganda Minister, a peaceful resort where he could work and relax. The so-called official residence was at his disposal for life. It may seem surprising that in the eyes of the City Fathers an official appointment should have been seen to be for life, but in the case of Reich Minister Goebbels they proved to be right. He too was convinced that his life would not exceed that of his office. In any case he willingly accepted the offer.

Castle Lanke was a peaceful lakeside retreat, surrounded by a forest of pine and fir trees stretching for miles. There was no noisy industry in the vicinity, road traffic was sparse, and above all there were no hordes of day-trippers. The so-called castle was in fact hardly more than a manor house, and on account of its relatively modest size could only serve as a weekend retreat for a family like that of the Goebbels.

So Goebbels, who already owed 100,000 marks (at the then current value) to his publishers, raised more money in order to have another large, modern, very tasteful country house built on the opposite shore of the Bogensee. The cost was estimated to be 500,000 marks, but in the end it ran to some two million (to reach today's [1978] value this sum should be trebled). This did not worry Goebbels, however, since he took the view that this official residence did not belong to him personally, but to the City of Berlin, so that the City should bear the expense. Unfortunately for him the Finance Minister, Count Schwerin von Krosigk, declined liability, an admirably courageous gesture for this minister from the previous administration to have made. A crisis between the two ministers developed, but Schwerin von Krosigk stood firm. Then the film industry jumped in and made good the one and a half million marks which were lacking.

Goebbels, always so superficially correct, did not allow the money to be offered to him simply as a gift. The house at Lanke was given out to be the property of the German film industry. When the beneficiary died, the estate was to be used as a place of retirement for elderly and needy film actors. In the event Lanke is today a boarding school for communist youth.

Goebbels modestly named his new property 'House on the Bogensee'. The building was equipped with every known modern technical device, with air conditioning and huge windows which opened and closed electrically. There was central heating in all the rooms and of course a cinema.

The lust for power and hedonistic extravagance gained increasing hold on the one-time restrained and financially scrupulous Propaganda Minister. By 1937 the fine villa in the park of the Ministry of Agriculture, which had already been rebuilt once, no longer satisfied him. Goebbels cleverly obtained an order of the Führer whereby the house was to be demolished and a truly imposing structure erected in its place. He called it a palace because Hermann Göring had a palace. And as Goebbels no longer had any inhibitions whatsoever with regard to the treasures of the State Galleries and museums, many celebrated pictures from the National Gallery, and valuable carpets from the Art History Museum, found their way into this palace. In fact the residences and summer resorts of most National Socialist ministers, as well as the offices of the leading authorities, were all lavishly furnished in this way. Later, after the fall of France, many things were brought from Paris for this same purpose. So the once penniless Goebbels now had the use of six residences, since he had two, both at Schwanenwerder and at Lanke. When war broke out they were all immediately provided with an air raid shelter, each comprising a smaller, fully equipped dwelling. While numerous families were bombed out of their homes and many thousands had no proper roofs over their heads, Goebbels, each night of the war, had several beds at his own disposal.

While Goebbels was the one who acquired the houses or had them built, Magda had to furnish and equip them and manage the households. For this purpose she received 5,000 marks a month from her husband. It sounds an enormous figure, equal to 15,000 marks today. It was never adequate. Though Magda was very clever with money, she was not a perfect housewife. She did not plan ahead, but allowed matters to take their course. Her parties were always somewhat chancy affairs, and for anyone in the know, like Ello Quandt, nerve-racking experiences. Tea was often not ready when the guests arrived; soup occasionally came cold to the table; the cutlery might be wrongly placed. However, the conversation was always so animated, the atmosphere round the Minister so stimulating and highly charged, that guests were oblivious of such minor failings. Magda never made wordy excuses if anything went wrong; she just carried on as if everything were normal.

To her staff Magda was kind and generous. She trusted them and left them a free hand. Such confidence is not always justified, and now and then Magda would discover how shamelessly they stole from her, what quantities of wine and whisky disappeared from the house, as well as bed linen and cutlery. From childhood she had been accustomed to converse openly and freely at table with family and friends. Even as the wife of Dr Goebbels, Magda relied upon her staff not to repeat conversation overheard at his table, until she learned with indignation that half Berlin was quoting what a few days previously had been said at a meal with close and trusted friends.

Magda was not soft-hearted, sentimental or highly sensitive. Lack of self-control in herself or in others annoyed her. At one time she had a housemaid who suffered from a poor memory, and the few things which the girl did remember were invariably done wrongly. Magda rebuked her and threatened her with dismissal, whereupon the unhappy girl went into the kitchen, turned on the gas tap and lay down beneath it. Luckily she was quickly discovered. Magda ordered her to pack her bags and leave. 'How anybody can be so lacking in self-control,' she remarked, 'as to try to commit suicide because of a well-earned rebuke, I cannot understand. It is absolutely stupid.' The girl fell on her knees and wept. But Magda was adamant; the girl had to go, and left with three months' wages in advance. Ello, more tender-hearted, found the girl another, more suitable job.

One of the most remarkable of Magda's characteristics was her iron self-discipline. Her personal daily routine, regulated almost to the minute, would seem almost painfully exacting, and all the more surprising as she never planned for the days ahead. No matter how late she went to bed and whatever the circumstances, whether she felt well or not, she would rise at the same minute and go through all the stages of a punctilious toilette and make-up routine: forty-two strokes of the hairbrush, always the same number of minutes for her teeth from right to left and up and down, and so on. She got herself ready in an astonishingly short time, and never left her room in disorder. Even the closest members of her family never saw her other than perfectly groomed. She disliked the slightest personal negligence, never failing to change for lunch and dinner or to renew her make-up completely before going out.

Her intelligence was never in doubt; she was if anything too serious-minded. Although always ready to laugh at others' jokes, she herself was not one to joke or to generate a carefree, lively atmosphere. Light-hearted banter was beyond her, and she was quite unable to counter the scornful remarks which her husband so enjoyed making at the expense of others, and more especially at her own.

In her judgment of people, particularly in later years, when she had become embittered, she was intolerant. From time to time she would drop people with whom, for quite trifling reasons, she was angry or disappointed. But she always remained steadfastly loyal to those with whom she had ever been closely connected.

In the second half of the war, when defeatism was punishable by death, trustworthy witnesses secretly informed the Propaganda Minister that Günther Quandt had on many occasions expressed it as his view that Hitler was leading Germany straight into the most frightful catastrophe in all her history. Goebbels was furious; he considered this seditious and wanted to order Quandt's immediate arrest. He would then have been brought before the *Volksgericht* (People's Court) and would most certainly have been executed. Magda met Quandt in secret and persuaded him to be more discreet. She was then able to reassure Goebbels to some extent, and Quandt survived. Had Magda not intervened, his fate would undoubtedly have been sealed, like that of so many other opponents of the regime.

Her general loyalty explains her staunch adherence to her convictions once she had adopted them. In 1930 Magda had bound herself to National Socialism, and thereby to Adolf Hitler, and she remained faithful to both until her death. As wife of the Propaganda Minister she sharply criticized much that took place, poked fun at National Socialist institutions, and was contemptuous of many of the subordinate leaders of the Party, but never once did she allow the thought to arise that she no longer believed in what the Party stood for. Ello Quandt was the only person to whom Magda ever voiced any real doubts. For example, in 1938: 'When our generation has gone,' she lamented, 'there won't be any culture in Germany, no mirth, no real joy in life. Instead there will only be discipline, blind obedience, regulations, commands, B.D.M. and K.d.F. [The League of German Maidens and Strength through Joy].'

She did not hesitate to voice her occasionally highly perceptive criticisms even in front of Hitler. With a boldness which startled all those present, she would attack him, particularly when he made disparaging remarks about women. He owed his rise and his position, she reminded him, not least to the votes of women. It was irresponsible of him to deride women; moreover, he had deliberately lowered their status in Germany, and failed to change the law so as to eliminate discrimination against them. When he tried to contradict her she interrupted him angrily. 'The German woman,' she declared emphatically, 'has the right, Sire, to receive more consideration from you.' Adolf Hitler hastily changed the subject.

In 1939, when she was having marital difficulties, Hitler fell short of the chivalrous rôle in which she had idealized him. 'The Führer,' she said to Ello resentfully, 'was a little lance corporal, and that is what he has remained to this day. He will never be anything more than a little lance corporal!'

She remained true to her faith in Buddhisim to the very end. Most remarkably, she spoke to nobody except Ello Quandt about what may well have been her firmest belief, not even to those who otherwise were nearest to her in life. And even Ello was unable to say how serious her attachment to Buddhism really was. All we do know is that from when she was a young girl until the day of her death Buddhist writings were always to be found at her bedside. She read them only at night when everything around her was quite still.

In spite of her enlightened mind, Magda was superstitious, at times almost primitively so. She often consulted gypsy fortune-tellers, who without exception prophesied that between the ages of forty and forty-five she would meet an unnatural death. When the end was approaching, she remembered and spoke about this prediction.

Magda had no interest in sport. Although in both her marriages she had had a country house near the water, she was unable even to swim. When she did go in the water, which was seldom, she would cling tightly to the boat – 'like a sack of potatoes,' mocked Goebbels. She showed not the slightest interest in driving a car, and even less in walking, tennis or golf. It was only in 1939, during the crisis in her marriage and through her friendship with Hanke, that she learned to ride. As with everything else that she undertook, she then pursued the art of riding with great energy and whole-hearted commitment, becoming an excellent horsewoman, devoted to Mausi, her favourite horse.

Basically Magda was a very healthy woman, but her severe mental suffering reacted on her physical condition, even affecting her heart. Towards the end of the war, Magda suffered, without any previous symptoms, from a suppuration of the Trigeminus facial muscle. She underwent two operations and bore severe pain for several months, in spite of which Goebbels would not permit the doctors to prescribe morphia.

12

Glamour and Delusion

Magda bore seven children in all. Each of their names began with the letter H: Harold, Helga, Hilda, Helmut, Holde, Hedda and Heide. No explanation exists as to why they all have this same initial letter. Remarkably enough, the names of her two stepsons also began with H, though the boys were much older and already baptized before Magda became the second wife of Günther Quandt. The children were all healthy including Holde, who was born two months prematurely and was sickly at first.

All Magda's children were lovely to look at, graceful and captivating. Outwardly they scarcely resembled their father at all, and as far as it was humanly possible to judge there appeared to be no danger of their having inherited his moral disposition.

Magda herself once described to her friend Ello the various temperaments of some of her children. She imagined that they were all grown up and married, and had suddenly learned that their spouse had deceived them. She then pictured how they would each react:

Helga   would seize a revolver and shoot the unfaithful husband out of hand, or at least try to.

Hilda   would collapse altogether, sobbing and weeping, but would soon appear to be reconciled if her husband expressed remorse and swore to be faithful in future.

Helmut   would never believe that his wife would deceive him.

Holde   would never quite get over the infidelity but would be too proud to reproach her husband. Finally, through the breach of confidence on the part of her husband, she would go to pieces altogether.

Hedda   on the other hand, would give a peal of laughter and say, 'Come here, you rascal, and give me a kiss.'

Goebbels was a good, loving and proud father. He worshipped his children. Neither he nor Magda believed in corporal punishment, so none of the children knew what it was to be given a good hiding; nevertheless their behaviour at all times was exemplary. When there were no guests they ate with their parents, who allowed them to chatter as much as they liked. Both parents would listen with interest to what they had to say. They were diligent without being coerced, learned quickly, and were not in the least stand-offish with other children. Though himself inordinately vain, Goebbels would not allow his children to consider themselves better than their playfellows.

For this reason they went to the local school at Schwanenwerder. During the last year of the war when, owing to the bombing, they lived at Castle Lanke, they were taken by pony cart to the primary school at Wandlitz. Nobody at that time, not even Goebbels' keenest political opponent, would ever have dreamed of attacking innocent children. Goebbels, of course, could not forbear from criticizing the teachers and their methods, but he refrained from doing so in front of the children. Neither did he interfere with what they were taught, protest about impositions, or make a fuss if they were detained. He occupied himself often with the children, and played games of make-believe with them; he was pleased by their intelligence, which occasionally bordered on precocity. As far as politics were concerned he left them quite alone. None of the children received any kind of Party political indoctrination, except his stepson Harold in the early days. None of the girls joined the B.D.M. (League of German Maidens), and this at a time when practically every German child of comparable age was compelled to belong to the B.D.M., the *Jungvolk* (German Youth) or the Hitler *Jugend* (Hitler Youth).

It flattered Goebbels' vanity to be seen walking with his children from the Ministry, along the Wilhelmstrasse, to the Hermann Göringstrasse where, behind the wall of the park, his city palace lay hidden. He was fully conscious of the publicity value of such appearances.

Holde was the least lively of the children. By nature quiet and withdrawn, she was often roughly pushed aside by the other much more ebullient children. 'You are silly and a nuisance', they teased her. Holde suffered from all this until eventually it was noticed that she would creep away by herself and cry. Goebbels, whom no one could accuse of being sentimental, was, strange to say, deeply touched by this. From then on he took this child specially under his wing, and she repaid him with a moving devotion.

He remained deaf to all Magda's pleas not to rouse the children from their beds when he came home late at night, and take them with him into the salon. Magda would wring her hands in vain while the children jumped for joy, as their father shepherded them in their night clothes into the cinema, sat them in the front row, covered them up and let them watch a film, even foreign films of which they could not understand a single word. Afterwards he would get each child to describe exactly what he or she liked about the film and the individual actors. When Helga commented about Otto Gebühr: 'He acts so fantastically that you hardly notice that he is an actor', her father remarked that Gebühr had never received a better tribute.

As time passed and Goebbels succeeded in establishing his primacy over the various sectors under his control, the instinctively negative side of his character asserted itself more forcibly, even among his intimate friends and within his own family, and not least in his marriage. He rarely went on trips accompanied by his wife, and would drive round Germany and Italy by himself. He took Magda with him on a tour of Greece in 1936, when the Greek government gave them a magnificent reception, but in the later years of their marriage Goebbels and Magda each planned their own journeys at different times. The reasons for this are not clear. Any other man but Goebbels would have been proud and happy to go about in public with such an elegant, beautiful, cultivated woman as Magda. She spoke several languages fluently, and could have won the German minister much popularity abroad.

As the years went by Goebbels' pride in his wife diminished as his own self-esteem expanded. He became so outrageously vain that he grew jealous of Magda, fearing that people's attention would be diverted towards her and away from himself. Soon she was no longer allowed to accompany him when he drove in his huge Mercedes to a first night at the theatre. If she wished to attend the performance she had to go later in a separate car, which she usually chose not to do; but if she did, she was rarely permitted to sit beside him in his loge.

However much all this hurt her feelings, she did not complain. To herself and others she sought to explain his conduct on the grounds that he was the one in public life; she, fortunately, could please herself.

Goebbels found it hard to accept the fact that when in the company of Hitler and Göring he attracted less attention and earned less applause than the Führer and his even more popular Reich Marshal, with his magnificent uniform and glittering array of decorations. It angered him unduly to be ousted in popular acclaim by theatrical celebrities or sports heroes. However much in his heart of hearts he despised the masses, he nevertheless wanted to be idolized by them.

On one occasion it happened that he was leaving a theatre at the same time as Max Schmeling, German world heavyweight champion, fresh from his victory over Joe Louis and at the peak of his fame. The crowds surging round the popular boxer cheered him and demanded his autograph, while the Propaganda Minister, largely ignored and very much put out, climbed into his car. From that day on he hated the good-natured, worthy Max Schmeling and pursued him with his dislike. He dared not let it be openly remarked, since the Führer had warmly received the world champion and congratulated him. While at the outbreak of war nearly all the leading sportsmen were granted exemption from the calling-up order, and in any case never came into the firing line, Goebbels took care to see that Max Schmeling was among the paratroopers who made the landing on Crete, when more than half of Schmeling's fellow fighters perished. He also instructed the press not to acclaim the former world champion as a great war hero.

How far his personal vanity went, even in very small matters, is shown by his dread of having to wear glasses – a dread that he shared with Hitler. Why the wearing of glasses should have been considered by the Nazi hierarchy as such a sign of inferiority, even as being unmanly, is puzzling. In any case both Hitler and Goebbels had to wear glasses for reading; indeed both had such poor eyesight that documents which they had to read in public were transcribed on a special typewriter with extra large type, and both needed glasses to read them just the same. But it was absolutely forbidden to photograph or to film them while wearing them.

Although Goebbels proved himself to be extremely courageous during the early period of struggle – a fact which has never been disputed – later, as a minister, he was always exceedingly cautious, living in continual fear of assassination. He was regularly guarded by Criminal Investigation officers; police patrolled the surroundings of whatever house he happened to be living in. It is significant that he never allowed himself to be guarded by the Nazi S.S., only by the reliable, mostly older, permanent civil servants. His heavy Mercedes was unobtrusively armour-plated and was also equipped with bullet-proof tyres. This would not have been enough to protect him from hand grenades or a bomb, however, only from revolver shots.

Looking back it is surprising to realize that no attempt was ever made on the life of Joseph Goebbels. It must have been recognized by internal opponents of the National Socialist regime, as well as by those abroad, that, next to the Führer himself, Goebbels was the driving force of the Third Reich.

Like the Führer, Goebbels was unable to speak any foreign language. In Hitler's case this is not surprising, since he attended only a provincial primary school at a time when standards were much lower than they are today. But Goebbels matriculated brilliantly and continued to study thereafter for many years. Languages did not appeal to him, however, and the compulsory French, English and Latin which he learned at school he had meanwhile mostly forgotten. As a result he was unable to read any foreign newspaper or to converse with a visitor from abroad without an interpreter. The explanation for this deficiency, of which he must have been conscious, can be sought in his overweening pride, which would not permit him to take first steps as a beginner, making mistakes and speaking haltingly. He preferred to manage without languages. When listening during the war to Churchill speaking on the radio, or to the B.B.C. enemy broadcasts, he would nod his head at times, or smile, or otherwise seek to convey the impression that he understood the English or French spoken text. It is quite possible that he did indeed grasp something, perhaps enough to be able to guess the rest. Occasionally he would glance through English newspapers with the look of a man who was reading with mounting interest. At other times he would insist on receiving all important articles in the foreign press in German translation.

Unlike Magda, he was a witty and often highly amusing conversationalist. His strong point was irony, which he enjoyed working up to a pitiless cynicism. He appreciated the witty remarks of others, and could laugh until the tears rolled down his cheeks. He liked jokes to be risqué or downright erotic, although he hated obscene or coarse behaviour.

In his youth he had been strictly brought up as a Catholic, having been intended by his parents for the priesthood. But as a student he had renounced all religious belief, becoming an outright atheist. It was only at Magda's insistence, at a time when he was still prepared to meet her wishes, that they were married in church, but where the children were concerned Goebbels got his own way and none of them was baptized. In spite of his anti-religious outlook, however, he maintained great respect for the Catholic Church and its organization. Within the family circle he spoke repeatedly of its rock-like power.

If the N.S.D.A.P., [he would say] had such a tradition behind them, such blindly devoted adherents, such a splendid leader, such rigid, well-defined principles, equally satisfying to the apathetic mass of the people and the spiritual élite, National Socialism could conquer the world without so much as a stroke of the sword. Unfortunately we lack all that which has enabled the Church to endure, in spite of many setbacks, for two thousand years, and which I am convinced will enable her to endure for a long time yet.

However much he attacked priests and other ecclesiastical dignitaries in public speeches and the printed word, in private conversation Goebbels would often express his admiration for their steadfast faith and courage. 'There is no getting through to such people,' he complained respectfully, 'what can you do with people who submit to imprisonment, even to execution, rather than yield? You are powerless against such stubbornness – and can merely raise your hat to it!'

'That's exactly what I think,' agreed Magda.

At the time of his spiteful press campaign, when Goebbels referred to monasteries as hotbeds of unnatural vice and accused the Benedictines of serious currency offences, a diplomatic reception was being held in the Kaiserhof Hotel. Goebbels was offered a glass of Benedictine, but declined. Thereupon François-Poncet, the French Ambassador and later High Commissioner, noted in the diplomatic corps for his satirical wit, who was standing near by, said laughingly: 'But Minister, this morning you swallowed a whole monastery and now tonight you're afraid of a little Benedictine!' Goebbels liked the joke so much that he would often repeat it to his guests.

As far as one can tell, Goebbels had no beliefs at all. People still living, who were part of his immediate circle or his household, agree absolutely about this. To him all human existence was nothing but chaos. He considered himself one of the very few great intellects capable of surveying and mastering it. This attitude explains to some extent his fantastic delusion that he was godlike; gradually he became Goebbelist, instead of nihilist.

Goebbels had no liking for orderly, meticulous office work; he was always a man of impulse, improvising from one occasion to the next. He only ever gave his staff broad guidelines, leaving them to interpret these and put them into effect. In this respect he was a most popular chief. He himself would outline the plan of campaign; he would then leave implementation to ministerial officials, judging the latter solely by results, and concerning himself only marginally with the methods by which the results were achieved. With such a lordly work style ministerial affairs did not by any means absorb his tremendous capacity. He had much more time to spare than one would have imagined possible for a minister with so much responsibility. A great part of the time thus gained he spent in consorting with stars of stage and screen.

It was not until towards the end of the 1920s that it became customary for actors to be accepted in prominent social circles. Eminent opera singers or leading theatrical personalities might occasionally be encountered in a large country house, an embassy or a duke's palace, or at a state reception, but only if they enjoyed a worldwide reputation. Film actors were scarcely recognized for some fifty years; American stars such as Mary Pickford, Lilian Gish, Ramon Navarro and Douglas Fairbanks would stay in Berlin without even the American embassy taking more than fleeting notice of them. They were merely entertainment artistes, it was said, and their job was to amuse cinema-goers. Even if they earned millions of dollars, high society still ignored them.

This rigid attitude had begun to be relaxed before Joseph Goebbels' appearance on the world stage, but with his customary astuteness he quickly seized the opportunity offered by the changing times for his own profit and that of his regime. It was thus through the efforts of the new Minister for Information and Propaganda that stage and screen artistes, hitherto kept at arm's length, became socially acceptable.

It is difficult to judge his actual motives. His approach to favourites of the general public made him popular, even among those who otherwise did not like the Nazis. He also believed that 'show business' personalities who, like himself, had previously been rejected by society would be more easily manipulated. In particular, he felt, certain inhibitions on the part of the ladies would more easily be overcome.

In this he was mistaken. Much to his regret he found more often than not that the actresses whom he gathered around himself enjoyed solid middle-class family lives. With a few exceptions, they did not go in for casual affaires, as so often supposed. However, both Hitler and he always felt more at ease with personalities from the entertainment world than with leading economists or generals. They were versatile people, stimulating and witty, receptive to animated, pointed conversation. Moreover, they were mostly good looking and well-dressed.

In order to attract artistes within his orbit, Goebbels founded in 1935, in the beautiful old Rathenau-Villa in the Skagerratplatz, a social centre for German members of the entertainment world, a modern club with reception rooms, dimly lit cocktail bar, winter garden, dance floor and beer cellar. The architect Benno von Arendt, whom Goebbels had appointed National Stage Designer, skilfully directed the club. It quickly became known as the Artistes' Club, a meeting place for all notabilities of stage, screen and press, anybody in fact, who was more or less well-known or otherwise had good connections. Curiously enough, no questions as to membership of the N.S.D.A.P. were asked; known critics of the Third Reich came and went, even those whose Aryan background left something to be desired. Young people with diplomatic connections were particularly welcome to join, whether belonging to the German Foreign Office or a foreign embassy.*

Goebbels frequently turned up at the club at a late hour to finish off the evening in the company of his 'showbiz' friends. He was scarcely if ever accompanied by his wife, preferring to go there with one or two male members of his own immediate staff. He would then smilingly survey the assembled guests, peering slightly. Benno von Arendt understood perfectly which actresses were most likely to arouse the Minister's admiration. Those who caught his eye would be immediately introduced to him. He would joke and laugh, captivatingly charming.

Any outsider knowing nothing of conditions in Germany behind the scenes, nothing of summary arrests at dead of night, could

---

*Since I fell into the former category I, too, had a membership card. I have an unforgettable picture of the much-envied man seated on a damask-covered divan between two very lovely, daringly decolletée women, while the small but excellent Broadway orchestra played jazz.

scarcely have imagined a better picture of cosmopolitan life. Everything in this milieu, down to the aquarium surrounded by tropical plants in which exotic fish were lazily swimming, was exactly typical of all that which, day in, day out, Goebbels' controlled press dished out to its unsuspecting readers as plutocratic decadence.

Those darlings of the public of the 1930s, well-known beauties of stage, cabaret or screen, would now like people to believe that it was only under duress that they were prepared to accept leading rôles in Goebbels' big propaganda films, that all their efforts to sneak away to the harmless boards of provincial theatres were in vain. According to the memoirs of certain former popular idols, during the years when Goebbels reigned supreme they were forced to live in Berlin, to film in Babelsberg and to collaborate in Goebbels' propaganda films for Hitler's Reich. They emphasize how reluctant they were to work for him, thereby earning, incidentally, fabulous salaries. Worse still, the man whom they all claim to have detested wanted to be the lover of so many of them.

The truth is that while Goebbels did pursue many women, many more than he could possibly have taken an interest in others quite obviously set out to win his favours, and did so in public on many an evening in the Artists' Club. He in his turn loved to invite women guests to his table at the club, to Schwanenwerder, to his Lanke Castle estate – and such men as he could not avoid inviting because they happened to be the husband or fiancé of one of the coveted women. But he had no scruples whatsoever about inviting a woman without her husband, particularly if the husband were away on duty. In the case of film personnel, or others dependent on him, it was easy for Goebbels to arrange for the absence of inconvenient men. When the lady in question declined, Goebbels would be very much put out. 'I simply cannot understand,' he once said to a well-known actress, 'why you are so virtuous and won't come alone. After all you have already had four men . . .'

'Yes, of course I have had four men,' replied the lady firmly, 'but I was married to each of them.'

Goebbels never extended invitations to distinguished, really interesting men. Magda tried to make up for this by giving afternoon parties to which famous artists and writers were welcomed, amongst whom were the well-known portrait painter Professor Hommel and the Swiss writer John Knittel, whose *Via Mala* was Magda's favourite book. Goebbels' children were particularly fond of

General Rommel, who never failed to call when he was in Berlin.
Another frequent guest at Magda's tea-table was Crown Prince
Umberto of Italy.

13

The Festival on Peacock Island

The most outstanding of the many social events which Goebbels organized was known as the Festival on Peacock Island. This turned out to be his biggest social fiasco.

It took place in 1936, the summer of the Berlin Olympic Games, on the beautiful island in the Havel, formerly the site of the summer residence of King Frederick William III and Queen Louise, which remained in the possession of the Imperial family up to 1918. The island, a fairly large one, consisted entirely of well-kept parkland with primaeval tree plantations. The castle itself was well over a hundred years old, small and unassuming in character, consistent with early Prussian taste. When, therefore, Goebbels decided to hold a big festive function there, on the occasion of the Olympic Games which were attracting illustrious visitors from all over the world, the castle was suitable only for use as a cloakroom for his guests.

For the occasion, the picturesque island was connected with the mainland by a pontoon. The latter was stabilized throughout the night by thirty Pioneers★ who stood in dinghies to the right and left of the bridge bracing the steel hawsers with their outstretched arms. Hundreds of guests in evening dress or in glittering uniforms, with beautiful women on their arms, crossed the bridge to the ball past the men in field grey holding taut the ropes.

Throughout the momentous summer of the Olympiad one

★German youth organization.

152

function succeeded another. Each of the heads of the Reich – Hitler, Göring, Ribbentrop and of course Goebbels – staged his own impressive event. Goebbels and Göring in particular vied with one another to offer the world something quite unprecedented. A multitude of internationally famous guests – kings, crown princes, presidents, ex-kings and prime ministers, the Duce naturally, multi-millionaires, maharajahs, oil kings and capitalists – all congregated in Berlin for the famous games. The gnomelike son of the works foreman invited them one and all, and they all came. They wanted to see with their own eyes this Goebbels, Europe's Mephistopheles, the crippled genius and his lovely wife.

Three thousand guests in all accepted invitations for the evening, a select company of great names: all the foreign ambassadors and envoys in Berlin, all the prominent personalities of the National Socialist state, generals, admirals, celebrities from opera, stage and screen, writers and people from the media, leading sportsmen, champion riders, dozens of German princes – some who had ruled at one time, and many who had not. Two of the former Kaiser's sons came, and William III's only daughter, the Duchess Victoria Louise, with her husband, the Grand Duke of Brunswick and Lüneberg, and her daughter, later Queen Frederica of Greece, and Prince Bernhard of The Netherlands with Juliana, today the Dutch queen.

The Führer's old guard were there, as well as the muscle men from Goebbels' early days, group leaders, brigade leaders, S.S. unit leaders in their becoming dress uniforms of black bedecked with silver, S.S. *Reichsführer* Heinrich Himmler, who was later to become one of the most fearsome mass murderers of all time. Many a guest was to be found on the island who had either commanded a detachment or had given orders to shoot on the occasion of the Röhm revolt. An untold number of gatecrashers came too, some bearing forged invitation cards and others managing somehow to slip through the barriers. It was a mixed company, and, as the night wore on, this became ever more manifest.

Lining the pontoon bridge right and left, and along the path through the park all the way up to the castle of Queen Louise, stood a row of slim young girls holding aloft flaming torches. They were dressed as handsome young pages in close-fitting white breeches and satin blouses. They wore white powdered wigs and high-heeled shoes with buckles; white lace cuffs hung from their sleeves. Obeying orders, they smiled charmingly into the faces of the guests.

The extensive island park was brilliantly illuminated. Four

thousand lamps were suspended among the ancient trees, as if an army of coloured glowworms had settled all over the island. Three large dance floors had been laid out on the lawns, each with its own orchestra. Brightly coloured tents were equipped as bars, hundreds of tables had been set out in the park and along the shore of the Havel. Barbecue charcoal glowed in bronze vessels, ice buckets proliferated, the widest assortment of drinks was everywhere available.

The long white-covered tables strained under the weight of an immense variety of mouth-watering delicacies: huge mounds of rust-red lobsters, dishes of caviar, oysters, salads of all kinds, cold turkey and partridge. Tail-coated waiters, menservants in livery and ushers, proffered plates.

Champagne glasses were filled and refilled, except in the case of those who for the sake of simplicity made themselves independent by carrying several bottles under their arms.

The magnificent spectacle of men and women in ceremonial dress became yet more colourful as the slim pages, the satin-clad girls, began to mingle with the guests. It soon transpired, however, that only a few of their number were dancers from the State Theatre, the majority being chorus girls and others from night clubs.

Up till now the festival, although overcrowded, had nevertheless remained a consistently impressive official occasion. But soon a few of the men had shrieking girls on their arms, others had girls on their laps, and yet others could be seen slinking off into the bushes in pairs. Things became generally disorganized. Sedulous adjutants attempted vainly to restore order. Hapless ministerial officials tried to pacify agitated individuals. But the muscle men, familiar with uproar from the early party meetings in Berlin had not forgotten how to deal with interlopers, and put their former skills into practice once more. Bottles were hurled through the air, tables with all their contents were overturned. Pandemonium reigned. Diplomats, ministers, generals and industrial magnates took to their heels. There was no longer any question at all of propriety. Magda had slipped away at the first signs of disorder. Goebbels ran helplessly to and fro; not even he could subdue the evil spirits he had himself invited.

Lower ranks of the S.S. guards, waiters, all sense of duty gone, and flighty girls now dominated the brightly lit island. Full bottles were being seized, later to be thrown empty into the lake. Whole plates of food were thrust into napkins to be taken home surreptitiously. From the bushes came squeals of delight, giggly laughter and the sound of glasses clinking. The night wore on and grey morning began to dawn, but the high jinks still continued, and it was not until midday that the last reveller was evicted.

So ended the mammoth festival on Peacock Island, the most notorious social scandal the Third Reich had seen. Magda wept for shame, her husband fumed, the Führer was indignant, and all who hated the Nazis sniggered.

The next evening Göring's own festival took place. Guests were carefully selected; the hospitality consisted of beer, sausages and Bavarian cracknels. There was soft music and decorous dancing on polished parquet. Disciplined personnel from the ranks of the Luftwaffe were freely at the host's disposal, sophisticated officers were in command. Göring's event was a great success, to Goebbels' intense mortification.

Soon afterwards, during the Biennale in Venice, at the World Film Festival in which Goebbels, as supreme patron of German films, was expected to participate, he had more bad luck. It was his practice to take with him to receptions his chauffeur and personal bodyguard. As both men wore decorative uniforms they were taken for officers by the Italians. For the most part they were orderly and respectable, but on one occasion the chauffeur drank too much, grew noisy, and pestered a lady-in-waiting to the Crown Princess of Italy. The foolish drinker was identified as chauffeur to the German Propaganda Minister. Sobered down, the chauffeur maintained that Goebbels himself had given him the invitation to the official reception. So the responsibility was pinned on the trusted friend of the Führer. Much indignation followed; spiteful tongues even suggested that the Reich Propaganda Minister had purposely introduced the uncouth fellow in order to affront Italian royalists.

Others who loved to attend festivals, at the expense of the State, were Gauleiter Wagner and Christian Weber, Hitler's old fellow campaigner and banner-bearer at the Feldherrnhalle. Both were working in Munich, newly designated with the honorary title 'Stadt der Bewegung' (City of the Movement). Neither of these men could by any stretch of the imagination be called terror-raising thugs, but they brought disgrace on themselves and the regime by the unorthodox festivities which they organized, such as the opening of the Centre for German Art, which turned out not unlike the affair on Peacock Island.

But Christian Weber put all previous achievements in bad taste to shame when one summer evening in the Nymphenburg Castle park, to the sound of classical music, he staged a quadrille on horseback by bareback women riders, all stark naked. Today this might not be regarded as so unseemly, but forty years ago to appear nude in public was scandalous in the extreme. Magda was clearly heard to say, 'What a shameful thing to do in public . . . but a stable-hand like Weber does not know any better . . .'

14

Plots and Projects

Hitler was becoming increasingly reluctant to mix with his ministers and party leaders. The reason for this may be sought in the mounting battle of intrigue which the most powerful figures in the party waged between themselves. Every opportunity to exchange a word with the Führer was used to gain advantage for themselves or to blacken rivals. Dissension, jealousy, resentment and striving for power seem to flourish uniquely under a dictatorship.

Hitler soon wearied of the perpetual squabbling of his henchmen – though it also suited him to exploit their rivalries for his own purposes. During his leisure hours he preferred the company of men who did not abuse every conversation with him to incriminate others behind their backs. It was one of Hitler's many failings, how-ever, that he himself was not immune to intrigue and insinuations. Eva Braun, for example had in this connection no little influence.

Among the few who knew of Hitler's relationship with his '*Tschapperl*'* was Magda. But she was never on good terms with Eva Braun, who was not quite so sweet and unassuming as was later generally claimed. She seldom appeared in public, but within Hitler's immediate circle she criticized his guests and at the same time expected deference and respect from them. Magda was not prepared to give this deference. She was aware that Eva's insinuations, insofar as they concerned personal and not political matters, were taken seriously by Hitler. 'That's all we need,' she complained to her sister-in-law, 'that this little girl, too, should begin to intrigue.'

Although Eva bought her clothes from the eminent couturier

---

*Austrian dialect word for sweetheart.

Romatzki, she did not look so well in them as Magda, who had long been used to wearing model clothes. On one occasion during the 1936 Party rally in Nuremberg somebody in a group of women which included Magda let fall the remark that 'Eva Braun looks frightfully insignificant again today'. The comment reached Eva Braun's ears and resulted in a tearful complaint to her protector, Adolf. It was quite impossible to ascertain who among the women had made this disparaging remark, but though Magda was not the culprit it was sufficient for Hitler that she was present. All the women who were witnesses of the incident were in disgrace, and Magda more so than the rest.

Hitler seemed to have completely forgotten what Magda had done for him long before in the Reichskanzlerplatz. After the Nuremberg episode he sent her no more invitations, came no more to the house, took no further interest in the children. Magda suffered greatly through this, and sought an opportunity to clear the matter up. She asked Hitler's adjutant Brückner to fix an appointment for her. She wanted to make him understand that she was completely innocent. All in vain. Hitler left orders that he did not wish to see Frau Goebbels. Most probably Eva Braun was behind this ridiculous severity, not because of the stupid Nuremberg remark, but simply because she was jealous of the more elegant, more intelligent and better educated woman.

From this time on, for more than a year, Magda did not exchange a single private word with Hitler. He took no notice of Hedda's birth, nor did he send Magda congratulations on her birthday or greetings at Christmas as had been his practice. No presents arrived at the house any more. Magda was beside herself, furious at the unmerited slight and indignant at Hitler's ingratitude. This conflict was never completely resolved. The ice only gradually melted, as the war and other events supervened.

Additional factors may also have entered into this otherwise incomprehensible rejection of Magda by Hitler. She was possibly too outspoken on those occasions when the Führer, at home with the Goebbels' family, was himself actually criticizing the National Socialist State, his very own creation. This would happen mostly at the end of his monologues.

When Hitler reached the end of such discourses, he sometimes invited comments; occasionally he would tolerate criticism, even stand contradiction. Once Magda ventured to condemn the egalitarianism, the proletarianization (she called it training), which the lads in the Hitler Youth and the girls in the League of German Maidens were being subjected to. She explained to Hitler how very much more tolerantly and sensibly things were being handled in Mussolini's Italy. In the Duce's Empire, girls in the Fascist Organization wore becoming uniforms, and consideration was paid to their femininity. No attempt was made to deprive them of respect for religion and tradition.

The Führer listened patiently to all this, and finally said that he had often tried to eliminate the military aspect, the exaggerated masculinity, from the Hitler Youth, and more especially from the League of German Maidens, but without success. 'The spirits which I myself conjure up,' he quoted, 'will pursue me always. You have no idea, Frau Magda, how the intention behind my orders changes by the time it reaches the last troop of girls.'

When Ello drew his attention one day to a cartoon in Streicher's *Stürmer* which was in particularly bad taste, adding that she thought the paper was a real disgrace, particularly because of its effect on foreign readers, Hitler shrugged his shoulders: 'It's only Streicher's hobby, I wish him joy of it.' Magda once spoke disparagingly about several articles in the *Völkische Beobachter* which was, after all, an official news-sheet of the N.S.D.A.P. To the general amazement Hitler, with a dismissive gesture, replied: 'The *Völkische Beobachter* has now sunk to the level of a local gazette!' Whenever anything seriously wrong was mentioned in his presence his only excuse was: 'In the great upheaval affecting our nation of eighty million people, something is bound to misfire, there are bound to be some drawbacks. It will be all the same in a hundred years.'

On one such occasion Hitler talked about the setting up of the association *Lebensborn* (Fount of Life), partly through voluntary contributions by S.S. members, but mainly through State subsidy. Its objective was to provide for the upbringing of the illegitimate children of S.S. men, as well as those born of 'racially valuable' mothers. What for Hitler was of paramount interest was the fact that these children had no parents. The fathers did not bother themselves about them, and they were taken away from the mothers at birth: 'Those children growing up there,' said Hitler, 'are State property, since they are not linked with a family. The National Socialist State replaces their parents and they are bound by duty to the State. Their whole upbringing is directed towards that end, that at all times they are prepared to serve the State with all their might ... yes, they even learn to die for the State.'

Magda's motherly instincts were outraged as she listened to Hitler speaking in these terms about children as State property. 'No State, not even the best, can replace its parents for any child.'

Ello Quandt was even more indignant, 'My Führer,' she protested unwisely, 'you can't do that – breed children for the State! You yourself have neither wife nor child, so in your case certain human feelings are atrophied. What you are proposing is against nature. Things like that will never work out!' Goebbels, Magda and the other guests froze. They had never heard Ello speak out so boldly before. Hitler contemplated her fixedly across the table as if seeing her for the first time. Then he shrugged his shoulders and changed the subject.

Though Hitler did not hold her words against her, he obviously did not forget them either. A few weeks later, at a party in his house, he turned to her suddenly and said: 'Frau Quandt, you are a lovely, very attractive woman, still quite young, divorced and therefore free. Why have you not married again? You are cut out to make a man happy . . .'

'Because,' laughed Ello, 'I have not yet met the right one.'

'Then I will make it my business,' said Hitler, turning serious all at once, 'to find a man for you. A lovely young woman ought to marry.'

'My Führer,' replied Ello, audaciously rejecting his suggestion, 'I would like to decide for myself whether and whom I marry.'

'You've had time enough to think about it. It is your duty to marry again.'

'Duty to marry? *You* say that to me, my Führer, *you* who when among your friends joke about the marriage tie? I have had three children and think that I have thereby done my duty. Please allow me to keep the golden gift of my freedom – that same freedom that you so carefully guard for yourself.'

Hitler stared stonily ahead. For a moment it seemed as though he were about to give way to an angry outburst, then suddenly he relaxed and gave a peal of laughter, 'I must bow to this piece of truly feminine logic. But I don't approve of it naturally. You really are incorrigible!' Ello breathed again. She felt as if she had just withdrawn her head from a noose.

Joseph Goebbels, too, was haunted by constant mistrust even of his closest colleagues and relations. One morning he summoned Ello, who the previous evening had been their guest at Schwanenwerder,

Magda Goebbels acting as official hostess at a reception in the great hall of the Reich Propaganda Ministry during the International Motor Show in Berlin

The riding competition at the Berlin Horse Show. On the grandstand, left to right: (first row) Dr Goebbels, Magda, Hildegard Meissner (the author's mother); (in the background, standing) Dr Lipper, Lord Mayor of Berlin, and Frau Lipper; (far right) Dr Otto Meissner, head of the Reich Presidential Chancery

The visit of Crown Prince Paul and Princess Olga of Yugoslavia to Dr Goebbels at Schwanenwerder on 3 June 1934. Goebbels' children present flowers to the royal couple, watched by Dr Goebbels and Dr Otto Meissner

by telephone to his offices at the Ministry. She was kept waiting in the reception room for two hours, time which she passed understandably in a state of nervous apprehension. She was then allowed to enter. The Minister's greeting was curt. Giving her a penetrating look across his enormous desk, he said sternly: 'You have been passing on to your Jewish doctor the contents of confidential conversations which have taken place in our family circle!' Ello Quandt was startled and asked him how he had come by this allegation.

'A well-meant letter gave me this information.'

'May I see it?'

'No, you may not,' continued Goebbels haughtily. 'You don't need to see it, neither do you need to lie. What was mentioned in the letter, what you have passed on, is what was actually mentioned in our house.'

Ello was in a very ugly situation. She could not categorically deny so unspecific a charge. 'It is obviously an anonymous letter,' she declared, 'and the proper place for them is in the waste paper basket. Moreover, it could equally well have been one of the domestic staff who overheard what was said at table.'

· The Minister tightened his lips. 'The letter is not anonymous by any means. And don't think that your imperturbability is convincing. The guilt lies clearly with you . . . you don't seem to realize the seriousness of the position.' He screwed up his eyes. 'We have stood a lot of men up against a wall . . . that could also be your fate!'

Ello Quandt was struck with fear. 'Doctor, if you don't tell me at least what you are charging me with, how can I possibly grasp the seriousness of the situation? Your massive threats against me, a defenceless woman, are out of all proportion to the charges of the mysterious denouncer. I consider it monstrous on your part to treat me, a friend of your wife for so many years, like this. I demand that you read me that letter and name the writer!'

What she had least expected then happened. Joseph Goebbels showed her the letter. She read it hastily and was at once relieved. It contained only hazy innuendos; the alleged indiscretions were not at all clearly formulated. In fact they were so oblique as to be scarcely palpable. 'Was that all, Doctor? Have you made such a to-do just for this?'

'No, not at all,' replied Goebbels, 'but I can't say more now.'

'Good, Herr Minister, now I know for sure. You only wanted to sound me out. You know yourself that there is absolutely nothing behind it all.' Goebbels was indignant and he started to shout: 'What's the idea? It could have been my duty to hand you over to the Public Prosecutor.'

'You do just that . . . then I should have an opportunity of defending myself and the writer would have to creep out of his cowardly hole. It would suit me perfectly.'

'Hold your tongue,' he commanded, in the same tone as before. 'Don't you ever dare to enter my house again. I will see that you don't go to the Führer's house any more either. In any case, you don't appreciate what an honour it is to be my guest or that of the Führer. You can tell everybody from me why you are not invited any more.'

'Good' said Ello, 'I shall'. Having said which she stood up. outwardly calm but inwardly trembling.

Goebbels would have liked to press his visitor still harder, but he accompanied her to the door, and kissed her hand in parting, in the usual way.

When the door had closed behind her, Ello burst into tears, and stumbled through the spacious ante-rooms to the exit. Deeply troubled by the brutality of such treatment, she drove home through the dense confusion of the Berlin midday traffic. When she arrived home, an urgent message from Magda awaited her. Would she please come immediately to the clinic, where she had just suffered a miscarriage.

Magda was in a very grave mood. Ello assured her that she had never been so indiscreet as to pass on anything that was mentioned in the Goebbels' household. Magda promised that nothing would ever happen to her; as long as she, Magda, was alive Ello need have no fear of Goebbels.

In fact nothing more did happen. Certainly Ello kept away from the Goebbels' family houses for a bit, but after several months had elapsed she gave in to Magda's pleas and again accepted invitations to Lanke, Schwanenwerder and the palace behind the Wilhelmstrasse.

Goebbels received her as if the conversation in his office had never taken place. For Ello the incident was a wholesome lesson. She was now alerted to the incalculability, the mistrust, the unscrupulousness of Goebbels.

It would be a mistake, however, to assume that the head of the Promi was unpopular with his fellow workers. Respect for his intelligence and his indisputable achievements were all the greater the less his subordinates had to do with him directly. But he was hated by a few of his closest colleagues, including Secretary of State

Karl Hanke and later his successor Naumann, his keenest adversaries. They knew much more than Magda of his private life. And both Hanke and Naumann also knew how two-faced he was, that he himself did not believe the propaganda which he and his ministry disseminated. They hated him above all for this. They themselves believed in what they had accepted office to do. Loyal if naïve, they held to their supposed ideals until the Third Reich collapsed in blood, tears and ruins. An unbeliever, a cynic and an egocentric like Goebbels seemed to these two men and many others to be a heretic, a traitor.

Nevertheless, there were many, especially those not in his immediate vicinity, who had every reason to be very satisfied with the brilliant Minister for Information and Propaganda and grateful for the many small and large benefactions which, one way or another, he bestowed on all his fellow workers at the Promi.

Foreign journalists and press correspondents in Berlin would have nothing to do with him, on the other hand; Goebbels simply did not understand how to treat them. An arch-manipulator of people in the mass, he did not take the trouble to handle foreign press representatives in the right way. He scoffed at the idea of the freedom of the press, as recognized at that time in most countries, and thought to prevent foreign criticism by expelling on the spot correspondents who reported in an unfriendly way about the Third Reich. But he thereby invested the victim in the eyes of his countrymen with the crown of martyrdom. In this way the American columnist Dorothy Thompson, who later became world-famous, owed her swift climb in her career to the German Minister for Propaganda, inasmuch as she was the first woman among the journalists whom he banned from the Reich.

In order to enhance the prestige of National Socialism in America, Goebbels hit upon the incredible idea of engaging America's best known publicity expert, Ivy Lee, to campaign on behalf of the Third Reich in the U.S.A. Mr Lee's organization served American industry in various ways, including the publicizing of new products, such as the latest type of car, or perhaps occasionally an actor. It did not do this solely through press announcements or similar methods, but made very effective use of indirect means: a wealth of editorial reports on the product in question, graphic reportage, sending speakers out to the provinces, and a thousand other tricks of the propagandist. This enterprise would naturally cost a few million dollars, but Goebbels was prepared to pay. His apparently useless overseas propaganda swallowed up 200 million marks a year in any case.

Mr Lee's son came to Berlin for discussions at Goebbels' request. The crafty Goebbels invited young Lee to his house, where Magda did her best to win over the important guest to her husband's side. The master of the house tirelessly exerted all his charm. But the young man was no fool and made enquiries elsewhere. What he learned, and perhaps saw for himself behind the façade of the Thousand Year Reich, seemed to him to make publicity on its behalf fundamentally difficult. Matters did not progress, and the great propagandist's inspired plan for a vast publicity campaign in America came to naught.

The Minister for Propaganda now endeavoured to rid the imprudently chosen word 'propaganda' of its prejudicial implications. He placed a strict embargo on the use of the word in commercial affairs. What tradespeople did was to advertise, what foreign governments did was to agitate, what German organizations outside the N.S.D.A.P. attempted had to be referred to as publicity. In this way Goebbels thought to ensure himself a monopoly of the word 'propaganda'. Was he not, after all, in his own view, the only man on the globe engaged in propaganda? His kind of propaganda naturally towered above agitation, publicity and advertising.

Goebbels was always making mention of the fact that his ministry cost less than any other that Germany had ever had. Not only did it not cost the State a penny, but it earned good money for the Treasury. In fact it supported itself on the fees received from radio. Fees at that time, were high; the operating costs of the radio stations, with their still somewhat primitive broadcasts, were ridiculously low by today's standards. So after outgoings had been met, a surprisingly large sum remained in hand. Radio fees furnished the funds for films – Goebbels' indulged favourite. More than once he had declared that it did not matter whether the German film industry made a profit or not, the main thing was that it should be outstanding.

Goebbels was unquestionably opposed to war, not on moral grounds, which he did not recognize, but because he was intelligent enough to perceive the dangers of a Second World War for Germany and more especially for National Socialism.

'A shrewd man should not let a war happen,' he used to say on every suitable occasion. He saw at once how much prestige Adolf

Hitler lost when it was realized that he was actually planning to start one.

But first the Great German Reich had to be united. The Führer's successors would come from the élite, from members of the Teutonic Order and from the Hitler Youth, as well as from the School of Prussian Junkers (noblemen) of the élitist S.S. Guards. Hitler then proposed to restrict himself to the role of consultant. At first he thought of giving the Thousand Year Reich a throne, no doubt because of his youthful veneration for the old Emperor Franz Josef of Austria–Hungary. Hitler for a long time considered that monarchy represented the form of national State most appropriate for the German character – though emphatically a monarchy based on National Socialism and thoroughly permeated by it. The imperial power and the National Socialist Party should coalesce and be one entity. The divide between the old inner German kingdom and the principalities was a thing of the past.

The Führer had not yet made up his mind as to who should be monarch. He thought first of the Hohenzollerns: not the ex-Kaiser of course, nor the Crown Prince, but perhaps one of the sons or grandsons. Prince August Wilhelm of Prussia, second son of the Kaiser, was an early, much-publicized prominent member of the N.S.D.A.P. For a time Prince Wilhelm also wore the somewhat unbecoming uniform of an S.A. group leader. Other young princes of the Prussian House clearly belonged to the movement. Hitler believed, and among his intimates expressed the view, that the best thing would be to train up from boyhood the most gifted youngster of the Imperial House, making sure he was thoroughly imbued with National Socialist ideals. If he proved worthy, he should then be proclaimed emperor, but he should not be given power until he attained full maturity and developed political convictions on an international scale. Until such time Hitler himself would lead Germany, or delegate the leadership to a triumvirate composed of his three closest associates.

Hitler evidently realized that he himself and his generation would only survive if he succeeded in uniting National Socialism indissolubly with national tradition. He was convinced that deeply rooted in the German ethos was a romantic longing for the old Imperial Majesty, and that he could best consolidate his system and so immortalize himself if he were one day in the cathedral at Aachen to set the crown on the head of a young descendant of the Imperial House. One evening in Dr Goebbels' house, Hitler actually depicted the whole scene in the cathedral at Aachen down to the smallest detail, thus realizing in imagination the crowning achievement of his own life.

To what extent the whole thing was just a fantasy will never be known. It is in any case doubtful whether Hitler understood the dynastic problems which would have ensued from the choice between Hohenzollern and Hapsburg. Moreover, there were the very popular Wittelsbachs in Bavaria and the Guelphs in the former kingdom of Hanover.

Goebbels endorsed these ideas; for a man of his talents, there could hardly be a more grandiose opportunity than the coronation of an emperor, and that under the symbol of the swastika. What a fabulous consummation of the Third Reich! To organize effectively such a magnificent spectacle would indeed constitute his most noteworthy triumph.

The fact that these plans gradually receded further and further into the background until finally, after 20 June 1944, they were completely reversed, was due to a number of factors. In the first place Hitler and his subordinates, unaccustomed to power at the start, grew so self-confident that they became less conscious of the lack of tradition. The adulation of their entourage and the perpetual acclamation of the crowds whenever the Führer appeared allayed their concern for the future of the National Socialist State. Added thereto were the experiences which Hitler and his entourage endured at the hands of other monarchies. Hitler's visit to Rome in May 1938 and his stay at the royal court finally put an end to all his ideas about the restoration of the German Empire.

On the occasion of the State visit to the Eternal City, to King Victor Emmanuel III, who had recently become Emperor of Abyssinia, only very few ladies accompanied the German party. Hitler was well aware that with most of the ministers' wives, and particularly those of the Gauleiters, he would make a very poor show. He could well imagine that the royal courtiers and ladies-in-waiting (disparagingly referred to as 'ermine bugs' by Dr Goebbels), would extract the utmost malicious joy out of any lapse in etiquette on the part of a National Socialist lady and would tittle-tattle about it among themselves. It was a well-known fact that Benito Mussolini, Duce d'Italia, never allowed his wife, the worthy Donna Rachele, to accompany him to a reception at court, because the 'ermine bugs' could not forebear from making spiteful remarks about the farmer's daughter from the Romagna. Of course, the Führer put Magda

Goebbels' name at the top of the list of German ladies, but she was unable to go as she was expecting another baby. So there only remained, apart from Emmy Göring and Lore Ley, wife of the Reich *Arbeitsführer*, the wives of the more cultured ministers.★ The arrogant, mostly hopelessly degenerate members of the Italian aristocracies thought that none of the German guests of their king understood even a few words of Italian. They therefore voiced their indiscretions quite freely.

Occasionally caustic replies were provoked by tactless questions on the part of the Germans. For example, one German woman enquired of her Italian partner at table, Prince Massimo, Governor of Rome, whether he could indeed prove that his family tree went back to the time of ancient Rome. His earliest ancestor was supposed to be the Roman military leader Cunctator Maximus. 'What do proofs signify anyway,' replied Massimo in German, 'when we've been told so in our own nurseries for more than 2,000 years?' My mother overheard this response. She was seated between two gentlemen who knew no German, one French and the other English, while her partner opposite could converse in neither of these two languages, so my mother spoke Italian to please him. Whereat Prince Massimo clamped his monocle in his eye, stared at my mother and said, 'My word, you are a *real* lady!' This shameless remark reveals what he thought of the other women who accompanied Hitler.

One scarcely known curious fact of the Hitler story is that Eva Braun travelled to Rome, not in the Führer's special train, but in the through coach of an express train, under another name. Eva Braun was never invited anywhere, but she always received seat tickets for stands along the route where the cars of celebrities were to pass.

When eyewitnesses speak of Hitler's visit to the Quirinal, it is difficult to avoid the impression that the monarchy there was digging its own grave. Numerous embarrassing and comic incidents took place behind the scenes during seemingly magnificent occasions, most of which never reached the ears of the public outside Rome.

The elderly stupid courtiers made their guests aware by countless pinpricks how they were regarded on account of their origin. This court society, together with the royal family, lived in another, completely different world, a world that had had its day, where

★Among these was my mother, who spoke three languages.

personal merit signified nothing, a long succession of mostly unimportant ancestors everything.

After one day Hitler was so fed up that he wanted to break off the visit and return home. Mussolini implored him to stay, saying, 'Have patience, I too have to be patient.' So for the sake of his friend the Führer stayed, but he got increasingly agitated by all that he saw. It angered him that twenty-year-old princes sat near the King, whilst elderly, deserving military leaders were placed at the end of the table. On the occasion of a military parade, in which the royal couple as well as Hitler and Mussolini participated, no chair was provided for Mussolini. He was expected to stand since it was not customary for the Prime Minister to sit in the presence of the King. So Hitler offered his seat to Mussolini. The courtiers all looked askance.

When after a concert Hitler reached up his hand to the platform to the great Italian singer, Benjamin Gigli, the whole court gasped in horror, because the King was forced to do likewise. Never before had the King reached out a hand to a performing artist. After this incident, Hitler, settling back in his seat, turned to Dr Goebbels and Bouhler and whispered quietly, 'Now, how was that?'

During a review of troops Hitler demanded of the King of Italy, 'Why do your generals, who conquered an empire for you, have to stand at the back of the loge, whilst court officials sit in the front row?'

Hitler returned from Rome full of disgust with all monarchies. As they crossed the Brenner he turned to his henchmen. 'Actually,' he said, 'we ought to be very grateful to Fritz Ebert, indeed to all the Social Democrats of 1918, for getting rid of the German princes for us.'★

It is unfortunate that of all places Hitler visited the court of Rome, whose rejection of the dictator Mussolini was so blatant. Had Hitler come to know the royal families of London, Brussels, The Hague or Scandinavia, he would have met modern monarchies better adapted to current social conditions.★★

'What a pity,' said Magda, when she heard all about the visit, 'what a pity. He will now drop all thoughts of a throne for Germany. It was a lovely idea, and would have legitimized our Third Reich.'

★As a result of this, Hitler immediately afterwards enquired of my father what pension Frau Ebert, as widow of the first president of the Weimar Republic, was receiving. On getting the reply that it amounted to about 500 marks a month he shook his head. 'See that she gets more – if possible double it.' As far as I know, definite instructions to this effect were given, but an increase of only just about a quarter was possible, although her pension was gradually increased year by year within the scope of general increases in salaries. My parents and I remained in touch with her until her death.

★★In this connection, Francisco Franco had proved infinitely wiser than his German confrère. He first made Spain into a kingdom minus a king and then concerned himself with the training of the king-to-be, thus sparing the nation the violent upheaval of succession to the dictatorship which would have involved much bloodshed.

15

Casanova

Many women who came into contact with Goebbels during his time as minister have since asserted that he was somehow attractive. None, however, was able to explain subsequently precisely why it was that he influenced women so strongly.

Sceptics will, of course, insist that it was because of the power he wielded, because his official position brought women, particularly actresses, under his jurisdiction. Nevertheless, it cannot have been just power which caused so many women to fly like moths to the lamp. Hess, Göring, Himmler and many others in the highest rank were powerful, but they did not attract women in the same way. Goebbels certainly combined intelligence with charm. And he had adequate time at his disposal at the right moment, one of the most important prerequisites for pleasing women. He was a brilliant talker, had a deep, thrilling voice, and used to make the most acceptable compliments with all the assurance of a somnambulist. He was brutal, charming, crude and attractive at one and the same time. Moreover he knew how to make gifts. He would never bestow great baskets of orchids. Instead he noted what each woman's favourite flower was, realizing that a bunch of lilies-of-the-valley, even a few violets, could convey more than a large nondescript arrangement.

He paid a lot of attention to the gifts he made to Magda. He liked best to give her something when she least expected it, thus achieving maximum effect. He would take note of anything which she particularly admired or mentioned. Long after she had forgotten about it, there it would suddenly appear on her table.

During the war, Terboven, the Reich Commissioner for

Norway, was a guest at the Goebbels' house. When he mentioned the large Norwegian fur producers, Magda enquired how many skins were required to make a mink jacket and what they would cost. Terboven told her, but the number and price were too great. 'What, as much as that!' she exclaimed, 'That's out of the question.' A few weeks later, Goebbels pressed a parcel into her hands. 'Just a trifle I ordered for you, dear,' he said, 'a foot muff in cat fur for the car!' When Magda untied the string, more than a hundred beautiful mink skins met her eyes.

As so often happens, Magda was one of the last to learn of her husband's love affairs. While the Propaganda Minister's licentious conduct was notorious throughout all Berlin, she still believed in his fundamental loyalty. An escapade here and there would be brought to her notice, but this did not worry her. She had after all sanctioned this before their marriage. She also received many anonymous letters revealing her husband's infidelity, but these she just threw into the waste paper basket. When, however, she overheard some remarks of his adjutants which pointed in the same direction, and she too received certain clear indications, she broached the matter openly with him. 'Harmless little flirtations,' he replied, brushing aside her misgivings. 'Fleeting affairs which are always falsely attributed to well-known men . . . nothing at all to worry about.'

A few weeks later, the English and French press published accounts of the amours of the Reich Minister for Propaganda. There they were, with a wealth of detail, names, dates and circumstances in black and white, so that even Magda could no longer doubt. Bitterly disillusioned that he had lied to her, she tackled him once more. This time he reacted very differently from what she expected. He not only admitted his lapses but considered his behaviour fully justified. He reminded Magda of the conditions on which she had married him, that he should retain the freedom to pursue his erotic interests. Magda left him without a word and disappeared back to her room. After that the subject was never again referred to.

Outwardly Magda came to terms with the outrageous demand that she should put up with her husband basking in the company of attractive actresses. She resigned herself all too quickly and settled for the rôle of understanding companion, thus encouraging him to go further in his indiscretions. She devoted herself far too much to her children, although there were two nannies in the house. Looking back, Ello considers that Magda became too much of a housewife, a little plump and just a 'good little mother'. Goebbels himself believed that she consoled herself with her social position and was content merely to accompany him on official occasions. He had no idea how she really felt, how completely she could feign indifference. The truth was that Magda suffered intensely. Outwardly it was all splendour and prestige, thanks to her husband's powerful position, but in fact she was desperately unhappy. The Minister's affaires in the last years before the war were legion. It would be taking things too far to recount them all, however, and tactless to mention names, for the lengthy list contains the names of actresses still highly regarded today.

However, some women who have been linked with Goebbels in fact rejected his advances, preferring to put up with innumerable difficulties rather than to comply with his wishes. Contrary to all the rumours, and in spite of all his efforts, Goebbels failed to make a conquest of Jenny Jugo, the well-known actress, who was happily married to Friedrich Benfer. Although invited alone by Goebbels, she was bold enough to let Magda know beforehand that she would not come without her husband and asked her to include him in the invitation. So it transpired. Goebbels then went to a great deal of trouble to inveigle her into a tête-à-tête, but she cleverly evaded him and diverted the conversation on to a harmless plane. Finally, he had to accept that he was not going to get any further with Jenny Jugo.

Goebbels also suffered a defeat at the hands of the actress Anneliese Uhlig, which was all the more embarrassing as the young girl shortly afterwards placed herself at Magda's disposal as a confederate in her marriage crisis. She was able to prove from experience the shameful means employed by Goebbels; having one's career impeded, perhaps even destroyed, being shadowed by the secret service – such were the least of his threats when met with opposition.

In order to save himself from being taken unawares, Goebbels had had a small but tastefully furnished bachelor flat set up adjacent to his office in the Ministry, with a salon, bedroom and bathroom. A system of bells unobtrusively mounted near his desk notified adjutants and commissionaires when he did not wish to be disturbed – also when he wished to be interrupted.

The Minister would on occasion neglect his duties to the point of irresponsibility. He even kept foreign diplomats, who had made definite appointments, waiting in the ante-room without apology. Not all of them put up with it. Some went away and made official complaints to the Foreign Office about the treatment they had received.

He paid even less consideration to his wife. In Schwanenwerder, where the so-called adjacent 'citadel' was available for such amorous visits, Goebbels would go off in the direction of his studio with a lady friend before Magda's very eyes, making the childish excuse that he wanted to play the young lady a couple of gramophone records. 'He is a devil,' said Magda to Ello Quandt, scarcely able to control herself, 'he is completely heartless.' But whenever he called, she responded. In spite of everything she would always love him.

It seemed to please Goebbels to shock his entourage, and as time passed he paid even less regard to the public in whose spotlight he stood. It is quite possible that it amused him to get his virility talked about in this way, his outward appearance in this respect being so unconvincing. 'Louis XIV of France and Charles of England and the victorious Napoleon had as many women as they wished and all the people still worshipped them,' he declared.

Quite unconcerned he would leave his car, recognizable on account of its number plate, standing all night outside the house of one or other of his lady loves. Soon all Germany knew of the abundant sex life of the nation's chief propagandist – in which capacity he made a mockery of the Nazi exhortation that people should lead wholesome family lives. Numerous jokes about the excesses of the limping devil were to be heard on all sides. The 'goat of Babelsberg'* was one of the most popular names for him. For his coat of arms it was maliciously suggested that the sex-mad 'Giftzwerg' (foul-mouthed toad) should have the picture of a tadpole assigned to him – the tiny creature which consisted chiefly of a snout and a tail. If anybody wished out of caution to avoid mentioning his name when talking confidentially, he would just say 'the tadpole'.

While Goebbels' rivals in the Führer clique pointedly drew attention to his failings, idealists in the N.S.D.A.P. waxed indignant about his lack of consistency and the bourgeoisie were shocked by his cynicism, whereby he wrecked his own and others' marriages. He gave opponents of the National Socialist system in Germany, and above all the foreign press, a rewarding target. The ordinary man, too, increasingly dissociated himself from him. His plutocratic life style alienated the very people whom he had won over for himself and for Hitler only a few years earlier.

So gradually Joseph Goebbels became an almost unbearable burden to Hitler.

*The film studios (chiefly those of the U.F.A.) were located in Babelsberg, near Berlin. From these, so it was said, the Minister found his stars – and starlets.

16

The Baarova Scandal

Enough scandal already existed to bring about Goebbels' downfall. It was generally expected that he himself would finally set the ball rolling (which was indeed what actually happened), and that it would come about on account of the Czech actress, Lida Baarova. This affair, common knowledge at the time throughout Germany, was the subject of gossip everywhere, embellished of course with much conjecture. The public saw it merely as one of many, perhaps the most shameful affair of the ministerial woman-chaser. In fact it was much more; it was a genuinely passionate affair, quite different from all the previous ones.

The Baarova scandal had far-reaching political ramifications of which only a few people were aware. Ello Quandt, Magda's only trusted friend, her support from start to finish, was among these, and after the war she was the only surviving person who knew the whole story. Even Frau Behrend* who was present when Ello told me about it, was astounded at many of the incidents, which showed that Magda had not involved her own mother in it at the time.

The actress Lida Baarova was Czech by birth and nationality, but lived for professional reasons in Germany, the film industry in her own relatively small country offering few opportunities consistent with her ambition and talents. Baarova (who is still living) was dark, fairly short and extremely slender, very pretty and spirited. For the great film public her Slav nationality gave her an exotic appeal. She

*Frau Friedländer reverted, at Goebbels' request to her maiden name of Behrend to eliminate the Jewish connotations of Friedländer. (Translator's note)

lived with the actor Gustav Fröhlich. Their marriage had been fixed for an early date, and their liaison was regarded in film circles already as marriage. Fröhlich had recently acquired a villa in Schwanenwerder, quite by chance close to Goebbels' large estate. He was engaged in converting it into a comfortable home for himself and his future wife.

Goebbels came to know Lida Baarova during a visit to the U.F.A. studios at Babelsberg, in order to see a few shots of the Paul-Wegener Film *Stunde der Versuchung (Temptation's Hour)*, in which Gustav Fröhlich and Lida Baarova played leading rôles. That was shortly before the Berlin Olympic Games of 1936.

Goebbels was immediately fired with desire for her but learning that she was closely involved with Fröhlich he proceeded with caution. Since the celebrated actress had long been living in Gustav Fröhlich's house, the Minister could hardly invite himself to tea, normally his first step. So he started off with car drives with her in the countryside around Berlin, then invited her to call on him at the Ministry, at first ostensibly to discuss film matters and then entirely for private reasons.

The Minister's fervent friendship with the lovely Czech actress was revealed to his adjutants on the occasion of a journey to Prague. Goebbels was incautious enough to take Lida Baarova with him and to stay with her in the same hotel. With characteristic lack of consideration, this happened to be on the same day that Magda's daughter Hedda was born.

Although the 'tadpole' had no compunction whatsoever about being seen in artistic circles and at private parties with Lida Baarova, it was two whole years before his wife learned of the relationship, or more strictly speaking, before Magda grasped that this was not just one of her reckless husband's many escapades, but rather a serious threat to her marriage.

Since Goebbels well knew that his wife could not just accept the affair if she learned how serious the relationship was, he camouflaged his friendship with great skill. Usually silent about his affairs, he spoke openly about this one. He did not find it easy, he admitted to Magda, to remain loyal to her where this attractive woman was concerned. Nevertheless he had resisted temptation because his beloved wife was shortly expecting a child. Just as in any mawkish novelette, Magda floated on a cloud of bliss as she listened to her faithless husband swearing that he had been true to her. Full of pride she said to the dumbfounded Ello, 'Joseph and I are now just as close to one another as ever before. It makes me so happy that he is resisting temptation and being true to me.'

At that time everybody except Magda had long known how deeply Goebbels had become involved with Lida Baarova. In spite of all the disappointments and lies, Magda still wanted to have faith in her husband. She must have been the only person in interested circles throughout Germany who for many months knew nothing of the famous slap on the face which Gustav Fröhlich was supposed to have dished out to the Minister of Propaganda. The news of the resounding blow on Dr Goebbels' thin cheek spread like wildfire round the country, indeed round the world. It became the favourite theme of countless cartoonists, abroad. In Germany it passed from mouth to mouth by way of *double entendre*. Magda heard about it in the end and asked her husband whether there was anything in it. He laughingly replied that naturally the whole thing was a slanderous bit of backbiting by his enemies.

Although the story was music in the ears of most people, unfortunately it was not true. The infuriated Gustav Fröhlich did not slap the face of the goat of Babelsberg but that of Lida Baarova, to her utter amazement. It was at the time when the Minister's relations with the lovely actress were still in the early stages. Gustav Fröhlich had already heard whispers, but did not believe Lida to be capable of such flagrant perfidy.

He waited one evening a few metres away from the entrance to the Goebbels' villa in Schwanenwerder. When Fröhlich saw the warm embrace with which his beloved took leave of Goebbels, anger overcame him. He rushed forward, tore open the car door, which till then had remained closed, pulled the indignant lady out and slapped her face. All this happened in such quick succession that the Minister and his chauffeur could only look on helplessly. The actor then disappeared unmolested. A few hours later Lida Baarova was told to leave his house at once.

Fröhlich's action was an unheard of piece of audacity. To have dared commit an assault on the beloved of one of the heads of the Thousand Year Reich! An ordinary actor to have maltreated the lady friend of 'his' minister, and that in front of the latter's very eyes! Who could hope to escape retribution after such an outrage?

Gustav Fröhlich did. He was not arrested, nor secretly liquidated, nor did he fall victim to a car accident, nor hurtle in the dead of night from his balcony window; what was even more amazing, he was not obstructed in his career. Goebbels, who had so often impeded or completely destroyed the artistic careers of women who resisted his advances, allowed to go unrebuked the man who had struck the woman he passionately loved in his presence.

Possibly the actor's anger had impressed him. He may have felt that Fröhlich had a right to relieve his feelings. What is more probable, however, is that Goebbels appreciated the weakness of his own position, and recognized the miserable rôle he had played in the incident. A gentleman should never have permitted another to strike a woman in his presence. The lover should have intervened, whether or not, like himself who was physically much weaker, he was worsted in the mêlée. It must then have seemed wiser to him to hush the matter up as far as possible, thus making it impossible for him to take any steps against Fröhlich.

How the rumour got around that he himself had received the blow cannot be established. In any case it was willingly believed, which was very likely the intention of the author, and gave rise to much laughter and malicious wit.

One day in the summer of 1938 in Schwanenwerder the Goebbels were entertaining a few guests, among whom were Ello Quandt and Lida Baarova. The Havel shone like a mirror beneath a cloudless sky. The Minister had recommissioned his yacht *Baldur* and invited his guests to take a trip on the lake. Goebbels never bathed in public because of his rather unsightly physique, so he lay in a deck chair in the bows of the yacht. Near him in a wicker chair sat Lida Baarova. Unlike Goebbels, who was fully dressed in a white linen suit, she had on a very scantily cut two-piece bathing costume. At that time such an exiguous bathing dress was most unusual.

Magda and Ello had made themselves comfortable on deck by the cabin. From their superior position they could not avoid looking down on the Minister and his friend. In vain Ello sought to distract the attention of her sister-in-law, who was giving signs of increasing distress, by remarks about passing vessels, or trivial everyday matters. Suddenly Ello noticed that behind her dark glasses tears were pouring down Magda's cheeks. Since Magda was not known to weep, Ello realized that something was seriously wrong. She urged Magda to unburden herself, Magda hesitated, then made Ello promise faithfully not to repeat what she was about to say. Magda proceeded to confide what had been notorious for a long time, both throughout Germany and abroad. 'Lida Baarova is Joseph's mistress,' she whispered.

Had Magda not looked so desperately unhappy, had Ello been less sympathetic, it would really have been quite a laughable matter. But not wishing to make Magda more unhappy than she already was, Ello said that everybody knew, were in fact tired of talking about the hateful scandal. She tried to dismiss the matter as just one of his many light-hearted affairs. Magda shook her head; it was obvious that she was very well aware how serious the matter was. She explained to Ello what had happened a few weeks previously.

One day Joseph had phoned from Berlin to Magda in Schwanenwerder to say he would be home for tea, adding incidentally that Frau Baarova would accompany him. Goebbels often made such visits, bringing women guests with him. Magda prepared the tea table and looked forward to her visitors coming, as she had been feeling lonely in the last few days. Her husband arrived in his most benign mood, bringing her flowers and greeting her almost respectfully. Frau Baarova, too, showed her best side. They chatted for about half an hour, then Goebbels turned to Magda and said, 'I have something very serious to discuss with you. Frau Baarova and I love one another.' Lida confirmed this promptly, with considerable emphasis. 'Yes, indeed – we love each other.'

Magda put her tea cup down and looked fixedly at her husband with the strange woman at his side. She felt as if the ground had opened up at her feet. Before she had really grasped what was happening, Goebbels went on: 'You naturally are the mother of my children and the wife who belongs to me. But after so many years you must of course understand that I need a lady friend, I mean a steady and serious friend.'

Magda's indignant silence he took for consent, or he persuaded himself that it was so. As Magda rose to leave, he got up too. He put his arms around her. 'I knew I could rely on you, dearest Magda,' he cried, 'you are and remain my good old wife.' The 'good old wife' was not more than thirty-six years old. But Lida Baarova was just twenty-four. Immediately afterwards the radiant 'young couple' took their leave and drove back together to the city.

As Magda recounted all this to her friend, Ello's indignation over Goebbels' proposal to his wife knew no bounds. Shaken, she enquired how Magda could ever consider such an abysmally vile request. Her sister-in-law gazed out over the lake and woods beyond, looked up into the empty sky and shrugged her shoulders.

I don't know. Joseph is, when all is said and done, a most extraordinary man. One has to admit that, and I say so to myself very often. A firm commitment to the Baarova, whom he obviously really loves – a, as he calls it, second wife – will perhaps hold him back from countless other affaires, affaires which might ruin him and affect his position. I will try to stick it out, will seek to understand him. Perhaps if I am magnanimous enough I can still keep him by me. One day even his love for the Baarova will come to an end. If I leave him now, I shall have lost my husband for good. So I must hold on to Joseph for later on. When we are both old, he will be mine again.

Ello shook her head. There was nothing more to be said. She knew that Magda was deceiving herself, and that she confronted a situation which would in time become untenable.

Meanwhile the Minister had the yacht turned round and the *Baldur* ploughed through the water at top speed. It was on this return trip that the two women openly clashed for the first time. They met accidentally in the small ship's cabin. The actress had gone there to change from her scanty swimsuit into a tea-gown before landing. Magda wanted to comb her hair before the mirror. They were together in the cramped little room for no more than a few minutes, but that was long enough.

It is not known what was said, nor what happened, but when Frau Baarova emerged on deck, dressed once more, she looked as though she had been mortally offended. The Minister perceived at once that something untoward had occurred, but did not enquire after the reason for Lida's injured look. In uneasy silence they climbed up from the shore of the lake to the house. Magda hurried immediately to her room to change for the evening. Benno von Arendt, the stage designer, and his wife were expected for dinner. Goebbels, Lida Baarova and Ello Quandt remained in the lounge.

Although the actress continued to wear an injured look, Goebbels refused to take any notice. Suddenly Frau Baarova clutched at her heart, threw her head back and began to breathe heavily and in jerks. The Minister was now forced to say something. 'Is anything wrong, dear lady?' 'Yes,' nodded the barely conscious artiste, 'I'm always taken like this if I'm upset.' More exasperated than concerned, the master of the house offered her his arm to lead her into the adjacent salon. There he made her lie down on the sofa. Ello Quandt followed them both. Lida Baarova was after all Magda's guest, and for good or ill Ello had to keep up appearances and look after the Minister's 'second wife' for Magda's sake.

Goebbels had sat down on the sofa by Frau Baarova and decided to ask her what was the matter.

'I couldn't believe my ears what she said to me,' gasped the sufferer.

'Who?'

'Who?' repeated Frau Baarova. 'You can well imagine *who*, Minister.'

He could indeed.

Meanwhile Ello approached the ill-used artiste with a glass of water and two tablets. When Frau Baarova had swallowed them, Goebbels said, 'Come and have a little fresh air, it will do you good,' and again proffered his arm. The tablets had apparently quickly taken effect. Frau Baarova stood up. Ello realized that they would use the opportunity to discuss Magda and decided to follow the pair, who had gone on into the garden a little ahead. But Goebbels had instructed the manservant at the door, who now stepped forward, saying firmly, 'You can't go out there now.'

Ello was about to protest vigorously at being so brusquely treated in her sister-in-law's house, when the arrival of the von Arendts was announced. She turned back into the room and greeted them. Before long, the Minister and Frau Baarova returned from the garden, the Minister welcomed his guests, and Ello asked the film actress whether she felt better.

'I'm absolutely fine,' laughed Frau Baarova exultantly. She looked it; her face was radiant, her pink cheeks glowed.

'Yes,' said Ello to Joseph, 'a walk in the garden with the master of the house is the best medicine.' Things seemed to bode ill for Magda.

Magda came down to the meal, during which it was obvious that she had sustained a serious defeat. Both her husband and Lida Baarova behaved as though she were not there. They spoke to each other, ignoring her completely, paying no attention whatever to her timorous attempts to join in the conversation. But Frau Baarova in her arrogant mood went too far. They were discussing actors and actresses when with a dismissive gesture Frau Baarova exclaimed: 'For goodness sake, Anny Ondra, that silly nanny goat – who would ever wish to look at her stupid capers?'

Ello became angry, but said with apparent icy calm: 'Frau Baarova, it ill becomes you to speak of Anny Ondra like that. She has become world famous by her own efforts, without any patronage whatever. Moreover, she is highly respectable, a versatile, talented woman. She is a friend of mine and I can't bear to listen to you passing judgment on her in this impertinent and thoughtless way.'

There was silence at the table. Frau Baarova, obviously furious, was about to answer back sharply, but at a look from Joseph held her tongue. Magda stayed aloof. When later she tried to bring the conversation round to small talk, she was sharply interrupted by her husband and then by Frau Baarova, so obviously that even third parties could not but notice the rebuff. Immediately the meal was over, Magda excused herself to her guests and disappeared. Ello followed her. In a stifled voice Magda blurted out: 'I can't stand it any longer. I've made up my mind to get a divorce.'

'Quite right, Magda. It can't go on.'

When the guests had all departed Goebbels appeared in Magda's room. He was excited and reproached her angrily for insulting Frau Baarova. Magda calmly and with apparent unconcern told him that she wished to have a divorce. 'I can quite see,' she added, 'that your suggestion that I should have this woman to live in my house is not going to work.'

Joseph, still under the influence of Frau Baarova, made the unforgivable mistake of not taking her seriously. He laughed, told her not to be hysterical and departed without another word. But Magda was not the sort of person who, having once made up her mind about such a significant matter, would procrastinate or back down. It was not an easy matter to get a divorce, however. If Goebbels refused – which he obviously would on account of the unwelcome publicity – a lengthy, difficult process would follow. It would be up to Magda to sue. A charge of adultery would have to be proven. When warned that she would have to produce the evidence in court, she shrugged her shoulders. 'But everybody knows,' she said, 'everybody in Germany is talking about it and the foreign press gives all the details.'

Bit by bit she came to understand how difficult it was to provide legal proof of what she herself knew for a fact, and what so many people were talking about. It was only when discussing the matter with her most intimate friends that it emerged with startling clarity how cautiously, indeed cunningly, the Minister had for years conducted his many affaires.

His adjutants, his chauffeur and above all the housemaid would naturally side with their employer. Nobody could get a word out of them. A wealth of names were available and many more could be conjured up. There was infinite gossip about the numerous affaires of the insatiable womanizer, but it was quite another matter to prove any of it in the eyes of the law.

In her predicament, and quite out of the blue, Magda found an

ally precisely where least expected – in the very heart of the
Minister's entourage. A few days after she had decided to get a
divorce, a private showing in the Goebbels' cinema in their city
palace of the French film of the Dreyfus affair, *J'accuse,* was taking
place. Goebbels was as usual seated in the front row with Lida
Baarova at his side. Magda had ostentatiously taken a seat in the back
row. Just as the lights were dimmed Secretary of State Karl Hanke
came and sat down in the seat next to her. When the lights came on in
the interval, Goebbels did not find it necessary to withdraw his
fingers from the hand of Lida Baarova. Everybody could see – and
everybody did. Even Magda. She stared spellbound at the two hands
intimately entwined.

Hanke grasped what was passing in her mind. So in his faulty
French, on the one hand referring to the film and on the other to the
Minister's scandalous behaviour, he said firmly, '*Moi aussi* . . .
J'accuse!' (I too, I accuse!)

Magda turned slowly round and looked at Hanke in astonishment.

17

Oaths and Conspiracy

A few days later, Secretary of State Hanke, Magda and Ello Quandt met together in secret, thus initiating Magda's conspiracy against her husband, in which the Minister's closest colleague betrayed his chief, but out of a sense of honour and with a clear conscience.

'To begin with, dear lady,' said Hanke, without any beating about the bush, 'you must collect all the evidence against your husband that you possibly can, otherwise all your efforts to get a divorce will be unsuccessful.'

Magda knew how true this was. 'But how do I get it?' she enquired helplessly.

'Through me,' declared the Minister's Secretary of State succinctly. He kissed the hands of both women and departed.

Karl Hanke was a man of few words. Magda still doubted whether he would really dare to help her. But Hanke was risking even more than she surmised. They met again some days later, this time at Ello Quandt's house, which became the headquarters of the conspirators. Hanke took a sheet of paper from his pocket. 'I can bring conclusive evidence, dear lady,' he declared, 'that the Minister has had a liaison with all the women whose names are on this list – in some cases, still has.' The two women listened with horror as Hanke read out the names on the extensive list. They had expected some surprises, but the list of names Hanke read out was so staggering, so outrageous, that it seemed impossible that it be true. 'I know,' said Hanke, interrupting himself, 'that you find it hard to believe, but I and two other reliable people are prepared to swear to this list in every detail – even in court.' Saying which he returned to his list and continued to

183

read out names. When he finally came to the end, all three looked at each other in silence. Suddenly Magda began to laugh, a wild, hysterical, uncontrolled laugh. Hanke laughed too and Ello joined in. In the view of the length of the list there really was no other possible reaction.*

The following day Hanke went once more to Ello's house. Magda asked him to arrange an appointment for her to see Adolf Hitler privately, as soon as possible, without any third party being present. Hanke agreed to do so.

But Goebbels had sharp ears, or perhaps microphones hidden at suitable points. In any case he learned that his wife wished to see the Führer and to speak with him in private. He hastened out to Schwanenwerder and demanded an explanation. 'I forbid you to have an appointment with the Führer,' he stormed. 'I forbid you to go on spying on me, and I forbid you to think of divorce. The Führer would never permit his Propaganda Minister to be divorced.' Magda, who had by now recovered her spirits, laughed at him.

'The Führer's job,' she countered, 'is to look after Germany, not my marriage. If he won't permit the divorce, what does that matter? The Civil Court is the ultimate authority.'

'Nobody,' screamed Goebbels, 'nobody will dare to appear as witness against me.'

Furiously angry, Magda threw caution to the winds. 'Oh yes,' she cried, 'Ello will stand by me. She will tell the truth and say what must be said. She has promised me solemnly.'

'We shall soon see about that,' said Goebbels, as he banged the door behind him.

A few hours later a car with two of the Minister's adjutants drew up before Ello Quandt's front door. She was not in but they learned from the staff that she had gone to a film première at the Gloria Palast in the Kurfürstendamm. As Ello all unsuspecting came out of the cinema, she suddenly saw two well-built, determined-looking men at her side. She was directed to follow them quietly. A seat in a black Mercedes car parked in front of the cinema was silently indicated to her. She felt as if a menacing dark cloud had gathered over her head. 'Where are we going?' she asked as unconcernedly as she could.

---

*A few ladies who have published their memoirs during the past decade should be very grateful to the late Ello Quandt that she consistently refused to satisfy curious journalists and to mention names from her exceptionally good memory, as this would have undermined so many assertions of virtuous resistance to the lust of Joseph Goebbels.

'The Minister wishes to speak with you. We have to take you as quickly as possible to Frau Kimmich.' Frau Kimmich was Dr Goebbels' sister who was married to the film producer Kimmich, and living in a suburb of Berlin.

Ello was somewhat relieved as Maria welcomed her warmly, but the young Frau Kimmich had no idea at all what it was all about. 'My brother wishes to speak with you alone,' she said artlessly. 'It seems to be very urgent.' Saying which she conducted Ello into the sitting room and left her alone with Goebbels.

Goebbels rose from his chair as Ello entered and came towards her. 'What have I done to you,' he enquired in a coaxing tone, 'that you take such a hostile stand against me?' Ello perceived at once that he was on the defensive. 'Would you expect,' she replied firmly 'that I would ever take sides against Magda, who has been my best friend for close on twenty years?' The Minister's face looked stern, but he could not find a suitable reply. He paced up and down in agitation for a few minutes then suddenly halted in front of her. 'You'd better mind what you are doing,' he shouted. '... if we are divorced all Europe will tremble.' In spite of his threatening manner, his statement was such a grotesque exaggeration that Frau Quandt ventured incautiously to ask, 'But Doctor, please tell me, aren't you exaggerating? What has all Europe to do with your marriage? If Magda divorces you, you have only yourself to blame – the Continent has nothing to do with it!'

Goebbels stared at her. Ello realized that she had perhaps gone too far. 'What in God's name have I done?' he demanded with an expression of injured innocence. 'What are they reproaching me with? These wild viragoes when they get hysterical cause no end of trouble. After all I am only doing what every other man does. I *have* a lady friend; well, what's wrong with that?'

Ello had long known that this man had no morals. She also knew how much it meant to him that the public should not see through him. 'It is certainly not unusual,' she replied, weighing her words carefully, 'unfortunately it is even quite usual for successful men as private individuals to have a lady friend. On the other hand, the National Socialist movement, which you also represent, demands through its propaganda, which you yourself put out, loyalty in marriage, a happy family life for parents and children. As the Führer himself has so often rightly said, wholesome family life is fundamental to a nation. But apart from that, every married woman has a right at least to expect tact and consideration from her husband. It is not *what* you have done, Dr Goebbels, but *how* you have done it that makes it impossible for Magda to go on with the marriage.'

Goebbels turned pale. 'Aha! you say that I don't show any tact or consideration?'

'Yes I do and I must. Moreover, Frau Baarova is extremely foolish. She goes about boasting of her connection with you. Even in front of perfect strangers she speaks of "Joseph" or "my beloved". She exerts influence through you which goes far beyond anything which a powerful man like you should allow such a friend to do. Lida openly boasts that you neglect your wife for love of her – and of course it's true in every respect.'

To Ello's amazement, Goebbels looked quite crestfallen. He must have realized that she was unduly well informed. He knew full well that she spoke the truth and perhaps surmised that she knew more than she was willing to disclose at the moment. 'Frau Baarova,' he said finally, after a long and awkward silence, 'is as much a victim of this emotional conflict as Magda or myself.' Ello realized that he was just making an excuse to get away.

'Frau Baarova's troubles don't interest me at all. Lida is your friend, Magda is mine. Understandably enough she can't put up with this situation any longer.'

The Minister changed his tone. 'Promise me at least,' he pleaded, revealing the extent to which she had disarmed him, 'that you won't aggravate the situation. Please dear Ello, do all you can to prevent a divorce.'

Ello did not reply. His face softened; overlooking her silence and assuming an unctuous manner completely foreign to him, he bowed, kissed her hand and accompanied her to the door. He had obviously forgotten that only an hour earlier he had had his wife's best friend picked up from the street with every indication of summary arrest.

Immediately after this conversation Goebbels drove out to Schwanenwerder to Magda with a view to reconciliation. Placing a bouquet of roses in her lap, he promised her never to see Lida Baarova again. He was visibly relieved that Magda had received him and listened to him. She made no comment at all, and Joseph, bidding her a tender goodbye such as he had not done for many years, hurried to his car – and drove straight to Lida Baarova.

Whilst Magda temporized, not at all disinclined to forgive him if he honestly intended to keep his promise, every doorman in the Propaganda Ministry and every extra in the film industry knew that he continued to deceive his wife as shamelessly as ever. With a surprising degree of self-delusion, Goebbels believed he could rely on the loyalty and discretion of his staff. In fact their sympathies lay wholly with Magda.

Not long afterwards, Secretary of State Hanke again talked with Magda and Ello. He began by laying on the table photocopies of letters which his chief had written to Lida Baarova. From the dates and from the text it was evident that a close relationship still existed. But there was still more to be gleaned from these love letters than just the continuation of the relationship. The Minister had obviously promised to marry his beloved, since in one of her letters she had written: 'Does it still hold good – can I still count on what you promised me?' To which Goebbels had replied with a definite 'yes', underlined three times, with his characteristic green pencil.

Magda read the letters through in silence, then with a despairing gesture threw the bundle back on to the table. Hanke rose, bowed and left the two women alone with the letters. Ello, who had been closely observing the Secretary of State, remarked, 'You know, Magda, Hanke is in love with you.' Magda appeared not to have heard; in any case she did not reply. The two women carefully went through all the evidence again, as Magda wished to establish whether perhaps Hanke might have exaggerated in order to bring about the divorce for selfish reasons. Ello repeated more firmly this time that she was convinced of Hanke's love for Magda.

Magda was genuinely surprised at Ello's opinion. She had thought of much else but certainly not of that. 'You do imagine things, Ello. He is a respectable man, indignant at what Joseph is doing to me.' Then she added, after a pause, 'He is in fact behaving chivalrously, as men used to do, when one could still look up to them.'

While Hanke might have been behaving chivalrously towards Magda, as far as Joseph Goebbels, his chief, his patron and his friend of many years, was concerned, it was gross betrayal. Goebbels trusted his old associate implicitly, and although he was usually most cautious by nature he allowed his private correspondence with Lida Baarova to pass exclusively through Hanke's hands. So Hanke alone held the key to the dissolution of the marriage, and hence the switch for releasing the biggest scandal that had ever occurred within the hierarchy of the N.S.D.A.P., indeed within the government of the Great German Reich. However much Goebbels was seen in public with other women, however much gossip there was about his affaires, adultery could only be conclusively established if such letters were produced to the court in divorce proceedings. Indeed, just one of the letters would be enough.

All the same Goebbels thought he knew exactly what he was doing. He firmly believed that none of the compromising letters could ever reach court while his faithful colleague was in charge of them. But Hanke continued to photocopy the letters or bring the originals to Magda for her to see before sending them on.

Whether Hanke was a modern day knight or a despicable traitor is a matter of opinion. Perhaps he was in the first place a romantic. Much in his later behaviour betrayed a naïve idealization of ancient chivalrous tradition. The son of a Silesian engine driver, he had through diligence and natural talent become a technical instructor until swept along by swift political promotion. Hanke and Goebbels both bridged two social classes, the proletariat and the bourgeoisie. At the time of the marriage crisis between Joseph and Magda, Imperial Germany with its rigid code of class distinction lay barely twenty years in the past, but it was already enshrined in memory as a golden era. Current novels and films were particularly slanted in favour of aristocratic society, the world of the nobility, of officers and gentlemen, which those romantically inclined sought to emulate. The then relatively young Karl Hanke could well have been such a one, Ello Quandt believed, in looking back.

Unlike his chief, Hanke did not strive within the new ruling class of the National Socialist regime after power, money and fame. He yearned instead after that genteel world which no longer existed and with which he was only familiar from books, the world of amateur riders, the officers' mess and student fraternities. Their code of honour fascinated him, and perhaps he now fancied himself at last caught up in a real romantic adventure. He would play the leading rôle such as he had always dreamed of; a knightly hero, he would stand at the side of a beautiful lady of rank being shamefully deceived. He was drawn therefore to Magda, since she represented what he most admired – a real lady. To rescue her he would risk his honour and his life, as any gentleman would have done in olden times.

Without betraying Hanke, Magda could not again approach her husband about his continued relationship with Lida Baarova. Goebbels would merely have denied everything. But as luck would have it, a new climax in the crisis was reached. Magda, with some friends from Schwanenwerder, had driven to the city to see a performance of the Cabaret of the Comedians. As she entered her reserved box, she found herself sitting immediately next to Dr Goebbels in the adjacent one, with Lida Baarova. Five hundred pairs of eyes were turned on them, usurping all interest in what was happening on the stage. Here in public for the first time Magda deliberately snubbed her husband. She turned and left the theatre immediately. As Ello remarked, one could feel that everybody's sympathy was with Magda.

The next day Magda asked her husband to come to Schwanen-werder to talk matters over. As he could not deny that he had again appeared in public with Lida Baarova, Goebbels confined himself to assuring Magda that all previous relations had in fact been broken off. He had merely wished to protect his beloved from the '*Schadenfreude*' (malicious joy) of her fellow artistes, by letting himself be seen with her in public once again. He insisted that it was the duty of a gentleman like himself to protect Frau Baarova from the gossip of those who could not forgive her for once having been his friend.

Magda, who knew from his letters that every word was a lie but could not say so without compromising Hanke, demanded firmly that he should drop all such ideas of gentlemanly duty. Joseph heatedly refused. Then, declared Magda categorically, she would insist on divorce. They quarrelled violently. Finally the Minister declared that if he was forced to choose between the love of his wife and his duty as a gentleman towards his erstwhile lady friend, he had no alternative but to shoot himself that evening. Magda's reply left him thunderstruck. 'A bullet in your head would be the best thing,' she said calmly, 'the best thing for the family and for Germany as well.'

Goebbels turned pale, limped, his head drooping, to the writing table, took a loaded revolver from the drawer and stuck it in his coat pocket with the safety catch released. Magda watched him with horror. He hesitated a moment at the door, but as Magda failed to throw herself on his neck and plead with him to go on living for the sake of the children and for Germany, he bowed slightly and departed with the words, 'Farewell for ever.'   Scarcely had the door closed than Magda collapsed. She began to weep hysterically and to imagine herself guilty of her husband's suicide. In spite of his constant betrayal, it seemed to her that she had driven the father of her children to death. Dashing to the telephone, she rang his various residences and enquired for him. An hour elapsed before she was able to ascertain that he was at the Ministry. He was taking a bath, said the adjutant, and whistling. 'I was worried,' explained Magda, concealing her relief. 'My husband was not feeling well when he left.' 'You can feel quite reassured, dear lady,' came from the other end of the wire, 'the Minister is in the best of spirits. We have both just had a good laugh.' The next day she learned from Hanke that Joseph, having taken a bath, had driven out to Lanke to spend the rest of the evening with a lady friend. Not Lida Baarova this time, however; he deceived her as well as his wife.

From then on, events in that summer of 1938 moved fast. Magda held her husband in contempt and was more than ever determined to bring to an end her shameful marriage. When she received a further bundle of love letters from Hanke which Goebbels had recently written to Lida Baarova, she forced him to make the most dramatic of his pronouncements hitherto, revealing to her that she had indeed been living with a monster for the past eight years – though, in spite of everything, she had loved him.

'I have got absolutely reliable proof,' she began, 'that you never intended to part from Frau Baarova. You have kept the relationship going all along. Now we must finish with each other. I hate all this play acting, these lies, this hypocrisy.' But Goebbels still continued to deny the facts. He claimed to have sent Lida packing, and to have erased all memory of her from his mind.

'I can't believe a word you say,' she countered angrily. 'I know you to be incapable of speaking the truth.'

'What do you wish me to do to make you believe me?' he cried despairingly. Then, after a pause, he flashed her a look of triumph: 'Well all right, I give you my word of honour.'

'Your word of honour? That's not worth anything. It's all lies with you.' Magda's voice was full of contempt. Goebbels stiffened. His lips went pale and for a whole minute he remained speechless.

'What are you daring to do to me?' he groaned finally. 'Magda, you doubt my word of honour? That's a dreadful insult. But I will take it, because I love you. Tell me, what must I do to make you believe me? There is truly ... nothing more at all between Lida and me!'

In Magda's handbag was the letter which he had that morning written to tell Lida that he would call on her that evening. 'So swear to me on the lives of our children that you have actually broken with Lida Baarova and will never take up with her again.' He will never do it, she thought to herself. He can't do it; now at last he must confess and release me. But Goebbels went across to the bureau where photographs of his five children stood in silver frames. With a meaningful gesture he placed his right hand on the picture of his eldest daughter, and while Magda looked on with a feeling of dread in her heart he said in his deep, vibrant voice, slowly stressing each word: 'I have for a long time past had no relationship whatsoever with Frau Baarova, this I swear on the lives of our children.'

When Goebbels had sworn his frightful oath, he turned to Magda, still standing in the middle of the room with a stony expression on her face. 'Do you believe me now?'

'No,' she screamed, and ran sobbing from the room. Goebbels went out to his car and was driven back to town.

That night at 3 a.m. Magda went to the house of her sister-in-law. Without saying a word, she fell unconscious to the ground. Looking pale and strained, she sat a little later in the armchair, smoking one cigarette after another. Finally, she said, 'The best thing would be for me and my children to die.' After she had calmed down a little and given Ello an account of the events at Schwanenwerder she went on, 'Can you begin to understand how anyone can lie so fearfully? Why go on? I will let myself be divorced. He is a devil and I made him my god.'

18

Goebbels falls into Disgrace

The next day she acted; Magda summoned Hanke and together they examined all the evidence which had been collected. It was enough, more than enough. A few actresses found the courage – and it really did require courage – to offer to act as witnesses for Magda in the divorce proceedings. In writing and by statutory declaration they described the threats and other unlawful means by which the Minister had forced his attentions on them.

So extensive were the proofs of adultery that they would have been conclusive in any German divorce court. But neither Magda nor Joseph were private individuals who could simply make application to the court for their rights. For both, Adolf Hitler was their Leader and Supreme Judicial Authority. This is so in all totalitarian states, more especially so when the litigants themselves are members of the State hierarchy. If Hitler vetoed it, there could be no divorce, even if lawyers held a different opinion.*

Magda, like Joseph, knew therefore that the road to separation lay only through Hitler. Hanke had the courage to confess he was the traitor, well aware that he was thereby gravely risking both his career and his life. He undertook to warn Hitler by dropping hints as to what was happening, and was instrumental in arranging an

---

*Hitler had in no fewer than six cases arbitrarily refused to allow a divorce purely on the grounds that the number of divorces among his ministers and party leaders was above the average, and this situation could not go on. Moreover, he had also forbidden the divorce of my sister, who had to wait until after the collapse of the Third Reich to get her freedom.

The wedding of Maria Goebbels to the film producer Max Kimmich at Schwanenwerder on 2 February 1938. Front row, left to right: Hilde Goebbels, Helmut Goebbels, Dr Joseph Goebbels, the bridal pair, Helga Goebbels, Frau Goebbels (mother of the Minister); second row, left to right: Herr and Frau Kimmich (brother and sister-in-law of the bridegroom), Magda, Count Helldorff, the Chief of Police, Ello Quandt, Karl Hanke, Countess Helldorff, Harold Quandt

A State reception for the Italian Foreign Minister, Count Ciano. Adolf Hitler conducts his visitors through the main gallery of the new Reich Chancellery

Secretary of State, Karl Hanke. Following his conspiracy with Magda against Goebbels, he was transferred from the *Promi* to be Gauleiter and Oberpräsident of Lower Silesia

Gala night at the Berlin Opera House. Front row, left to right: Leni Riefenstahl, Magda Goebbels, and the Italian Ambassador, Cerrutti. Standing, left to right: Prince Christian von Schaumburg-Lippe, the actor Willi Fritsch and Dr Goebbels

interview for Magda with the Head of State. This time Hitler received her at once, with a charming smile. Contrary to his usual practice he himself did not speak, but listened attentively.

Magda spoke for a full hour. She showed him all the written evidence and finally told him about the blasphemous oath which Goebbels had sworn on the lives of their children. Hitler was horrified. Already much about the affaires of his Propaganda Minister had reached his ears. He had put most of it down to the idle talk of jealous rivals, to agitation on the part of political opponents. He had received reports from the Gestapo, but had considered them insignificant escapades which he was inclined to overlook.

To Magda's disappointment he was even now less indignant over the behaviour of his minister as a husband than over his negligent attitude to his duties; above all he was horrified that his minister had kept a foreign diplomat waiting in spite of a previous appointment having been made, while he was entertaining a lady in an adjacent private room. Hitler also got very heated over the unscrupulous way in which Goebbels had exploited his official position to force women who resisted him to be compliant. He showed a certain amount of understanding for Magda's suffering, it is true, but the attendant circumstances which could possibly have political consequences concerned him much more.

Finally Hitler told her that he wished to turn the whole matter over in his mind. Then, with friendly words of comfort and exhorting her to be patient, he accompanied her to the door of his vast office.

Next day he summoned Goebbels. Little is known of the interview, as Hitler and Goebbels both kept quiet about it – hence the many conflicting accounts. The Führer appears to have repeated Magda's allegations. Goebbels is supposed to have laughed at every point, putting it all down to the hysteria of an all too sensitive woman, whose nerves were under constant strain through frequent pregnancies.

To reinforce what he had said, he offered the Führer his word of honour, and although he had perused Magda's supporting documents Hitler appears as a result to have believed his minister more than the latter's wife. He held out his hand to Goebbels. 'All right, then, Doctor. There is no question of a divorce. But do all you can to reconcile your wife.' Goebbels emerged from this battle the victor.

'The Führer will not permit a divorce,' he announced to Magda, 'so we must go on putting up with each other.' In despair, Magda consulted Ello and Hanke. The latter, indignant at Hitler's attitude, took it upon himself once more to have a word with the all powerful head of the Greater German Reich. Amazingly enough, this initiative was far more successful than Magda's visit. Hitler held Hanke in high esteem. He was a quiet man, who led an exemplary life, above all an idealist committed wholeheartedly to National Socialism. The Führer no longer faced an excitable woman but a calm man who deserved to be trusted, and who was moreover the closest colleague of the accused husband.

Hanke repeated word for word what Magda had already alleged; with practical, impartial thoroughness he submitted all the evidence, thus convicting his minister not only of a series of adulterous liaisons, but also, what would understandably weigh more heavily with Hitler, of having given a false word of honour to him, the Führer himself.

When he had convinced Hitler, Hanke went still further: 'These are not romances, my Führer, but infamous acts. Joseph Goebbels has betrayed our ideals. The whole world is laughing at us, since that same man who advocates our cause at the top of his voice himself treats it with contempt. In the past in a thousand speeches Goebbels has asserted that any actress who wishes to make a career for herself in Germany must first go to bed with the Jewish film producer. Today Goebbels himself is the greatest film Jew.'

Hitler banged the table hard with his fist and screamed that Hanke was quite right. Yes indeed, his minister had lied to him. Even by his handshake Goebbels had perjured himself.

From then on Joseph Goebbels was in the deepest disgrace. The Führer only received him officially, and then as seldom and as briefly as possible. Although Goebbels in growing despair repeatedly requested personal discussion, Hitler always refused with icy severity. The Minister was not allowed to take meals with Hitler either in Obersalzburg or in Berlin. He was also notified that he was persona non grata at the Führer's evening parties.

The sensational news of Goebbels' downfall, his false word of honour and his banishment from Hitler's circle, flew like wildfire round Berlin, evoking sheer delight on all sides. Daily, almost hourly, Goebbels' dismissal as minister was awaited. The 'tadpole' was regarded as an outlaw, his political career in jeopardy. Soon it was whispered that he was applying for an appointment as ambassador to Tokyo. But apart from Magda nobody else knew what Hitler had said to Hanke: 'Where women are concerned he has no scruples, he even lies to me. But where it is a question of politics, I can rely on my Goebbels. Besides, I shall be needing him again soon.'

Since Adolf Hitler needed Joseph Goebbels he could not permit his divorce. There had been too many divorce scandals in the hierarchy already. Particularly in the case of the Minister for Propaganda there could not possibly be any question of divorce; his wife and her five enchanting children were so well known in public. So the Führer arranged for Magda to see him once more. He explained quite frankly that he now believed every word that she had said to him at the first interview. But he had to ask her, in the interests of Germany and the N.S.D.A.P., to refrain from a divorce.

Magda shook her head vigorously and said nothing. Whereupon Hitler said that he would be satisfied if for the present she remained outwardly with her husband. She could make any condition she liked as long as a scandal, which would provide Germany's enemies (meaning the enemies of National Socialism) with so much fuel for spiteful talk, was avoided. Magda realized that she could do nothing against what was in effect an order of the Führer. She would at least state her terms. In the first place she demanded the expulsion of Lida Baarova.

That same evening Julius Schaub, Hitler's adjutant, went to the actress's house and told her that she had to leave Germany within twenty-four hours. Frau Baarova suffered an attack of hysteria, which quickly developed into a heart attack. Dr Morell, later Hitler's very controversial personal physician, was summoned. He came and gave her sedative injections. Goebbels did not come. The unhappy woman appealed to her friend for help, but the beloved was not available. He was detained out of town on official business, she was told. So Lida Baarova left the country of her artistic and personal success, humbled and alone. She never again saw the man who had promised her marriage and whom she doubtless loved. Joseph Goebbels did not lift another finger for her; he neither wrote nor sent her a greeting. He feared for his own existence.

Since by the prompt banishment of Lida Baarova Hitler had proved that he was prepared to fulfil every acceptable demand on Magda's part an agreement was made which of its kind was possibly unique. This took place after further talks between Hitler and Magda, at which Secretary of State Hanke was also present, but not Joseph Goebbels.

Magda undertook to remain for one year outwardly Frau Goebbels, and to appear on important occasions at the side of her husband. When the year expired she would be free to sue for divorce from Goebbels, and would then be able – irrespective of what might have happened in the meantime – to adduce the same grounds against her husband as obtained at present.

During the interim or waiting period, she would continue to live in Schwanenwerder. Only with her permission could Goebbels go there to see his children. If, after the year had expired, Magda demanded a final separation and Goebbels was divorced as guilty party, Magda would have care of the children, receive a considerable sum as income and be able to keep Schwanenwerder as her home. Hitler declared that he himself was prepared to guarantee that the conditions of the agreement would be adhered to.

At the close of this long interview, Magda said that she would like the various stipulations to be legally drawn up, preferably by the lawyer who would act on her behalf in the divorce proceedings.

'As you wish,' replied Hitler, turning cool, 'provided you can find someone who is ready to risk appearing against my Propaganda Minister.'

The well-known Berlin lawyer, Dr Rudolf Dix, expressed his willingness to take on this hazardous enterprise. He took the view that in the event of divorce proceedings materializing Dr Goebbels would not stand as Reich Minister, but merely as the defendant husband, with the same rights and obligations as any other party to an action. Dr Dix therefore drew up the legal document embodying the various points agreed between Magda and Hitler.

To his astonishment Dr Dix was given to understand that at the end of the waiting period there would be no divorce proceedings, even if Magda still insisted on separation. Rather Hitler himself would dissolve the marriage. Magda was agreeable to this. According to National Socialist interpretation of the law, Hitler stood above the law. His decision, being paramount, replaced every law. Adolf Hitler took the view, shared by the compliant Magda, still faithful to the 'Ideal', that any dissolution of marriage decreed by Hitler would be definitive.

Dr Dix, experienced legal expert that he was, would not accept this interpretation of the law. In spite of every pressure from the other party, he refused to include this passage in the agreement. Oddly enough, Hitler acquiesced. Perhaps he too was nervous at times of his godlike powers. He withdrew the condition and the clause was omitted from the contract. If it came to a divorce, there would be the usual proceedings before the court.

This agreement was signed by Hitler, Goebbels and Magda. The Führer's signature was understood to qualify as a guarantee for the enforcement of the settlement.

Goebbels later maintained that he hardly noticed what he was signing. In any case he made no comment. At the sight of the Führer's signature all criticism or objection on his part was out of the question.

When they had all signed Hitler broke the icy silence: 'When one has such wonderful children as you have, Doctor, and you Frau Magda, you should not separate. The best thing is for you both to live ascetically for a whole year, you Doctor like a monk, and you dear Frau Magda as a nun.' The remark was intended to be a joke but neither was in the mood for jokes just then.

'My Führer,' replied Magda, without even the hint of a smile, 'I have been living like a nun for a long time already.'

For Goebbels it seemed prudent to hold his tongue.

19

Interlude

During the year which ensued Joseph Goebbels clearly demonstrated that he could be even cleverer and more capable of self-control than his opponents conceded.

'Crafty Magda,' said Himmler, *Reichsführer* S.S., rubbing his hands with glee. 'She has got her husband in the net all right. He won't get out of that again. He'll get all tangled up and in the end throttle himself.' But it wasn't like that at all.

To start with, the Minister for Propaganda staged a big celebration for his staff, in the blue reception room, the oldest and most beautiful room in the former palace. Supported by Magda, he welcomed with a radiant face colleagues, friends and foes. At his side was his deputy and Secretary of State, the 'faithful' Hanke. The charming host, wreathed in smiles, behaved as though he had never heard of Hanke's treachery. As far as Goebbels' lady friends were concerned, he either dropped them altogether or covered their traces with such ingenuity that nobody perceived the slightest evidence. Even Heinrich Himmler, chief of the Gestapo, the greatly feared German secret service, failed to lure his hated enemy into a trap.

An attempt was made at this time to bring Lida Baarova back to Germany. It is not clear whether or not Goebbels had anything to do with the matter. In view of his cautious behaviour at that time, it hardly seems likely. More probably it was one of the leading film producers of that period* who arranged for Lida Baarova to come to

---

*Ello Quandt did not wish his name, which was well known, to be given. He was still living at the time she told me the story.

Babelsberg, for the sole reason that her particular type of acting was best suited to his current production. He may also have thought that bringing Baarova back would prove financially profitable.

In any case Lida Baarova was once more to be seen sitting in the lobby of the Hotel Adlon and driving through the gates of Babelsberg. Hanke learned straight away that the woman expelled by order of the Führer had returned. The Secretary of State knew, or thought he knew, where his duty lay. Accompanied by several S.S. men, and driving in one of the Promi's heavy duty vehicles he went out to the film studios at Babelsberg. It was just at the time of the mid-day break on a hot summer's day as the car roared through the gates. All the windows of the office buildings were wide open. Hundreds of extras and the technical staff were strolling languidly about in the grounds when, to their astonishment, half a dozen S.S. men suddenly emerged from the car and dashed up the steps to the executive suite. Soon excited voices could be heard coming from the leading producer's room, followed immediately by the sound of blows and the dull thud of a body flung against the wall.

A few moments later, the Secretary of State and his cohort stormed back to the car and departed. The film impresario, who is understood not to have uttered a word during the brutal surprise attack, naturally enough decided to avenge his wounded pride. He immediately despatched a friend belonging to the Führer clique to Colonel Gritzbach, Göring's adjutant, with the request that a duel with pistols be arranged between Secretary of State Hanke and himself. Whether Hanke, with his penchant for chivalrous romance and so for knightly duels, would have risked the doubtful experience of being shot at dawn on an open stretch of heath is not known. Hitler in any case decided that the time for that sort of gun play was long past. He forbade the duel and the matter was settled calmly. The impresario resigned from his post shortly afterwards. As an experienced film director he found a fresh appointment in a leading position in Paris during the Occupation; he later returned to Germany. Meanwhile Frau Baarova speedily disappeared once more.

In accordance with the agreement Goebbels was living in the palace behind the Wilhelmstrasse, working during the day in the Ministry, and in the evenings inviting only serious, respectable people to join him. His relationship with Hitler nevertheless remained cool.

Outwardly his manner was nonchalant, but inwardly he was suffering torment.

Magda for her part went on living in Schwanenwerder, as agreed. From time to time the Minister would ring up and ask whether he might come to see the children. On such occasions he would appear completely at ease. Magda nearly always managed not to be present, in which case he would express his regrets to the staff at having missed her. If she did receive him, he would take his place at the tea table quite naturally and chat lightheartedly. The fact that their parents were more or less living separately never seems to have occurred to the children.

Brick by brick, intelligently and energetically, Goebbels set about rebuilding his lost prestige. During the whole interim period he obviously had only one desire: to scramble up, slowly but surely, out of the depths of his disgrace.

With Magda it was quite otherwise. More impulsive and open-hearted than her husband, she behaved with a surprising lack of caution. While Goebbels was wearing the hair shirt of the repentant sinner, Magda reassumed her former rôle of beautiful society woman. 'I'm just beginning to realize,' she confided to Ello, 'what a big mistake I made all those years by being nothing more than a wife and mother. Now I'm going to show people that I can be something else.'* She had her hair restyled, dressed more elegantly, wore heavier make-up and went out much more.

She liked to be seen accompanied by Karl Hanke. Magda had known for a long time that Hanke adored her. He had proved himself to be a faithful, self-sacrificing, courageous friend deserving of her gratitude. Persistent suitor that he was, he now openly declared his love for her and begged her, after her divorce from Goebbels, to marry him.

But Magda did not feel so inclined. Hanke had mistaken her gratitude for affection. Magda felt with a woman's sure instinct that after the years with Goebbels, life with Hanke would not be satisfying. He was simple, honest, straightforward and well-mannered, an intelligent and hard-working man. But in many respects his education was deficient; he was no intellectual and lacked all sense of aesthetic

*It was about this time that the couturiers, chiefly Jewish-owned and spared so far by the Nazis, closed down. One of the last of these was Kohnen, where all the best-dressed women in Berlin society went for their clothes. Frau Magda, wife of the minister who carried out a permanent systematic persecution of the Jews, said to my mother: 'What a pity Kohnen is closing down. We all know that elegance will disappear from Berlin along with the Jews.'

appreciation. Magda could not forget his 'treachery', although she of all people had no right to reproach him for it. Certainly he had only done it out of respect for her; moreover, his action in so ignominiously deceiving his friend and chief had been in the interests of justice.

Among his friends Goebbels referred to Hanke as 'the dirty traitor'. Hanke heard of it and complained bitterly to Magda. He felt that he had behaved correctly and honourably. But Magda was so objective in her thinking that she could not bring herself to approve the betrayal.

Hanke was no life partner for Magda, only a stop-gap, a good friend. They spent a lot of time together, went often to dance at the Artistes' Club, were to be seen together at the theatre, at exhibitions and at race meetings. In the elegant, thoroughly dignified night club Ciro's, much frequented by the haut monde and diplomats, I myself saw Magda with Hanke a number of times. Normally such a well-known couple would have been the subject of tittle-tattle by those at other tables. But while most of the men thought the wife of the disgraced minister was behaving somewhat too provocatively, nearly all the women were on her side. 'She's quite right. She should show the "tadpole" that he's gone too far – the lecherous devil!'

Hanke was a good and enthusiastic rider and persuaded Magda to take up horsemanship. She took riding lessons with Tattersalls at the Zoo and kept a horse at Schwanenwerder. Always ready to throw her whole heart into anything she took up, she soon became an accomplished rider. The gossips naturally seized avidly on this new aspect of the couple's relationship, and they were soon looked upon by the Führer clique and in society as lovers.

There was not the slightest evidence for this assumption. Ello Quandt was emphatic that the relationship was purely platonic. There is much to support the view that Hanke and Magda, so very different in outlook and temperament, were just good friends – although it is undeniable that Hanke longed to marry Magda. Unknown to Magda he went one day to Hitler and asked whether the Führer had any objection if, after the divorce, he were to marry Magda. The Führer said he wished to wait until the stipulated year elapsed before making up his mind. If Magda still insisted on divorce, he had no objection to Hanke's plan.

Magda too, for a time, seemed to accept the idea of becoming Hanke's wife. 'I was terribly unhappy with the brilliant Joseph,' she said to Ello. 'Perhaps I can find some quiet happiness with a more ordinary but respectable type of man.' But when she learned that he had approached Hitler about the marriage, she changed her mind. 'That's definitely going too far,' she declared to Ello. 'He had no right to do that. Before I am free of the one marriage, I am being fixed up for the next. I'm going to be the only one to say what I want to do in the future and no one else.'

Hanke used to take a great interest in the children. In turn they all adored him. Magda's mother, too, had a liking for this suitor for the hand of her daughter, all the more so as she detested Goebbels. Hanke was charming to the old lady, always behaving very attentively towards her. As the year drew slowly to a close, Hanke repeated his offer of marriage to Magda and finally tried to persuade her to pay a visit to the pretty little house on the Grünewald Lake which he had just recently bought.

Goebbels was of course aware of the friendship. He had day-to-day business to conduct with his Secretary of State, and encountered him at social occasions, as well as at Schwanenwerder with Magda and the children. His inordinate vanity must have suffered greatly through this, but he managed to master himself and never uttered a word on the matter. He even brought himself to treat Hanke outwardly exactly as he had always done. Since his disgrace his position was still too vulnerable to risk causing a scandal over Hanke. He was only too well aware of the pleasure such a development would have provided for his enemies. Hermann Göring, for example, had been heard to say that he would rather see these two rivals going for each other than two rutting stags.

But the wily Goebbels wisely behaved as if he knew all about the relationship and indeed approved. He probably knew his wife well enough to feel sure that she would not go beyond the bounds of friendship at this particular time. Perversely enough, however, Magda wished to create the impression that she was doing so. 'I want people to gossip about me,' she said. 'I've been the loyal wife too long, the good mother who sits uncomplainingly at home while her husband deceives her with beautiful women.'

Basically Magda was deeply unhappy; she ate practically nothing, and had grown very thin. She was still lovely to look at, but it was clear that this would not last much longer. The outline of her face had sharpened, lines had begun to appear, and her complexion was losing its freshness. She used heavier make-up, and was smoking too much and becoming nervously restless.

Goebbels noticed what was happening; he felt, too, that he was increasingly consolidating his position. He drove out to Schwanenwerder more often than before, and sent Magda flowers and gifts. With the wisdom of the serpent he left her alone on Christmas Eve with the children and the Christmas tree. Naturally she wept, and equally naturally she laughed when he turned up next morning with a mountain of gifts and was given a tumultuous welcome by the children. When she casually mentioned that her car was not in order, a sparkling new Mercedes rolled up before the house the same day. 'A present from the Minister,' said the chauffeur from the works, handing over the keys.

More and more frequently it happened that Goebbels rang her from the city, asking her to join him on yet another official occasion. 'I don't intend to allow myself to be seen with him again,' Magda would say. 'He must not think that I'm sitting here waiting, ready to leap up as soon as he needs me.' There would then be a short pause: 'Shall I wear the blue or would the white with lace look better on me?'

If he had admired a certain dress, she would wear it again on the next occasion. If he said dove grey suited her best, she would hasten to the tailor to order a dove grey costume. She had once more fallen under his spell. Her friends noticed it, Hanke felt it, and Joseph Goebbels was sure of it. Magda herself, however much she tried to resist the idea, knew it as well.

In order to regain favour with Hitler and get closer to him again, Goebbels began to write a book on the Führer. It was to be called *Adolf Hitler, the Man*. But Hitler forbade him to do so. 'I don't want a man of such doubtful character to write about me,' were Hitler's words, promptly conveyed to Goebbels in secret, making him realize that Hitler was far from ready for a reconciliation.

Over tea at Schwanenwerder, he complained bitterly to Magda of this treatment. Magda thought Hitler was downright ungrateful. 'I've always known it, dearest Magda,' Joseph said, kissing her hand. 'You are the only one who really understands me.' When she heard that whenever her husband came to the Berghof, Hitler made him stay in the adjutants' house instead of in the main part as before, Magda was indignant. 'Joseph doesn't deserve such treatment,' she said angrily to Ello. 'He won over Red Berlin for the Führer. Hitler should never behave like that to him. That slimy rabble that Adolf surrounds himself with more and more these days will all be enjoying the joke.

By 'slimy rabble' she meant a host of important, active people who had succeeded in grouping themselves firmly round Hitler, encircling him like a sort of bodyguard. These included the bullying, working-class, secretive Martin Bormann; Hitler's highly controversial personal physician, Dr Morell; S.S. cavalry leader Fegelein, brother-in-law of Eva Braun; Leni Riefenstahl, who, since her successful film of the Berlin Olympic Games, stood in high favour; faithful, peace-loving, friendly Group Leader Joseph Schaub, since 1920 Hitler's personal aide; Adjutants Brückner and Günsche; the valet Linge and Erich Kempka, Hitler's favourite driver and chief of the entire transport supply service (car pool).

The twelve-month interlude had almost drawn to its close, and a decision now had to be made with regard to the Propaganda Minister's marriage. Goebbels had made every possible preparation for the outcome of this very private struggle. Throughout the whole interval he had planned his campaign so admirably that the issue was actually never in doubt.

Magda had gone to Bad Gastein to take the cure. Goebbels went off to the Salzburg Festival. It is not far from Salzburg to Gastein, so he drove over to ask Magda whether she would perhaps enjoy a performance in Salzburg. She would. During the journey in the car he exerted all his charm. Afterwards, alone together at supper in his private suite, 'Magda dearest,' he said smilingly, 'what is it going to be? Should we not get together once more? I really have been good for a whole year now.'

Magda had seen the question coming and had prepared the answer in her mind. 'No. I am going to be married.'

Joseph continued to smile. 'Oh! and to whom?'

'Hanke.' Magda's heart missed a beat, for of course it was a lie. For a whole second Goebbels appeared concerned. He was not sure at first whether she actually meant it or not. In any case he returned to the attack.

'Magda, we belong together – you know that.' He put on his sweetest smile, which he so rarely did, and took her in his arms. 'Hanke is not the man for you. You don't need me to tell you that.'

A little later that evening Magda phoned from Salzburg to Secretary of State Hanke at the Ministry and told him briefly that she was reconciled with her husband. At the other end of the line Hanke, bitterly disappointed, could hardly speak through his tears. She did not attempt to give an explanation for her decision, nor even to console him.

Hitler was extremely pleased when, in Goebbels' house, he learned of the reconciliation. Not unjustly perhaps, he gave the credit for the outcome of the struggle to his own understanding of human nature. Having frustrated the divorce, he now wished to be the one to consolidate the marriage afresh. But it was not so simple. Magda categorically insisted on certain conditions. Firstly, Hanke must be removed, but with dignity. His presence disturbed the reconciled couple. He was therefore promoted to be Gauleiter of Schlesien and moved into the Castle of Breslau; the honest son of a highly respected engine driver thus became the chief official in his native province.

Secondly, a list of people was drawn up who would no longer be welcome at the Goebbels' home; among these were the names of no less than thirty women, taken from the list which Hanke had submitted a year earlier. A further list contained the names of Magda's own friends whom she liked to invite and whom the master of the house was expected to receive in a friendly manner. By way of a special condition, the Minister was enjoined to treat his mother-in-law, the former Frau Friedländer, with a greater degree of civility in future.

Lida Baarova was again a victim. On Magda's insistence, Goebbels had to promise the Führer himself never to let her come back to Germany. None of those who had remained loyal to Magda during the marital conflict was to be persecuted or discriminated against. On the other hand, the Minister's personal adjutants who were accomplices in his affaires were to be transferred to remote units.

Finally, Magda should have the right at any time, whenever she so wished, to divorce Goebbels, and on the legal grounds obtaining before the interlude period. In spite of the reconciliation she could always get her divorce. She would then keep Schwanenwerder, have custody of the children and be in receipt of a substantial income.

This reconciliation agreement was drawn up in detail and signed by Magda and Goebbels, then by Hitler as guarantor. By the last days of August 1939 Magda had won a complete victory.

20

An Unmitigated Scoundrel

A few days later the Second World War broke out. Personal destinies lost their importance, and even ministers' marriages dropped into the background. The foreordained path of the German people took from that hour, in spite of many stupendous successes, its ever more swiftly winding course. Only a few far-seeing people realized how inexorably the war which had now erupted would plunge the Third Reich into the abyss. Nevertheless the first two years of war constituted an incomparable triumphal progress.

Under the pressure of ever greater decisions to be made, the Führer forgot his protracted differences with Goebbels – the latter's false word of honour, his execrable private life, all the worries he had had over the Goebbels' marriage. The outbreak of the Second World War completely redeemed the Minister from disgrace.

But Joseph Goebbels, far and away the best brains in the National Socialist hierarchy, had always feared war. On that fateful morning of 3 September when the declarations of war from England and France were received, Goebbels, to Hitler's surprise, with Ribbentrop, Keitel and other generals and ministers, present, said, 'Now we know how easily a world war can break out, but what will come out of it in the end, that we don't know.' Deeply concerned during those early days, according to Ello Quandt's recollections, Goebbels expressed these same doubts more than once when alone with his family.

Special formalities were no longer required for discussions between Hitler and his Propaganda Minister. Each morning and evening Goebbels was summoned by the Führer, or he could announce himself. If circumstances permitted, they would often share a meal. Magda for her part forgot much of the disappointment which Hitler had caused her – he had after all not come to her assistance out of a sense of justice and decency, but only for reasons of State and party prestige, which were far more important to him than personal sympathy. Her old loyalty to him was now restored. As a young girl she had lived through the First World War without any personal involvement, but she faced the present war with an almost fanatical love of the Fatherland. She was ready to suffer any privation and made genuine arrangements for sharing with her fellow countrymen the manifold restrictions to which the ordinary people were subjected. For nearly six months Magda endeavoured to run the household entirely on the basis of the food ration. For three months she even gave up her car.

However, in spite of such good resolutions, she was not strong-minded enough to withstand the bad example of other Nazi chiefs, who with a naïve lack of conscience continued to lead their own self-centred existences. When she saw how her friends and guests were evading the food restrictions and noticed that nearly all the wives of the party bigwigs were gliding past her in shining limousines, while she stood in a packed tramcar, she decided to opt for the privileges which were available to her, particularly as she had the excuse of again being pregnant.

The newly built ministerial palace in the large garden behind the Wilhelmstrasse had been completed. It was the third time within five years that the mansion had been reconstructed. It now had forty rooms, a truly princely residence, with a butler, and liveried footmen. However, on the outbreak of war all entertaining on a large scale was suspended. Invitations were only distributed within small groups and were renounced altogether during the three-week Polish campaign, when all the world waited with bated breath.

In Germany it was feared that while the greater part of the German army was tied up in Poland, the English and French would attack from the west. Goebbels himself knew that a breakthrough past the ramparts to the west – still incomplete and thinly manned – by strongly attacking enemy forces was altogether possible. Most probably such a breakthrough in the early stages would have decisively weakened the fighting power of the German Reich and, above all, the production of armaments. But the great Western democracies, unprepared for a war of such dimensions, roused themselves too slowly for effective action.

At the end of September Poland lay prostrate. The Führer, relying upon the impression which the lightning success of his armies would evoke throughout the world, clearly hinted in his victory oration that he would be prepared to negotiate with England and France in a true spirit of compromise, even before the war between them and Germany had really begun. Hitler was astounded when Paris and London gave him the cold shoulder. While the mass of the German people exulted over the rapid victory over Poland, blind to the suffering and loss ahead of them, Hitler was seized with profound disappointment and despondency. He had hoped for a reasonable peace treaty with the Western powers following the Polish campaign. But nothing of the kind was in sight; on the contrary, America's entry into the war was now to be feared.

One lovely October day, Hitler turned up quite unexpectedly at Schwanenwerder. He wanted to bring the children some presents, as he had forgotten a couple of birthdays. The children idolized Uncle Adolf and usually helped to restore his spirits straightaway. This time, however, they failed to cheer him. He remained depressed and taciturn.

'Yes, well, I must see how it all goes,' he observed, quite irrelevantly, to the Goebbels and Ello Quandt, as he was about to leave. 'We can only win this war by surprise tactics, must do exactly the opposite of what the enemy expect – those are our weapons.' And after a long pause he added the less than comforting remark: 'Ah, well, I expect I shall soon think of something!'

'But my Führer,' broke in Goebbels, eager to flatter, 'of course something will occur to you, and that for certain just at the right moment.' He laughed, intending it for a joke.

'Let's hope so,' murmured Hitler dejectedly, still refusing to allow himself to be cheered up. For a moment the leader of the Greater German Reich, lord over twelve million troops, stood bent and self-forgetting; then he muttered goodbye in a stifled voice and departed.

Goebbels accompanied him to his car. When he came back into the house he, too, had lost his confident look. As white as a sheet and limping more than usual, he paused in some agitation at the smokers' table and helped himself to a cigarette. 'Yes,' he said slowly, more to himself than to the two women, 'a great deal will have to occur to us. One victory doesn't last long, one victory right at the beginning.

What we need is a victory at the end. But ...' He didn't finish what he was going to say, and stood a long time thoughtfully regarding the flame of the lighter, forgetting even to light the cigarette.

During the so-called 'phoney war', that interval of six months between the Polish campaign and the occupation of Denmark and Norway, before the fighting in France began, the Goebbels found their peacetime living conditions almost completely restored. The Minister had new and very important duties, namely to prepare the German people psychologically for the rigours of war and the blessings of peace. He had to direct productivity in factories and workshops by means of skilful propaganda and stimulate the spirit of self-sacrifice and the readiness to contribute cheerfully. He succeeded admirably. Hitler had long recognized that the talents of the Promi chief were more effective vis-à-vis his own people than the rest of the world and had diverted the foreign propaganda away from him, transferring it to the Foreign Office and the Supreme Command of the army. Goebbels could now only exercise influence abroad indirectly, via the German press. And his centrally controlled and coordinated press was so boring that it afforded him little opportunity for making any impression on the enemy or influencing neutral countries. Notwithstanding that, during those first two years of war the Propaganda Minister was, owing to the gravity and importance of his duties, completely fulfilled, his talents and energies once again extended to the full. Thus he was able to resist the temptation to indulge in private amorous adventures.

Throughout that period he was a model husband and loving father. Within a short time Magda once more looked radiantly lovely; she forgave all his hurtful behaviour towards her in the past and was touchingly concerned for his personal well-being. All the same she remained on the alert to uphold her independence so laboriously acquired. If her husband, as he was wont to do made jokes at her expense, she would put him sharply in his place. 'What,' she would ask, 'does that stupid remark mean?' Or she would even deflate him with, 'I don't find you witty, only tactless.' But on the whole their family life was better than it had ever been before, undisturbed by any escapades on Joseph's part.

On 29 October 1940 Heide, the sixth and last child of the marriage, was born. The parents themselves called her the child of reconciliation. Heide was an adorable little creature; sadly her whole existence was bounded by war.

Harold Quandt, now a smart young man, had served at the Front since the war started. Neither Magda nor Goebbels made any attempt to withdraw him from any scene of immediate danger. As a paratrooper, Harold was a brave fighter, soon being awarded a decoration, the Iron Cross First Class. He fought in Crete, with Rommel in Africa and later at Monte Cassino, where he was badly wounded.

The relationship of Harold to his many half-sisters and his half-brother was always a particularly happy one. Whenever Harold came to Berlin on leave they made a tremendous fuss of him, their own war hero. Goebbels, too, had a pleasant relationship with his stepson and knew how to get on with him. Quite early on he had given Harold a motor bike, which his father Günther Quandt had replaced by a car as soon as the boy was old enough. Harold was a cheerful, boisterous young man, inclined to practical jokes. But as the fighting became harder and he experienced more of it he lost his youthful spirits, becoming as so many others of his generation, mature, even old, long before his time.

Soon after war broke out, air raid shelters were constructed at the Minister's orders beneath all his residences; they were complete before the first bombs fell on Berlin. Whenever a raid occurred, Goebbels dived immediately underground and insisted that all his family, domestic staff, guests and personnel did likewise. The paintings from the State galleries, worth about seven million marks, which had embellished the walls of his Berlin apartments, now adorned the cold concrete walls of the subterranean stronghold.

Yet once more the shadow of Lida Baarova loomed up. In March 1939, Czechoslovakia came under the 'protection' of the Reich, and Frau Baarova with it. During the war German forces were based in Prague, and Lida Baarova somehow earned recognition for welfare work undertaken on behalf of the occupying troops. Heinrich Himmler suddenly brought his influence to bear in her favour and petitioned Hitler to repeal the order against her. Hitler, having agreed for Magda's sake never to allow the lovely Baarova to come back to Germany, would not take a decision without her consent. He despatched Hanke's successor, Secretary of State Naumann, to Magda, asking her, in view of the altered personal and political circumstances, to consent to Frau Baarova's return. But Magda's reply to the Führer's request was a sharp refusal.

The actress was by now so far humbled that she wrote herself to Magda pleading for the past to be forgotten. Magda read the letter out to Ello. 'Can you really be so hard, dear lady,' wrote Lida Baarova, 'now that you yourself are happy once more? My only sin was to love a man who belonged to another woman and for that I have paid dearly. But I love Germany before all else and do not deserve to be made to suffer so. You alone can say whether I may return – I beseech you have mercy and allow me to do so!'

But Magda showed once more how hard-hearted she could be. She did not reply to the letter, and Goebbels never heard about it. 'Nobody,' remarked Magda to Ello 'ought to ask so much of me; it would only be the same old story all over again.'

Two whole years went by before Goebbels embarked afresh on a little affaire – or at least before it became known. This time Magda was the first to learn about it. The woman on this occasion was his secretary. Nobody took much notice if he were to be seen about with her or if she accompanied him on his travels or at weekends to Castle Lanke or Schwanenwerder. A minister's work is exacting; he may not even rest on Sundays; for such unremitting demands an assistant is indispensable. The fact that a young and pretty secretary was continually in his company was not of itself a matter for conjecture; the chief thing was that she was efficient.

Magda, however, saw her one night climbing up from the garden to her master's study. She was badly shaken by this discovery, which was entirely accidental. She had sincerely believed in her reconciliation with Goebbels, and thought that the grave problems arising from the war had cured him of his erotic propensities. She should have been shrewd enough to realize that neither reconciliation nor the gravity of war were really likely to stop him in the long run. Magda suffered an attack of hysteria followed by a nervous breakdown. 'Now I've really had enough,' she declared despairingly. 'I can't go through it all again. I will divorce him and I don't care how much of a scandal it causes.'

The next day she went to her lawyer and sought an appointment with Hitler. Ello Quandt tried to calm her, saying it was only a little bit of fun, as far as she could see. Joseph had far too much on hand to think of any serious commitment. But Magda was through; she wished to be free of him.

Ello lost no time in phoning Goebbels. He must drive out to his wife immediately and reassure her. And he must stop behaving so stupidly. The third year of the war, just beginning, was no time for such misbehaviour, nor for another divorce scandal. Ello advised him to tackle the problem straightaway since Magda was about to speak to the Führer. Goebbels calmly replied that it was all a storm in a tea cup. He could easily explain his young secretary's climb through the window. Still, he would drive out to Schwanenwerder to his dear but foolish wife, to save her from being too hasty.

Magda received him composedly, saying hardly anything at first. Goebbels waited for her reproaches so as to ascertain how much she knew. They were both beating about the bush. Ello recorded the remarkable dialogue that now ensued between deceiver and deceived.

'Good gracious! You don't usually come home as early as this, Joseph.'

'Now darling, may a husband not suddenly long to see his lovely wife for once?'

'How sweet of you ... but why the sudden longing?'

'You weren't very well yesterday, so I wanted to see whether you were any better.'

'So attentive of you, *Engelchen* ... but do tell me, had you no special reason for coming?'

'Quite honestly, yes, dearest,' he admitted, and Magda braced herself for a struggle. 'You know yesterday they made me frightfully angry again at the office. I do need your presence sometimes my dearest. You do me good, divert my thoughts. You really are the one comfort of my life.' He then suggested a walk down to the lakeside. Disarmed Magda agreed. And so instead of a bitter argument they enjoyed a peaceful stroll arm-in-arm around the shore of the Bogensee.

'That sly old fox got the better of me once again,' confessed Magda, regretting her weakness as he drove away. 'But it won't do him any good. Early tomorrow I will definitely go to see the Führer. I swear I will this time.'

The following morning at four o'clock war broke out with the Soviet Union. 'War has come once again to his aid,' thought Magda ruefully, as she learned the news on waking. 'But what is happening now will bring nothing but misery to all of us.'

The short-lived friendship between Adolf Hitler and Joseph Stalin had come to an end. The Propaganda Minister was thus able to throw off the fetters with which the Führer had all too long restrained him from dealing with the Soviet Union. He immediately turned the full blast of his propaganda machine towards the East. The guns of his press and radio speeches fired broadside on with unremitting vigour.

Goebbels was once more completely in his own peculiar element, again the wholly indispensable chief of psychological warfare. Nothing could assail him. Even Magda could not, and neither in fact could Hitler himself. So he did not bother to conceal his friendship with his young and pretty secretary. He could do as he liked with impunity. When he went too far and Magda demanded an explanation from him, he laughed the matter off. If she produced evidence he denied it. When she threatened to denounce him to Hitler once more he scoffed brazenly. 'The Führer has no time now to listen to complaints from hysterical women.'

He steadfastly refused to replace the secretary in question and continued to take her with him to Lanke or Schwanenwerder. Magda was compelled to share meals with her. She also appeared at small parties at the house, greeting Magda with a deferential manner, making a deep curtsey and kissing her hand, leaving onlookers to guess whether she acted in this way to salve her conscience or in derision of the mistress of the house.

But Magda, as is so often the case with wives who are much deceived, had many friends, among whom were others similarly treated by their own husbands. Together they formed a solid front against the adulteress. They snubbed her conspicuously, giving her censorious looks and making insinuating remarks about her. She was, in fact, engaged to a young man, generally regarded as a good match. Fearing that her fiancé might learn from one of the ladies about her disloyalty, she finally realized that she had no alternative but to ask Goebbels to be good enough to transfer her to another post outside Berlin.

It was a defeat which touched Joseph Goebbels on the raw. Not since his first love, Anka, had he been spurned by a woman. But his distress was short-lived and he soon consoled himself. 'It's no good,' confessed Magda resignedly to Ello, 'we've hardly schemed one little puss away, than the next one appears – and behind her are all the others. I have spoken frankly to Joseph. He was fairly reasonable and promised me not to have any more friends in the future whom I didn't like or who were impertinent to me. Now he's got one who so far is behaving herself and I must make the best of it.'

Ello Quandt could scarcely recognize the old Magda in this resigned attitude and told her so. 'What am I to do, Ello?' pleaded Magda, turning wearily aside. 'Look at me. I'm getting old. I often feel exhausted and I can't change matters. These girls are twenty years younger and have not brought seven children into the world.'

After a time she added, 'There are only two possibilities, as far as I am concerned. If we win this war, Joseph's prestige will be so high that I, an ageing woman, will be done for in any case. If we lose the war my life is finished anyway. I must bear the burden of this war at his side. Then everything will be finished; there is no way out for me.'

Magda now concerned herself more than ever with Buddhist teaching. She obtained new literature from Switzerland and immersed herself night after night in this, her own little world, to which none of her friends had access. If anyone tried to involve her in a conversation about Buddhism, she would sidestep the issue. Only once, when the son of a very good friend was killed, did she say to the mother: 'He is not dead ... he has gone on to begin a new life.'

'Do you believe,' she was once asked, 'in reincarnation?'

'Yes,' she said firmly. 'I do believe in that.'

She now faced her husband's amours with forced humour; she laughed at them, poked fun at him, and derided an adjutant who lent himself as a go-between. By chance she learned one day that her husband's current lady friend had been given the key to a passage usually kept locked. During the afternoon she had the lock changed. Next morning she casually enquired of her husband if he had had to wait a long time for his visitor. He muttered that he could take a joke and fondled her hand. Another time Magda arranged for one of the ladies much in the Minister's company to be telephoned on his behalf and told that the Minister would like her to wait for him at a crossing in the midst of the Grünewald, at eleven o'clock at night; the Minister's car would thus be able to pick her up unobtrusively. The unlucky lady was then left stranded in the dark, the rain and the cold.

Towards midnight, Magda glanced at the clock. 'Did you know,' she asked her husband softly, 'that Frau X has been waiting more than an hour for your car at the *Grosser Stern*? I had her sent there to cool off – in your name of course.'

Joseph was unconcerned. 'Oh!' he said calmly, 'but you really are ingenious,' and took no steps to rescue his misdirected friend.

'In marriage with you,' countered Magda, 'one learns to be like that.' Such jokes went against the grain with her; she made use of them merely as a remedy to forestall the dull resignation with which otherwise she would have had to accept her husband's persistent infidelity.

Magda gradually came to realize that his lack of self-discipline, his restlessness and his unscrupulous moral behaviour were pathological. To her it seemed incredible that a man who carried such enormous responsibility in the midst of the bloodiest war in the history of the world should be capable of leading such a reckless private life. Everybody, even Goebbels himself, knew that Germany's defeat would mean death for him. Yet while he was demanding such tremendous sacrifices from all the German people, he himself was not prepared to forego in the slightest his own personal pleasures.

So Magda began to despise him. She no longer loved him as she had once, she was no longer jealous of him or even hated him. 'Actually,' she observed one day to Ello, 'Joseph is, when all is said and done, the biggest scoundrel who has ever held the German people in thrall.'

21

Towards Disaster

As the war situation became more critical, particularly after Stalingrad and all-out total war had been declared, Goebbels was vested with increasing authority, and became still more influential. His rise in importance was balanced by the decline of that of his rivals.

Rudolf Hess, up to that time the Führer's deputy, had flown to England as an intermediary to negotiate peace – as traitor, or madman, to this day, who knows? Göring's Luftwaffe had failed; in spite of all the Field Marshal's assertions to the contrary, it had not been able to match the enemy's strength. Ribbentrop's foreign policy had turned out to be totally naïve, and he in consequence was practically finished. Of all the leading men in Hitler's court only Himmler and Goebbels had maintained, indeed consolidated, their positions. Army commanders were given field marshals' batons, fell into disgrace, but were soon hauled back into favour. Names zoomed like comets, only to be swiftly extinguished.

Goebbels' prestige was now at its peak. He was indispensable because he was full of new ideas. He understood the people, shamelessly abusing their virtues, their diligence and loyalty, their bravery and spirit of self-sacrifice. Equally shamelessly he exploited national weaknesses; for example, he made use of the German love of gossip to spread rumours. This had already proved particularly effective before the German attack on Soviet Russia. At that time Goebbels had had ten thousand little paper Russian flags printed in Berlin, presumably for Stalin's reception at the palace of the Reich Chancellor. Hitler and Stalin were to negotiate a Hundred Year Pact, leasing the Ukraine to the German Reich. Under cover of this readily circulated rumour, the surprise attack was launched on the Soviet Union, with whom the Third Reich was more or less in league.

Goebbels now decided to employ a similar practice with regard to the top secret, so-called wonder weapons. Everything which the German citizen confided about them, under the strictest pledge of secrecy, to his best friend, was thought up in the first place by Goebbels. The unique wonder weapon which Germany did in truth possess lay in the brain of the Minister of Propaganda; whispered propaganda was Goebbels' last resource. He played on this instrument with a degree of virtuosity never exceeded before or since. His newspapers had lost all credibility, at best his radio broadcasts were laughed at, but his whispered propaganda, which was only recognized by the intelligent few as 'made by Goebbels', was all too readily believed.

Goebbels successfully exploited the German propensity for mysticism and superstition. After the flight to England of his deputy, Hitler, furiously angry, wanted to incarcerate all astrologers, clairvoyants and fortune-tellers, simply because Rudolf Hess had consulted a Munich astrologer, and the lady's advice as to a favourable day on which to make the flight and achieve a safe landing had obviously proved sound. Goebbels arranged for her to come to see him. The clairvoyante's predictions were in future to be subject to his supervision – or she could expect trouble. Even after the death of the well-known prophetess, the Minister continued to use 'her' predictions. He made them up himself, so they naturally served the interests of the German Reich.

Similarly he made use of Nostradamus, the erudite scholar and astrologer, quoted by Goethe in *Faust*, who died in Paris in 1566. As Goethe had ensured Nostradamus's undying fame, his words were particularly credible. Quite fortuitously a passage in his prophecies was found to read as follows:

And war will break out in Europe on so vast and fearful a scale as never before. Death and destruction, conflict and bloodshed, will descend on princes and people alike, and press hard on the people of the middle kingdom until in the end the cities of Paris and London and those that be far to the East will be engulfed in a sea of flame. But that people which stands under the sign of the crooked cross, that people will triumph, to live in peace, prosperity and happiness, a proud dominion for a thousand years.

It goes without saying that Nostradamus did not write a word of all this. Goebbels himself was the author. 'Authentic reproductions' of the old prophet were secretly circulated, eagerly read and seriously believed. They were credible even to would-be sceptics, inasmuch as responsible men, solemnly averred that they had read these words in an original volume of Nostradamus of the year 1550. Nostradamus must indeed have prophesied thus, since it could be read in the leather-bound original volumes to be found in a number of State libraries.

The brilliant propagandist of the Thousand Year Reich had thought of everything. He was no dilettante. With all the facilities of modern counterfeit technique at his disposal, he had had a few folios from the mid-sixteenth century carefully copied and the operative sentences, in Latin text and Gothic script, laboriously inscribed on genuine parchment. Goebbels made the deception all the more complete by falsifying further passages in order to show that Nostradamus had correctly prophesied other things, such as 'giant fish which swim around in the sea with sailors in their bellies' or 'birds of iron'. When the forgeries had accomplished their objective, the volumes in question disappeared from the libraries, so that a more thorough examination was no longer possible. Because of the great value of such so-called presentation books which could not be taken away, but only consulted under supervision, even experts were deceived in this way by the Führer's Mephisto.

Sometimes he had inordinate luck, if one can speak of luck in connection with the finding of a mass grave of a few thousand Polish officers. From the graves of Katyn, Goebbels caused such a cloud of propaganda to rise that it enveloped not only Germany but half the world. Several commissions established incontestably that Stalin had had the officers executed by being shot through the base of the skull. Even the National Polish government in exile in London, although at war with Germany, held the Soviet government to be guilty. The English press also took sides against the Kremlin.

Goebbels made so much of the Katyn findings that in the end an expert from his ministry, when dining at Schwanenwerder, warned him: 'If you don't soon stop talking so loudly about Katyn, the people will begin to believe that we Germans were responsible.' 'No, no, certainly not,' replied Goebbels genially. 'It was definitely the Russians at Katyn – our mass graves are elsewhere!'

Goebbels, increasingly conscious of his escalating power, became less restrained even in his criticism of Hitler – though only in private, among his most intimate circle. Outwardly he identified himself with all Hitler's measures. When, in the winter of 1941, the German offensive against Moscow reached a stalemate and it was obvious that the Soviet Republic could not be disposed of by a *Blitzkrieg*, Goebbels blamed Hitler's misconceptions about Russia for the situation. Of course the Slavs were not the equal of the Germanic people, but they were brave soldiers, loyal to their country. With his crack-brained project to transform Russia, with all its inhabitants, into a sort of colony of the Greater German Reich, the Führer had dealt the liberating trump card to his great enemy Stalin. Hitler's inconceivable error transformed him from the brutal ruler of a nation which would gladly have been delivered from the harsh yolk of Stalinism into the resolute defender of his people.

From the winter of 1941-2 onwards, after the failure of the offensive against Moscow, Joseph Goebbels looked into the future with ever-increasing concern. He attacked Göring and Ribbentrop with unusual harshness. 'If we lose the war,' he grumbled to his family, 'that fool of a Göring is responsible, since he has not made the success of the Luftwaffe that he should have done -- and that conceited ass, too, that good-for-nothing Ribbentrop, who was only fit to peddle his wife's family's champagne around.'

Magda, too, became steadily more incautious. During a speech by Hitler on 9 November 1942 in the Beer Hall in Munich, to which she was listening with a group of friends, she suddenly stood up, switched the radio off and spluttered, 'My God, what a lot of rubbish.'

Goebbels appeared no longer even to fear Heinrich Himmler, *Reichsführer* S.S. and murderer of thousands. Although he knew that Himmler's secret police constantly listened in on his telephone calls, and that he and Magda and indeed all their friends were under continual observation, nevertheless he was firmly convinced that nobody would now be able to unseat him. Only one other, Martin Bormann, enjoyed greater confidence from the Führer than Goebbels; he was the only one whom Goebbels still had to fear.

Bormann had been one of Hitler's trusted intimates for a number of years; he was looked upon as Hitler's faithful shadow and was known to have his confidence. He understood Hitler, his weaknesses and susceptibilities, even better than Goebbels himself. He always knew what the Führer wished to hear, and made sure he heard it. Towards the end of the war, nobody had more influence on Hitler, or advised the Führer more fatally, than Martin Bormann. He was ruthless, brutal, persistent and determined. Bormann did not have any contact whatsoever with the Goebbels; he had no friends at all.

Hitler once again came often to the house of his Propaganda Minister. The war, as a subject of conversation, was avoided, each of the guests doing his utmost to keep off this, the subject nearest his heart. On 29 October 1942, when they were celebrating Goebbels' birthday at Schwanenwerder, Ello Quandt sat next to Hitler. She had laid her silver fox fur stole over the arm of her chair. The atmosphere was gloomy. A decisive outcome to the second year of the war in the East was still not in sight; the over-exhausted troops faced another severe Russian winter. Nobody spoke of it, but coming events were casting deep shadows ahead.

Hitler had been gazing spellbound at Ello's fur. 'Tell me, dear lady,' he said suddenly, 'do you realize that innocent animals are killed simply that you may wear this fur?'

Ello was on the point of saying that she found the killing of millions of innocent men on the battlefield far worse than the deaths of six silver foxes, but she restrained herself. 'I don't find the fate of foxes excessively tragic,' she replied.

Hitler reflected a moment or two then added gloomily. 'That's just what's wrong, that we no longer understand the tragedy of things. If only everybody realized that the destruction of only one life cannot be vindicated, so many things would be different and better.'

Ello found herself at a loss for a suitable reply. Was he referring to foxes or to men? And if he meant men's lives why had he started this war? Why did he daily sign so many death warrants?

On another occasion the conversation turned to a German emigré who had gone abroad to live for political reasons and had since returned to defend the Fatherland as a soldier, but who confessed to remaining, as before, an opponent of Hitler. All those present, including Goebbels, praised the attitude of the man, who of his own free will had hastened back to face extreme danger in serving Germany, although he rejected its leader. But Hitler remarked sullenly, 'I don't share your point of view. He who is against me ... is also against Germany.'

On the third anniversary of the Munich Beer Hall explosion* of 9 November 1939 Hitler explained to a small group of guests, among

---

*A few minutes after Hitler had left, after speaking at the annual 'Old Guard' party in commemoration of the 1923 Beer Hall Putsch in Munich, a bomb planted in a pillar behind the speaker's platform exploded, killing seven and wounding sixty-three.

whom were Magda and Ello Quandt, that he was convinced that Providence would protect him from becoming the victim of any attempt on his life. He described once again the course of events of the Munich plot, then covered his eyes with his right hand. 'I know that I shall not die,' he declared after a pause, 'before the historic mission is accomplished for which Providence has destined me. I shall never fall at the hands of an enemy.'

The longer the war continued, the more headstrong and stubborn Hitler became, less inclined than ever to take sensible advice. His fatal conviction that he alone was competent to make important decisions grew more pronounced. But instead of concerning himself with really decisive problems, the more catastrophic the situation became, he occupied himself all the more eagerly with minor questions. If his most trifling orders were not carried out precisely as he wished, he would work himself up into a state of as much excitement as if he had lost a battle. This lack of restraint in Hitler was a matter of increasingly bitter disappointment to Magda.

The following incident is typical of Hitler at that time. For a long-forgotten reason, Hitler had ordered that after three o'clock in the morning at the Berghof, near Berchtesgaden, no alcohol was to be served. One cold, snowy winter night, Colonel Schmundt had made the long journey from furthest East Prussia to Berchtesgaden without a halt. He carried an important document for Hitler and was due to return to East Prussia straightaway. He arrived at the Berghof at exactly ten minutes past three, and asked for a glass of champagne, which the orderly, in accordance with instructions, refused.

The Colonel turned to the S.S. adjutant on duty in protest. 'Who on earth begrudges a frozen soldier straight from the Front a well-deserved warming drink?' he demanded. 'The Führer certainly can have no objection to that.' The adjutant agreed.

'Bring the Colonel a bottle of champagne,' he ordered. 'I'll be responsible.' He had no idea what he had taken on. When Hitler by chance heard about it, he stormed with rage, and sent both the adjutant and the corporal who had served the bottle away to the Front. As for Colonel Schmundt, who had long since gone back to East Prussia, he rebuked him in a long letter.

'So it has come to that,' said Magda, when she heard the story. 'Three decent men disciplined on account of one bottle of champagne, and because they exceeded the time limit by ten minutes.'

22

Illusion and Reality before the Fall

By the beginning of 1944 Magda was growing increasingly despondent. She had long realized that Germany was not going to win the war, and that the Third Reich and all who had had any part in it faced with absolute certainty a grievous end.

It has all turned out quite differently from what the Führer promised [she confided to Ello]. He has failed because he has been doing the very same things which he himself previously fought against. He ridiculed the divine right of Kaiser Wilhelm and bitterly condemned the autocracy of the Czars. Yet how does he himself stand now? He regards himself as being just as infallible as all the potentates whom he so sharply criticized. If Louis XIV declared *'l'État c'est moi'*, well our Head of State is of the same opinion. He no longer listens to voices of reason. Those who tell him what he wishes to hear are the only ones he believes – they are the ones in the right. And all one can do is stand by and watch what is happening. It's all going to end badly – it can't possibly be otherwise.

Magda could never understand Hitler's attachment to Eva Braun, an association which became all the closer as failure and disaster approached. She was never able to establish a sympathetic relationship with the only woman who was close to the Führer for so many years. Hitler, burdened as he was with such enormous responsibility, had never been able to tolerate any woman around him who made claims for herself. Selfless devotion, patient self-abnegation, a companionship free from any problems, were all that he wanted. Magda no doubt put her finger on the matter when she said one day, 'He is not enough of a man to be able to stand a real woman near him.'

With the signs of approaching defeat ever more obvious, Goebbels in his own intimate circle showed surprising, in fact dangerous, candour. Any other person daring to say such things at that time would have faced summary execution in Plötzensee Jail. 'This Churchill,' he began one evening in front of a flickering fire at Schwanenwerder, 'is one of the most admirable figures in all English history. He has not only got courage, but great intelligence as well. Look here, see what a fellow he is. He dared to say to the public quite frankly, "I offer you nothing but blood, sweat and tears." Again, look how this man pulled his country to its feet after Dunkirk.'

This was followed by several minutes of complete silence. Nobody was bold enough to comment. 'But Churchill rules England,' Goebbels continued, 'and such candour impresses the English. The Führer and I could not inspire the Germans with the promise of blood, sweat and tears.'

At about the same time, in a speech over the radio, Hitler referred to Winston Churchill as 'an old whisky soak'. Goebbels, too, did not hesitate to vilify lewdly in his press the next day the same man whom he had praised to his friends the previous evening. Goebbels did not consider his ambivalent behaviour either immoral or incorrect. He was a deceiver, an illusionist, by vocation. No illusionist believes in the illusions he himself fosters.

Unlike Hitler, Goebbels listened daily to foreign broadcasts and read the reports submitted to him. He was anxious to keep himself well-informed; he insisted on being told the whole truth and never took it amiss. On the contrary, he was extremely annoyed if anybody tried to cover up anything that had gone wrong or to minimize a military failure. 'How can you influence the public,' he asked, 'if you don't even know what you've got to deceive them about?'

Statements of this kind demonstrate his cold intellectual attitude. He was also unbelievably cynical. 'It won't do,' he affirmed in the last few days of 1943, 'to pay workers more and more wages. Even in peacetime it is not possible. They will want butter instead of margarine on their bread and there isn't enough butter to go round. Just as it is not possible for every family to have a Volkswagen, so as to go out into the country on a Sunday; we have neither got the oil nor the space in Germany for everyone to spend Sundays in the country.' But in his propaganda, he promised that once the war was over every family would have a Volkswagen.

In the summer following the catastrophes of Stalingrad and El Alamein, at a time when night after night bombs were raining down on German cities and the people were seized by a growing feeling of despair, Goebbels was seated in the midst of a group of his friends on the terrace of his Berlin palace. The sun shone on the ancient trees in the park; a footman was serving refreshments and offering cigarettes. The Propaganda Minister, in a well-cut suit, leaned back in his garden chair and smilingly watched his children in their light summer clothes playing on the lawn. The peaceful idyll would have been perfect had there not been among the guests a lady who had just arrived from heavily bombed Hamburg. She described the fires and destruction, the long nights alive with flames, and insisted that nobody could continue indefinitely to put up with such monstrous suffering. The Minister wrinkled his brow. 'People can put up with a lot,' he countered ill-humouredly, 'more than you think. Our people can stand ten or even twenty years of war if need be. Think what the Prussians had to go through in the time of Frederick the Great.'

'But I ask you, Minister,' pursued the lady, anxious to defend herself, 'you can't compare the two things. In those days there were no bombs, there was no hunger, and armies were very small, relatively speaking. There was no conscription. In those days the only people aware of the war were those near the battlefields.' Goebbels stood up, an injured look on his face.

'Can't a man enjoy his Sunday in peace?' he snarled, and withdrew. Of course he knew about the hardships being endured by the population in the cities. He knew of the losses, the terror, the hunger and the cold arising from the war in the air. But he only knew about it, he himself did not experience it. The Promi chief, protected from the bombs, living far from the Front, was spared the horror, could only judge their effects theoretically at best.

Magda was an intelligent woman, realistic in outlook; among her friends she openly condemned the war as calamitous, had done so even before it broke out. But it was not possible even for her to grasp fully the privation and distress to which the people were exposed. She had had no first-hand experience of it.

In the Goebbels' palace behind the Wilhelmstrasse, as soon as the sirens began to wail, Magda accompanied her guests to a silent lift plunging fourteen metres deep beneath the surface. Emerging from the lift they faced a small, luxurious flat. The walls were panelled or covered with material and hung with valuable pictures, put there for safety. Thick carpets muffled the sound of footsteps. Upholstered armchairs stood invitingly around, there were roomy beds with soft mattresses and silken eiderdowns in the bedrooms. There was a bath with hot and cold running water, an all-electric kitchen with refrigerator, a well-stocked wine cellar, an air-conditioning installation – everything which went to make up a complete household. An oasis of comfort deep in the heart of the earth, guaranteeing the utmost security for the masters, for the war lords of the Third Reich and their families.* Each of the Goebbels' various households had been equipped, at enormous expense, with a similar underground dwelling.

Beneath twelve metres of earth and two metres of concrete, through which no sound of the air battle above could penetrate, it was quite impossible to imagine what the millions of big city dwellers were having to undergo, those who sat huddled together in tumbledown cellars, beneath water pipes which could burst asunder at any moment and flood them out. Pale with terror, peace-loving citizens crouched there together, while all around them raged a sea of flames, walls trembling and houses collapsing with a roar.

As Magda was driven through the city in her sleek Mercedes towards Schwanenwerder or Castle Lanke she could hardly be

*Just as the Goebbels family were protected from bombs and conflagration, so were the other leaders of the sinking Reich, as well as important government offices and administrative centres. A miniature dwelling with many comforts was to be found beneath Schloss Bellevue at the Zoo, the government's official entertaining centre.

From May 1939 my parents lived in the further left wing, and apartments in the bunker were available for them to use in emergency. The shelter had only just been completed when, on the occasion of a summit meeting with Molotov, an air raid, probably deliberately planned against Berlin, took place, just as the Soviet prime minister with an enormous entourage arrived at Schloss Bellevue. The Soviet minister, accompanied by his delegation, hastily descended to the agreeable subterranean apartments.

In September 1944 I too sheltered in the bunker with my father, as practically everything overhead was destroyed. There was a complete clinic down below with an operating room and all the necessary instruments. Only the most important accessories were missing – a doctor and his assistants with nursing sisters. My father lived in this bunker during the last few months, since life overhead was no longer possible. He had sent my mother and domestic staff away to our summer residence on the Schliersee. He lived on deep beneath the ground at Schloss Bellevue right up to the end, just before the encirclement of the city by the Russians. During the night of 20–21 April 1945, when it was just still possible, he left the condemned city on Hitler's instructions by way of a gap still open for a few hours, finally reaching Flensburg and Admiral Dönitz, who became nominal president of the rest of Germany after Hitler's suicide, and who negotiated the unconditional surrender. Following his brief period of government, which only lasted three weeks, Admiral Dönitz was arrested by the victors with all his staff, including my father.

expected to understand the anguish of the over-burdened, grey-faced, starving people who, after endless sleepless nights, were forced by the lack of transport to walk miles, sore-footed, to their work. Though Magda's meal tables were very simply set in wartime, she had not the slightest idea what it was like to be always under-nourished, to walk in worn-out shoes past repair, or to be without heating in the winter when the gas supply failed and no other source of warmth was available because of the lack of coal. Although she was probably one of the relatively unassuming and more discerning of the women of the 'thin-skinned upper crust', she lived neverthe-less under a bell of indestructible glass throughout the war.

One thing only affected her as it did millions of other mothers – worry about the safety of her son. Harold was in constant danger, possibly in even greater danger than the average fighting man among his contemporaries, because he was deliberately exposed. The Propaganda Minister did not wish his stepson to enjoy any preference or protection. Magda would have been a strange mother if for her part she had not, at least in secret, fostered the wish that he might. 'Joseph thinks perhaps,' she said somewhat bitterly to her sister-in-law, 'that it would be helpful, as far as his standing with Hitler and his general reputation is concerned, if one day he could get up before the public and announce that he had sacrificed a son to the Führer. But Harold is not his son.'

Although the relationship between Goebbels and his stepson was good, occasionally they disagreed. Through his experiences in battle, Harold had developed into a man, had learned to form his own opinions about the war and its leadership. On leave from Africa he openly criticized his stepfather. Calmly and factually, he faced the Reich Minister: he knew better what happened on the battlefield and how great was the superior strength of the enemy.

Like millions of other German soldiers, Harold Quandt, although aware of Germany's difficult position, still believed in the possibility of victory and continued to apply for dangerous postings. All the same he was the only one of Magda's seven children to survive. Badly wounded in Italy, he was captured by the English, finally returning to Germany in 1947 via Egypt.

When Goebbels raged against the spirit of defeatism in those who clearly foresaw the coming downfall of the German Reich, he acted solely from political motives. He knew for certain how matters stood. He had sought to prevent the outbreak of war, considering war a menace to be avoided at all costs by the National Socialist

State. He had desperately hoped that the war with England and France would be terminated at the conclusion of the brief Polish campaign. Now, however, after two winters in Russia, it was clear to him that victory, at any rate a true victory, was no longer possible. He by no means envisaged total defeat, but grievous years with heavy losses. Already by the end of 1941 he was pressurizing Hitler to instigate all those measures for total warfare which were in fact later promulgated.

He was also convinced that the enemy had missed many opportunities. In his opinion they could have been spared enormous losses of men, material and effort, as well as milliards in money, if they had accepted the heavy German setbacks in the East, particularly the catastrophe at Stalingrad, as suitable junctures at which to conclude an honourable peace with the German people, conditional upon the country being relieved of National Socialist domination, or upon the Führer with all his clique being made to disappear in some other way. Goebbels held the view that in such circumstances the National Socialist leadership could no longer maintain its authority against the army and the General Staff, nor indeed against the S.S. units, with whom the army, as a result of comradeship built up on the battlefield, stood, for the time being, in closer association than with the Party bosses. Being himself aware of all these factors, he could not understand why the enemy powers let slip their chance of bringing the war to a speedy end. He thought that possibly they would make the same mistake as the Führer in the campaign against the Soviet Union; he had missed his chance of winning the *Blitzkrieg* through his over-ambitious objective of delivering the Russians from communist tyranny and bringing the whole country under German domination as a sort of colony.

Because, towards the end of the Second World War, the enemy powers insisted on unconditional surrender, as well as the occupation and dividing up of the whole of the German Reich, the war was prolonged and the number of victims was doubled. Goebbels could not understand their attitude. It was in any case abundantly clear to him that he would in all circumstances be a lost man, even in the unlikely event of a compromise peace.

Goebbels looked upon enemy radio propaganda as dangerous only when it was particularly well done. The broadcasts in various German dialects which the B.B.C. transmitted regularly on certain weekdays were outstandingly good and therefore came into the dangerous category. The series 'Frau Wernicke in the Air Raid

Shelter' particularly fascinated the Propaganda Minister. He never missed a broadcast if he could possibly help it, and used to join in the laughter. Many Germans of the older age groups will remember those radio programmes in genuine Berlin dialect, in which a quick-witted Berlin woman would converse with other occupants of the house, sometimes in the air raid shelter, about all the topics of the day. It was all so clever, and so full of wit and humour, that one could easily have believed one was actually listening to a group of Berlin women, chattering and grumbling to each other.

Goebbels watched every anti-German propaganda film which had been captured or obtained through agents, even inviting guests to see these performances. Sometimes he found himself represented in them, mostly in a primitive and far from accurate fashion. In one of these films, however, he was so strikingly presented in appearance and manner of speaking that Magda cried, 'But Joseph, that's you yourself.'

'Yes, really magnificent,' Goebbels had to admit, 'a dangerous film, a hard nut for us. People who can do that sort of thing should be working for us .... We would pay them well, even in foreign currency.'

Magda was not in Berlin on the historic day of 20 July 1944, when the attempt on Hitler's life was made. She was in the Weisser Hirsch (White Hart) Sanatorium in Dresden. My mother was also in the sanatorium for a few days, and there she met Magda Goebbels for the last time. Magda appeared to be really ill, with dark shadows under her eyes and lines at the corners of her mouth. She looked completely despairing, and much thinner than formerly. My mother thought it was more a mental breakdown than a physical illness which had hit her so hard.

Magda suffered severely from pain in the right side of her face, in the Trigeminus nerve. It was a complaint from which she was never again to be wholly free to the end of her life. She was lying in bed with a compress on her face and a small radio on the bedside table when Ello entered. Observing tears running down Magda's grey, worn face she enquired anxiously what was the matter. 'Quiet, for God's sake, quiet,' the patient motioned to Ello. 'They have tried to murder the Führer.' Both women listened intently as Goebbels' voice announced that the Führer was unhurt, the revolt of a few criminal officers having been suppressed. Late that evening Goebbels rang the Weisser Hirsch. He spoke hastily, obviously agitated, and explained to Magda that it was all over and there was no need to worry. He mentioned that the conspirators had wanted to arrest him too, but had been thwarted through the strong sense of duty of a certain Major Remer. The time for clemency was now past. This underhand treachery on the part of an aristocratic clique would be severely punished. He then hung up.

Next day Magda learned through the radio that Hitler had vested her husband with the full plenary authority that he had wanted for so many years. His post was now that of Plenipotentiary for the Total Prosecution of the War. But it had come too late, as Joseph Goebbels, now so swiftly promoted to second-in-command, very well knew.

The last nine months of the Third Reich, the last too in the lives of Magda and Joseph Goebbels, were for those at the battlefront and those at home a time of agonizing suffering, of untold sorrow, horror and death. For Magda they brought a wealth of contradictory emotional experiences. Oddly enough her love for her husband returned once more in all its early strength, so shortly before the end. For Joseph Goebbels it brought an improbable late flowering of power.

Night after night more than a thousand bombers released their death-dealing cargoes over German cities, the losses among the civilian population were heavier than ever before, the smoking ruins stretched for miles, where previously housing estates, factories, cathedrals, railway stations and bridges had been. Nevertheless it was in these autumn months of 1944 that German armament production reached its maximum limits.

Far more guns and ammunition, armoured vehicles, aircraft engines, machine guns and other war materials left the ruined or hastily repaired factory buildings than ever during the relatively peaceful war years from 1939 to 1943. This economic miracle, made possible by the Plenipotentiary for the Total Prosecution of the War, called for enormous sacrifice. He had had vital production centres removed to tunnels or closed-down mines, thickly wooded forest land or rural estates. He summoned housewives to the conveyor belts and to man the anti-aircraft guns; he trained children to use bazooka missiles. Soon pictures of fourteen-year-old lads receiving the Iron Cross for bravery in front of the enemy appeared.

Trains ran, telephones operated, the distribution of food went ahead smoothly. Years later, commissions of enquiry set up by the conquering powers established that even the ceaseless terror raids from the air had not been able to disorganize for any length of time the war production of the Third Reich, nor the supply services of the hard-pressed Wehrmacht. What led in the end to the final collapse was the increasingly accelerated retreat on all fronts of the German military forces, thanks to the overwhelming superiority in men and materials of the enemy.

The assassination attempt of 20 July failed as the result of an improbable series of accidents which enabled Adolf Hitler to escape the time-bomb of Count Stauffenberg. Thereafter, when addressing the crowds or speaking on the radio, Goebbels would work himself up into such a frenzy of scorn and hatred as even Magda had never heard him do. 'The other Joseph,' said Goebbels privately to his friends, 'that is to say little Father Stalin, did the right thing. He was more intelligent than us. He not only exterminated those who were a danger to him but all those who could in any way have been dangerous. We were much too generous, showed much too much forbearance, were much too considerate. That's all done with now, once and for all. Whoever raises his head only a hand's breadth higher than he should, will get it chopped off!'

Now, even in his own household, nobody but Goebbels dared to speak openly. 'The Führer is much too soft,' he would scream, when he arrived back from the office. 'Every day I tell him to punish his critics with immediate death.'

'But what you are saying is dreadful,' protested Magda, appalled.

'What's dreadful? It is self-defence,' blustered Goebbels. 'These people approach us with a sharp hatchet. Should we wait for them in a tail coat and ask "What can we do for you, please?" No, there's only one way, to strike first.'

The Plenipotentiary for the Total Prosecution of the War not only had no mercy for the conspirators of 20 July, he despised them as well. He thought them stupid, dilettantish, muddle-headed, idle gossips. 'When the war is over,' he confided to Magda, in the presence of Ello Quandt, 'I will tell them one day how I would have organized the attempt. I guarantee it would have worked.'

The Minister's propaganda took on a note of pitiless severity. Now that the end was approaching, he once again had enemies in Germany, dangerous, resolute, desperate enemies. The time had come when he could once more, as before 1933, attack his own people unrestrainedly. His weekly articles in the *Reich*, the leading official weekly, were masterpieces of demogogic argument. Even his most embittered opponents at home and abroad eagerly awaited the Monday issue.

Something fresh always occurred to him. He always found a way to pick out from the gaping ruins of the Greater German Reich the signs of an early upswing, even a brilliant future. His style was all the more dazzling, the more ominous the outlook. He knew how, time and again, with apparent honesty to conjure up a mirage before the weary eyes of a nation on the point of exhaustion.

Some time previously he had invented the fable of the new weapon. Now, at a time when enemy tanks were invading the Reich from the east, west and south, he broadcast this 'news' with consummate skill. He rammed into the war-weary public that each day, each hour that they continued to hold out could and would help to bring deliverance. In fact, he did manage to raise the hopes of many at a time when all who were still capable of thought had long given up hope of victory, when ceaseless bombing attacks by day and night were demolishing German cities, when the battlefronts were being shattered like glass, when heightened terror of the Gestapo was rapidly spreading. He succeeded in creating the impression that the majority were behind Hitler's government, behind the regime of violence which had committed such stupendous blunders, such monstrous crimes.

Goebbels remained for the whole of that last winter in Berlin. In February 1945, as the Soviet army approached Lanke, Magda brought the six children and their two nurses away from the Lanke air raid shelter to Schwanenwerder. At no time did it occur to Joseph that it was high time to send Magda and the children to south Germany or somewhere in the Bavarian countryside. For ordinary families wishing to do so it was still possible, even if difficult, but for the all-powerful minister it would have been extremely easy.

Nearly all the refugees, evacuees and bombed-out people who fled to villages, small towns or remote spas in the south or west of unoccupied Germany managed to hold out fairly well until the end of the war. But the eight members of the Goebbels family stayed behind together.

During those final months Goebbels, whose ministry, unlike many other government authorities, had not been dispersed, carried out his official duties with all his characteristic dynamism. He praised, harassed and slogged as one possessed. He despatched to the Front every man who could possibly be released; as a result those who remained behind exerted every ounce of strength to make themselves indispensable. Because of a harmless piece of gossip, which at that time was regarded as dangerous, he recommended – or rather one should say he ordered – that a certain official in his household should be hanged before his fellow workers. At the last moment the order was repealed and the offender sent off to the Front.

Goebbels' own colleagues, who assisted him in inventing and propagating the myth of the new weapons, were not, of course, taken in by the baseless deception. In his ministry it was known that the manufacture of so-called wonder weapons, insofar as they were not altogether products of the Minister's imagination, had been started, and time and time again held up or brought to a complete standstill by enemy bomb attacks. The newly developed weapons could scarcely be put into service for yet another twelve months. In view of the shortage of raw materials and enemy air superiority, there was only a very remote possibility of their being produced and effectively used in sufficient quantities to affect the outcome of the war.

When Goebbels began to doubt whether the new weapons would continue to work as a propaganda trick after January 1945, he thought up something else. In spite of coming so near the end, this too was effective. He spread a rumour, by the well-proven whispering method, of a coming breach between the Western and Eastern allied powers, adding that secret negotiations were in train for an arms agreement between the Anglo-American authorities and Germany to enable the war to be continued jointly against the Soviet Union. Talk of the secret negotiations ostensibly on the point of being concluded was so skilfully disseminated, always passed on as coming from well-informed sources, that even this deliberate lie found ready acceptance.

But should the western allies fail to realize that it was their duty jointly with Germany to save Europe from Bolshevism, the tables would have to be turned. Soon tongues were whispering in the strictest confidence that negotiations of an even more secret nature were being held with the Russians, the purpose of which was to link up with the Russians and drive the Western powers right back to the Atlantic coast.

It is difficult to judge whether Hitler himself believed in the possibility of one or other solution. At the beginning of 1945, Goebbels still seemed to think it possible, in an almost incredible misjudgment of his opponents that London and Washington would, out of fear of Russia, make a pact with the German Reich. With this eventuality in mind, he drew up a sort of peace treaty. He was prepared to renounce all claim to Alsace-Lorraine and to be satisfied with the frontiers as they were before 1939, assuming of course a corresponding indemnity in the East. The parties to the new agreement would not on any account interfere in the internal affairs of Germany. Once peace was concluded, National Socialism would completely permeate life in Germany as a whole.

According to this plan, State and Party would be united in one solid block. The foundations would be reinforced much more invincibly than since 1933. The basis would be composed of manual workers, farmers, craftsmen and those working in service industries. All people, organizations, institutions and traditions which were not prepared to be wholly absorbed in the National Socialist totalitarian State would have to go.

At a tea party one day in the house of a well-known opera conductor, Joseph Goebbels unfolded plans for the future which took everybody's breath away. Mass murder of the Jews would be followed by massacre of the German nobility. 'When we have got rid of the last of the half-Jews,' Goebbels declared, 'then we must proceed to eliminate the aristocrats.'

'Do you really mean,' enquired a guest, 'that nobody may any longer bear a title?'

The minister wrinkled his brow. 'No, I didn't quite mean that,' he answered, 'since even without a title these people would still be the same. They constitute an alien element in the State, and as they only marry among themselves they intensify their degenerate proclivities. Like the Jews, they have international blood relationships and they will never cease to cultivate their own caste. They must be wiped out completely; men, women and children, all must be got rid of.'

'But *Englechen*,' cried Magda, horrified, 'do you realize what you are saying?'

'Oh! yes, I know it is a damned hard thing to do,' he replied, 'unjust to many, no doubt, but it can't be helped. It must and shall be.'

This horrific plan for the period after the war had been won was adumbrated by Goebbels at the end of July 1944. It is not altogether certain that he was really serious, since it occasionally amused him to shock his listeners. Goebbels only voiced his other thoughts to Magda. It is not known what these were, only that Magda confided to Ello: 'It is absolutely gruesome all that he says to me now, I can hardly stand it any longer. You can't imagine what dreadful things he oppresses me with and I dare not open my heart about them to anybody. I'm not supposed to tell anybody, but I must, if only you. Do you know he clings to me now, unloads everything on to me. It is all too much even for him. It is unbelievable – quite unimaginable.'

Magda was again ill, this time seriously so. Her nerves were stretched to breaking point, the tension manifesting itself in the form of an extremely painful suppuration of the salivary glands. In August 1944 an operation on the right side of her face had become necessary. There was only one specialist in this particular field, his practice was in Breslau and he could not get away. Breslau was the home of Gauleiter Hanke. So Magda had to go to Breslau, and Hanke went to see her in the clinic.

Hanke had been involved in the Polish campaign as an ordinary soldier. As this was just after his great disappointment over Magda she had, no doubt rightly, feared, that he wished to die, and had had some feelings of guilt on his behalf. But Hanke had emerged safe and sound and had been awarded an outstanding decoration. Shortly afterwards he took up his Gauleiter's post in Breslau and became attached to a young French lady, daughter of an aristocratic landowner in the Breslau area, whom he married early in 1945.

While Magda was in the Breslau Clinic her husband naturally visited her. The Gauleiter had unavoidably to receive him with full honours. In spite of the past, Hanke gave a magnificent banquet for Joseph Goebbels and his wife in Breslau Castle. At least it was intended to be magnificent; in fact it was not altogether successful. The guests were kept waiting at the table a long time before any food appeared, and when at last it was served the food which should have been hot was cold and cold was warm. Some guests couldn't find places, others had no spoons.

Back in the hotel with Magda, Goebbels roared with laughter. 'And to think,' he sniggered, 'that you very nearly became the Gauleiter's wife. What a joke that would have been.'

'If I had been Hanke's wife,' snapped Magda, 'it would have been a success.'

'Thank your lucky stars you aren't,' riposted Goebbels.

Magda and Hanke never met again. The career of the faithful henchman led briefly, right at the end, to the very topmost level.

On 1 May 1945 Hanke, following the deceased Hitler's testamentary dispositions, was appointed *Reichsführer* S.S. in succession to the traitor Himmler. At the same time Dönitz, the new President of the Reich, appointed him Minister of the Interior, although Hanke knew nothing of the appointment. Hanke did not take up either post because he was hemmed in in Breslau, bitterly defending the city to the utmost. There are several versions of his ultimate fate. Some say he was killed in Breslau. Others maintain that he shot himself at his desk as the city was in flames and unable to hold out any longer. Still others are sure that he left Breslau by air at the last moment to report to President Dönitz in Flensburg. En route his small aircraft had to make an emergency landing in Prague to refuel. The airport was occupied by Czech partisans who recognized Hanke and killed him. Rumours also persist that Hanke survived the postwar period and went into hiding.

23

Freedom Comes and Goes

In the last year of her life, when the world about her was threatening to disintegrate and the atmosphere was rife with premonitions of death, Magda Goebbels had, in the circumstances, the most unexpected experience. She fell in love once more.

Werner Naumann, Karl Hanke's successor at the Ministry, was the most dangerous enemy that Goebbels had yet encountered. It is a vexed question why Goebbels should, following Hanke's promotion, have appointed such a man as Naumann to be Secretary of State in the Ministry. Well briefed in every way, he must have been aware that Naumann was resolutely inimical to him. It could have been that in appointing him as his deputy he hoped to disarm him, or to be in a better position to supervise him effectively.

Naumann, superior in intelligence and more far-sighted than the worthy but credulous Hanke, had from the outset discerned the true nature of his chief. While Naumann admired his talent for controlling the masses and his sure understanding of the German mentality, he perceived clearly that these gifts of Goebbels were brought to bear empty of conviction or belief. Goebbels was, in Naumann's opinion, the very essence of evil, a diabolical genius, and he hated him from the start. He watched his chief closely, trying to probe his character, piecing the evidence together. Naumann was full of sympathy for Magda, tied as she was to Goebbels for good or ill. It never occurred to her that Naumann had set to work to overthrow the Minister at the first opportunity. No longer young, she was immensely flattered by his devoted admiration and grateful for the slightest friendly gesture to offset the inner torment, the weighty depression, created by the menacing outlook. To her astonishment she suddenly realized that she loved him.

Naumann was happily married with four children. Magda's contacts with him were confined to sharing a table at tea occasionally, or meeting at social gatherings in the evening. Yet every moment that she could be near him, the object of her almost teenage devotion, was filled with happiness.

These last few months of emotional involvement found expression, as had her first love, in the writing of verse. She read them out to Ello and then burned most of them. A few that she considered to be the best she sent anonymously to Naumann. None has been preserved, although in Ello's opinion they were masterpieces of their kind. The romance came to an end in December 1944 when Goebbels discovered her feelings for Naumann and summoned him to an interview. 'What's all this about?' he demanded imperiously. 'This is not the time for another Hanke affair. Things have changed.' Naumann yielded and broke off the friendship straightaway. Deeply disappointed at first with his behaviour, Magda later found much to excuse in it.

Even stranger and still more unexpected than Magda's brief unfulfilled love for Naumann was the conduct of her husband during their last winter together. Goebbels behaved as a loving, loyal husband and father. He turned once again wholly to Magda, his last support. He spent anxious evenings alone with her, stood long and thoughtfully at the bedside of his children. So many women had enjoyed his favours in the good days and profited greatly from their connection with him. His agony, his last victory, his ultimate defeat and finally his end he shared with Magda alone.

'Magda I beg you,' pleaded her mother, 'don't let this man destroy you altogether. He's ruined your life and shamefully deceived you.'

'I've got no choice,' replied Magda sadly, 'for me there is no other way.'

After her operation in Breslau in September 1944, Magda had gone into the Sanatorium in Dresden, in the hope of making a more rapid recovery. She still suffered severely, and apart from her husband and Ello, would receive no visitors at all. Goebbels used to drive over from Berlin to see his sick wife. He was taciturn and withdrawn. He didn't stay in the sanatorium with Magda but below in the Hotel

Bellevue. Nevertheless they spent much time together, nearly always just the two of them. On one occasion Ello was invited to join them for lunch in the hotel. Hardly a word passed between them. After the meal Goebbels switched on the large radiogram and they listened in silence to an orchestral concert conducted by Herbert von Karajan. 'How I envy that man,' murmured Goebbels, 'devoting his life to music.'

The battlefronts were closing in on Berlin. It was Goebbels who, once again, succeeded in delaying collapse for a few weeks, accomplishing through his skill at lying an almost unbelievable feat.

Goebbels' last great lie campaign was the 'Werewolf' saga.* The moment the enemy set foot on German soil, Goebbels called up, through countless radio broadcasts, those newspapers still in circulation, and whatever other propaganda outlets were still available in unoccupied zones, all those youths not old enough to enlist for military service, to form a juvenile underground movement. Secret tribunals mushroomed and camouflaged resistance groups stood ready to harass the enemy. These organizations and groups, claimed the Promi chief from his concrete bunker, would unleash a form of bitter guerilla warfare behind the troops in the fighting line. One of the most important duties of the Werewolves would be to liquidate so-called traitors and collaborators – that is to say those Germans who placed themselves at the disposal of the occupying powers for the purposes of reconstruction.

Goebbels must have been only too well aware that all such efforts would be fruitless. He was far better informed as to the true position than Hitler himself. This emerges clearly from his recently discovered diaries of the final months of the war, which show that he was under no illusion whatsoever. What hurt him more than anything else was the fact that the population of Rheydt, his native town, welcomed the American troops with great enthusiasm as liberators from the Nazi yoke. The German people would have

---

*The 'Werewolf' concept originated in ancient Germanic folklore, according to which a man ('*Wer*') enveloped himself in a wolfskin and in a moment of ecstatic frenzy turned into a wolf. Medieval warlords and later political extremists misapplied the early widespread Werewolf legend, organizing groups of fanatical guerilla fighters to harass and intimidate. This objective was usually successful up to a point and was finally made use of by Goebbels, although the German underground movement 'Werewolf' never actually became effective, or at most only to an insignificant extent.

nothing more to do with guerilla warfare, secret tribunals and the legendary Werewolf.

The enemy did, to a certain extent, fall into the trap prepared by Goebbels. Progressing rapidly, they gave full credence to the Werewolf myth. They seriously feared partisan attacks, increasingly the deeper they penetrated, and expected to suffer heavy losses as a result. They were not prepared for this sort of thing, so unlike anything the Germans had ever done before. Right to the end the victors believed in this lie of Goebbels, although the Germans themselves rejected it utterly. Hardly any in the foundering Reich seriously thought of proceeding as ordered with the formation of 'Werewolf' and partisan groups.

The consequences of this ultimate success of Goebbels were grave. While the Western allies halted hesitatingly at the frontiers, penetrating only slowly and cautiously into the heart of the Reich, the Soviet armies pushed rapidly forward from the East causing enormous suffering, an untold number of deaths and infinite sorrow.

Ello Quandt, who since 1943 had been suffering from a serious protracted illness and had gone for treatment into the Weisser Hirsch Sanatorium, was there during the epic enemy air onslaught on Dresden on 13 February 1945. The sanatorium and its surroundings outside the city on the hills above the Elbe were not directly affected, but the patients, among whom was the aged poet Gerhard Hauptmann, witnessed the horror to the full from their windows, saw the fearful sea of flames which within a few hours engulfed and destroyed one of the most beautiful of all German cities. Three days after the attack the ruins of Dresden were still enveloped in smoke, and the storm unleashed by the huge conflagration roared round the sanatorium, causing all the windows to rattle.

It was never possible even to estimate the actual number of victims, there were so many refugees from the conquered territory in the East among them. It is reckoned that the terrorist air attacks of English and American units, apart from the destruction of Dresden, claimed more than 100,000 lives. As the enemy had in effect won the war long before, it is impossible from the German point of view to give any reasonable justification for the Dresden holocaust.

Some three weeks after the attack on Dresden, at the beginning of March 1945, Magda came for the last time to the Weisser Hirsch. She wanted to see her sister-in-law, her trusted friend of twenty-five long years, to pay a final farewell.

On this occasion Frau Goebbels did not arrive in the shining limousine, but in the delivery van of a cigarette firm, sitting up front with the driver. It was definitely safer. Had anybody recognized her, even perhaps if she had been in a large chauffeur-driven car, she might well have been attacked at some blocked street crossing by a refugee half-crazed by hardship and despair.

On entering Ello's room Magda, at the end of her tether, threw herself exhausted on to the bed. Low-flying enemy bombers had attacked the van several times en route; more than once she had had to crouch down in a ditch at the roadside to shelter from the gunfire.

Ello Quandt, painfully supporting herself with the aid of sticks, started to weep. 'What in the world is going to happen to us now?' she sobbed.★

Magda pulled herself up with a jerk. 'Why, the new weapons,' she said confidently, 'they will save us. Only a few more days now. Fantastic things are being prepared. All at once the tables will be turned. It will come suddenly − victory!'

Ello regarded her doubtfully. Since she understood absolutely nothing about war weaponry, she immediately felt relieved. Magda would know what she was talking about. If anybody knew how the situation really stood, then it must certainly be the Plenipotentiary for the Total Prosecution of the War, who in recent times had kept no secret from Magda, but had told her everything.

Magda slept the whole afternoon, tired to death. Towards evening a nurse came to Ello and told her that Magda would like to see her. Magda was still in bed when Ello entered the room. Her blonde hair was loose, encircling her pale, sad face. She appeared to have recovered somewhat. 'Please Ello come and sit near me,' she pleaded, taking her friend's hands between her own, I have something to say to you. I lied to you at noon today. I spoke of wonder weapons about to be launched ... that's all nonsense, only a swindle cooked up by Joseph. We have nothing more, Ello, nothing at all. We are quite done for ... total defeat is now only a question of weeks. It could even come to that in the next few days. We have only one hope left − that the enemy powers will fall out with one another. That alone could perhaps save us − partially save us. Otherwise everything is finished. I, in any case, don't believe in miracles.'

She fell silent. Ello, too. She could only slowly grasp what Magda

★This last conversation between the two women follows word for word Ello Quandt's own report.

Lida Baarova with Gustav Fröhlich

Karl Hanke, Secretary of State and deputy to Goebbels in the *Promi*

Dr Werner Naumann, successor to Hanke as Secretary of State in the *Promi*

Discussions at the Economics Ministry. Left to right: Günther Quandt, Otto Meissner, Funk, the Minister for Economics

Magda Goebbels

The last photographs of the six children of Magda and Joseph Goebbels, taken at Christmas 1944. Top left, Helga, born September 1932; top right, Hilde, born April 1934; centre left, Helmut, born October 1935; centre right, Holde, born February 1937; below left, Hedda, born May 1938; below right Heide, born October 1940. All six were to die on 1 May 1945

The remains of Dr Joseph Goebbels in front of the bunker exit of the Reich Chancellery. He had instructed that his body, and that of his wife, should be burned, but due to lack of petrol and ceaseless gunfire, this proved only partially possible

had just been telling her. 'So the Russians will soon be here then?'

'Yes, they will.'

'Magda, what's going to happen to you and your husband, to your children?' she demanded, stroking her friend's hands tenderly.

'We shall all die, Ello ... but by our own hands, not at those of the enemy.'

'No, for God's sake, Magda, don't say that,' cried Ello, 'that's too horrifying.'

'Horrifying certainly,' admitted Magda calmly, 'but it's the only solution left.'

'No, there must be others ... the Russians are not here yet. There must still be some way of escape, at least for you and the children.'

'No, replied Magda firmly, 'for me there is no escape – and I am not looking for one.'

'But you can't, you must not die for that man who has so frightfully deceived you, whom you recognized long ago as a lying devil.'

Magda shook her head. 'The life that you will all live after the collapse won't be worth living,' she said, emphasizing every word. 'In the short or long term the whole of Europe will be overcome by Bolshevism. We were the last bulwark against the Red flood. As far as we are concerned, we who were at the head of the Third Reich, we must draw the logical conclusion. We have demanded monstrous things from the German people, treated other nations with pitiless cruelty. For this the victors will exact their full revenge ... we can't let them think we are cowards. Everybody else has the right to live. We haven't got this right ... we have forfeited it.'

'But you, you haven't. You are not guilty. Nobody can make you responsible.'

'Yes,' replied Magda sadly. 'I make myself responsible. I belonged. I believed in Hitler and for long enough in Joseph Goebbels. I belong to the Third Reich now on the verge of destruction.'

Ello tried again to protest, to convince Magda that even the victors' press had never written maliciously about her.

'You don't understand my position,' Magda insisted. 'Suppose I remain alive, I should immediately be arrested and interrogated about Joseph. If I tell the truth I must reveal what kind of man he was – must describe all that happened behind the scenes. Then any respectable person would turn from me in disgust. Everybody would be thinking that now my husband was dead or shut up in prison, I was prepared to slander the father of my six children.

Outwardly it would seem that at his side I have lived a glamorous life and benefited from all the power. No! As his wife I remain at his side to the bitter end. Nobody will believe that I really ceased to love him – perhaps I still do, against all reason, against all my experience of him. Whatever I've had to go through, Joseph is my husband. I must be loyal to him and must maintain our relationship to death and beyond. So I could never say anything against him, especially afterwards, after his downfall, I certainly couldn't.'

It was very still in the room on the heights above the Elbe, high above the rubble heaps of Dresden, on that evening in March 1945. Magda broke the silence. 'It would be equally impossible,' she explained, 'for me to do the opposite – that is to defend what he has done, to justify him to his enemies, to speak up for him out of true conviction. I couldn't do that either. That would go against my conscience. So you see, Ello, it would be quite impossible for me to go on living.'

For a long time Ello could find no words. Later she asked quietly: 'And the children? What will happen to the poor children?'

Magda covered her eyes with both hands. 'We will take them with us, they are too good, too lovely for the world which lies ahead. In the days to come Joseph will be regarded as one of the greatest criminals that Germany has ever produced. His children would hear that said daily, people would torment them, despise and humiliate them. They would have to bear the burden of his sins; vengeance would be wreaked on them ...'

Magda covered her eyes with both hands. 'We will take them believe that! Neither our enemies nor our countrymen would torment your children.'

'You forget, Ello, all that has happened. You know how I told you at the time quite frankly what the Führer said in the Café Anast in Munich when he saw the little Jewish boy, you remember? That he would like to squash him flat like a bug on the wall. Do you not remember that still? I could not believe it and thought it was just provocative talk. But he really did it later. It was all so unspeakably gruesome, perpetrated by a system to which I belonged. It has amassed such lust for revenge all over the world – I have no choice, I must take the children with me, I must ...! Only my Harold will survive me. He is not Goebbels' son and happily is a prisoner of the English.'

Ello still could not grasp it. 'But Magda, Magda,' she protested, 'you can't kill your own children.'

'Yes, Ello, I can . . . everything has been arranged. When things get to a certain pitch, they will be given a strong sleeping draught. Afterwards, I mean when they are fast asleep, ... they will be given an injection of Evipan or something, sufficient to ... to ...'

She could not go on, but it was quite clear to Ello that Magda intended to kill her children by injecting them with poison.

At the same time there still existed possibilities of rescue, even of safe and relatively simple rescue. Seven years later Ello Quandt told me that Günther Quandt offered his former wife a house in Switzerland. The children were to be taken there, and the generous Quandt was willing to provide for their upkeep and education. Ello was not quite certain whether the offer applied to Magda as well. There was even talk of an annuity for them all, which Quandt, through his excellent connections in Switzerland, was easily in a position to arrange. Ello could no longer remember the exact date of the proposal or whether Magda discussed it with her former husband. But Magda did not feel able to accept the proffered solution. Had she done so, it would have been a simple matter for Goebbels to have the children sent in good time to the neutral country. He had the means and the power to do so, right up to the last week or so.

'I can see from your face,' said Magda at the end of this last long conversation, 'how horrified you are by the thought that I am going to take my children with me when I die. But you forget, dear Ello, that I believe in reincarnation. They won't die, none of us die, we only go through a seemingly dark door into a new life.'

The next day Magda drove away through the ruins of Dresden, back to Berlin. Ello accompanied her to the delivery van of the cigarette firm. The two women were silent. Even if they had been able to speak, there was nothing more to be said. They had been such very close friends for over twenty-five years – a friendship such as only very few enjoy. Magda knelt on the upholstered seat and waved until she could no longer catch the smallest glimpse of Ello.

24

Last Days

The summer and autumn of 1944 was for the six lovely children of Magda and Joseph Goebbels a happy, carefree time. They had no inkling as to why their parents were so low-spirited, no presentiment of approaching doom; they were completely unaware of the advancing Soviet armies. Helga, who was nearly thirteen, pretty as a picture and highly intelligent, could make no sense of what was going on because no one would tell her anything.

Since the middle of 1943, the children had had a young governess, chosen by Magda from among six dozen or so candidates. Quite by chance it happened that shortly before I finished this book I made the acquaintance of Frau K. She was ready to talk about her experiences during the last few years in Lanke and Schwanenwerder, as well as at the very end in the Berlin city palace of the Goebbels family. Frau K had never before passed on anecdotes, rumours or gossip about the family to the press or to producers of so-called documentary films and television. And even to me she never mentioned anything of a political nature, or about the morals of the master and mistress of the household.

The children without exception were enchanting, in appearance as well as character. Helmut, the only son of the marriage, resembled his father in looks, but his manners were very much the opposite of those of Dr Goebbels. He was considerate and sensitive, a dreamer. This did not suit his father. When Helmut's teacher at the Lanke primary school reported to the parents that Helmut's promotion to a higher form was doubtful, the atmosphere at home became very stormy. This for his father was unthinkable. *His* son not intelligent enough, not capable enough or willing to go up into a higher class? He shouted angrily at the little boy and made him tremble, threatening him with dire punishment unless he did better. Magda intervened. She herself and the governess took the little dreamer in hand, two, three, four, five hours a day. Both understood him, and managed to shake him out of his dreamy ways into reality, with the remarkable result that he was not only promoted but gained astonishingly good marks.

Frau K described how Dr Goebbels, when with the children, never gave any indication whatsoever of the massive responsibilities he carried. He could always switch off completely. In the house and at meals a light, unforced atmosphere prevailed. The children were allowed to chatter to their hearts' content. At home the Minister of State was always relaxed and cheerful; he was never condescending and was much loved by the household staff.

He could be seen at his best when at table, said the governess, who used to sit opposite him at mealtimes. Then the abnormal manner in which he carried his lame foot and the fact that he was so short and ill-proportioned were not apparent. When in a cheerful mood, his face was not by any means bad looking; he had intelligent eyes and a charming smile. He was an animated, discursive conversationalist and had excellent table manners; his slender, well-cared for hands were particularly striking. The formidable energy, the amoral character, and above all the appalling brutality of which Joseph Goebbels was capable, were not immediately discernible.

Though he practically idolized his children, all six of them had one great drawback in his eyes: they were too well-behaved. He would have preferred them to be a bit wild, a bit unruly, more quarrelsome. He used to go out of his way to provoke them, mocking them and making all sorts of outrageous statements, in the hope of getting them to react strongly. He was delighted when one or other child took him up on something. On the other hand, he was greatly disappointed when they all calmly accepted what he said – which was particularly the case with peace-loving Helmut.

'On one occasion,' said Frau K, 'Goebbels had got all the children so worked up that they set on him, chasing him wildly round the room, darting under the tables, turning chairs upside down and so on. In the mêlée Helmut, who had crept under a sofa, managed to grasp his father by the foot, so that he fell flat on the carpet. The children danced with glee, Magda and the two aides present all laughed. Dr Goebbels, however, presumably conscious of his club foot, flew into a rage and shouted fiercely at the little boy.'

It was an ugly scene. Frau K remarked to Adjutant Schwägermann that this sort of thing on the father's part was really brutal. Goebbels overheard what she said, called her to one side and reproached her for making such a highly improper remark. Frau K stood up for herself and the children. 'You don't like it, Minister,' she said, 'when they are all well-behaved. Today you were able to create a rumpus and Helmut in his childish way showed fight and actually made you fall over – a victory for him in the scrimmage which you started. The gallant little fellow got the better of the all-powerful master of the house. A child does not consider what he is doing, he just uses his little strength for all he's worth. What do you actually want from the child, what else did you expect?'

Dr Goebbels beamed. 'Yes, looked at like that, you are quite right. I was in the wrong; I will make it up to him.'

The children remained at Lanke not only right through the summer and autumn of 1944, but over Christmas and well into the new year. Whenever Magda was not in a clinic, the sanatorium at Dresden, or in Breslau for the operation already mentioned, she too was at home in Lanke.

Life there was just like being on an island. At Lanke there was no sign at all of war, provided the family did not listen to the news on the radio or read the newspapers. Life seemed to go on just as in peacetime. Thanks to the local farmers, the other people in the area also had enough to eat. The refugees streamed through, and reports were heard about fallen or missing sons and husbands. In the house, however, everything went on more or less as before.

Magda, according to Frau K, was a many-sided woman. She had a basically cheerful nature and a light and agreeable social manner, especially with the household personnel. She remained optimistic until the situation had got past all hope. But during the last few months she was full of despair and often could hardly hold back her tears.

As a housewife she was no perfectionist. She would let the reins slacken for a time and then, quite suddenly, at intervals of about four weeks, she would become obsessed with cleaning and tidying everything. Her household staff were long used to this and took it calmly. All the curtains would come down, be washed and put up again; bookcases, furniture, cupboards and chests of drawers would be emptied and rearranged.

As far as the Goebbels' marriage was concerned, Frau K remained commendably discreet. In any case, Magda would always leave Lanke for Berlin at a moment's notice whenever Joseph needed her, even if it were only for an hour or two of companionship. Towards the end nothing would prevent her from making the journey, not even low-flying enemy planes, fighter bombers and bomb craters. The more infrequent the occasions on which the Minister could devote himself to his family, the more eagerly would Magda hasten to be with him. In spite of all their differences, in spite of all that had happened between the two of them, for better or for worse she was unquestionably bound to him.

Hitler did not come to Lanke any more. It was too far away, and, besides, with his own problems and the rapidly worsening situation he had more than enough on his hands. But Ello Quandt used to come quite often, staying longer each time. She was Magda's only woman friend. To no other person in her life had Magda opened her heart so fully; nobody else had been so close to her, or sympathized so deeply with her.

Frau Behrend, Magda's mother, came even more frequently and stayed longest, becoming in fact a permanent house guest. Their relationship, which had earlier been an affectionate one, had suffered under the stress of the years, steadily deteriorating as the war progressed. As Frau K explained to me, the cause of the ill-feeling lay clearly with Frau Behrend. She was an extremely selfish old lady, although she was perhaps not altogether to be blamed if her pent-up fears at the prospect of the coming disaster found release in hysterical outbursts.

She expected Magda, whose own worries were already more than she could bear, to do something positive to improve matters, and harassed her daughter day and night. When she failed to get her way, or Magda was unable to pacify her, she would threaten to throw herself in the lake. At times she would even burst into Magda's room in the middle of the night to tell her hard-hearted daughter please to send somebody the next morning to fish her body out. We have already seen how Magda reacted to a threat of suicide in the case of her former friend, Ernest. Frau Behrend naturally did nothing of the kind, and in fact survived her daughter Magda by some twelve years.

I later came to know Magda's mother well. She held her unhappy daughter's memory in great affection and mourned her deeply, but could not find a single good word to say about her son-in-law, Joseph.

On Magda's birthday in November 1944, on the stroke of midnight, all the children suddenly appeared in her bedroom. The little girls were dressed in long white party dresses, Helmut in a dark suit. They carried nosegays in their hands and packages tied with ribbon containing simple gifts they had made themselves. Magda, surprised and deeply moved by this unexpected demonstration by her family at such a time, dissolved into tears of joy. The children had barely another six months to live.

When asked whether, in her opinion, the murder of the children in the bunker had been planned long beforehand, Frau K gave a thoughtful denial. 'In moments of despair,' she explained, 'Frau Goebbels had hinted, so to speak, at the idea, if the worst came to the worst, but I never had the impression that she meant it seriously.'

Magda was at that time feeling optimistic again, and repeatedly expressed the view that, one way or another, something would turn up to save them. 'Just let's be patient a little longer, then we'll see . . .!' Her tendency had always been to let matters take their course, even where quite weighty problems were concerned, and then to try to solve them when it was already too late. So it may have been with this last, most agonizing decision. In any case, between Magda and the governess there was never any talk of a final parting with the children. Their fate still remained open on 23 April when Frau K had to tear herself away from her charges.

The six children, the governess and the house personnel, as well as Magda (most of the time), remained at the Lanke Castle estate until the end of January 1945. But time was running out. The children were becoming increasingly puzzled at the sight of the endless columns of wretched refugees trekking from the east to the Bogensee. The explanations they were given no longer satisfied them, particularly in the case of the thoughtful, intelligent Helga. The tempo of the fugitive hordes quickened daily; overladen vehicles collapsed and exhausted animals gave up; cumbrous baggage was dumped at the roadside. The German defence fell back before the relentless pressure of the superior Soviet forces. Reports of the behaviour of the Russian troops spurred the fugitives on still more.

From Berlin Goebbels ordered the removal of his family from Lanke to Schwanenwerder. All the household personnel went too, and Lanke was abandoned. In dead of night, with headlamps dimmed, the line of cars forged its way slowly, with difficulty, through the crowds of refugees towards Schwanenwerder on the Havel. There, for a brief three months, life resumed its even sway.

Dark clouds of smoke swirled above the capital; bombing attacks persisted almost daily; at night searchlights probed the sky. To the clamour of anti-aircraft guns was added the thunder of the detonating high explosive bombs and the plunging 'whoosh' of incendiaries. The children in Schwanenwerder were completely unaware that the anti-aircraft guns were being manned by young girls and fifteen-year-old boys.

Since February Schwanenwerder had become very crowded. Many friends and acquaintances had sought refuge in the two houses, including one extremely long-standing member of the party, Her Excellency von Dirksen, who, in her heyday as First Lady in Berlin society, had opened her house to the Führer of the N.S.D.A.P. long before the seizure of power. She was known as 'the grandmother of the Third Reich', a title which she herself did not repudiate. Death had spared her all too long, and still compelled her to witness the overthrow of the Third Reich whose beginnings she had so passionately furthered.

No bombs fell on Schwanenwerder; the spring of 1945 seemed lovelier than ever. Gaily coloured crocuses dotted the damp grass, bitterns sang in the reeds around the lake, bushes and trees unfurled their young green shoots. The bright sunshine sparkled on the expanse of water and wavelets gurgled round the stakes of the boathouse. But in the distance the thunder rumbled incessantly. 'Is that a storm?' the children asked, because they loved to watch the lightning flash across the water. It was no spring rainstorm, however, but the heavy barrage covering the Soviet advance towards the capital of the once great German Reich, Soviet artillery battering away at the last defences before Berlin.

By the middle of April the Russians had taken up their stand on the outskirts of the capital in the east, north and south. At night in Schwanenwerder the children could see a blaze of bright orange light flashing across the heavens. They marvelled that no rain followed, as was usual after a storm. Helga Goebbels, nearly thirteen years old, mature beyond her years, sensed that disaster threatened. She kept on asking whether the war was lost and if so where her parents would go with them all. It is doubtful whether Magda was able to reassure her.

The family remained unexpectedly long in Schwanenwerder. The Minister spent most nights as well as many evenings with his wife and children – occasionally, too, with guests – on the more or less undisturbed peninsula. Frau K spoke of their peaceful existence, hardly tolerable in the circumstances, so close was it to the doomed city, now surrounded on three sides by the enemy. The artillery reverberated ever more ominously; by night the glare in the sky became even more spectacular. When Helga or Helmut asked what the dreadful noise was and why there was so much smoke blackening the skies over Berlin, their mother told them that the Führer was overcoming his enemies and that everything would soon be all right again.

In the night of 18-19 April, the Russians tightened their grip on Berlin, now threatened with total encirclement. Magda telephoned to Schwanenwerder from the bunker of their city palace, sending word that the children were to come with Frau K back into the capital. A few trunks were hastily packed, and Frau Behrend tenderly embraced her grandchildren, one after another. Those members of the staff who were no longer required were given wages in lieu of notice. The houses in Schwanenwerder were left just as they were, fully furnished; they were later to be plundered time after time, but they escaped destruction by bombing or shelling.

The governess, Frau K, was one of the very few who now loyally stayed on with the family in the comfortable bunker under the city palace. It was becoming daily more difficult to calm down the children and keep them from worrying.

The twentieth of April, the Führer's birthday, was drawing near and the children, as in former years, were taking great pains to make some little gifts for Uncle Adolf. With the help of Magda and Frau K this was once more achieved, while high over their heads, the buildings of Berlin were being blown to pieces, and only two small gaps breached the stranglehold around the capital. This year, however, the children were not able to hand over their gifts themselves, since the way through the park had already become too dangerous.

25

Death in the Bunker

At the beginning of 1945, when the Ardennes offensive floundered, Adolf Hitler ordered the transfer of his headquarters from Ziegenberg near Bad Nauheim to the Reich Chancellery in Berlin. The chiefs of the Wehrmacht Operations Staff and the High Command of the army had to establish themselves in Zossen bei Jüterbog, a good hour's journey from the nerve centre, since the Chancellery was not spacious enough to accommodate them all. This was undoubtedly one source of the difficulties which in time brought about the complete breakdown of communications.

It is a simple matter to put down on paper that the Führer's headquarters were being transferred. What is actually involved, after sixty-four months of a war with extremely heavy losses on four fronts, can scarcely be imagined by the ordinary person in time of peace. It was Erich Kempka, who had been the Führer's personal chauffeur since 1932, who told me all about it. Since 1936 he had been in charge of all the Führer's transport, following the death of the long-serving Julius Schreck.

Kempka, one of the three or four remaining survivors, saw the Goebbels parents after the deaths of their children. He then managed to break out of the Chancellery and make his way to safety, amidst all the confusion, through the rubble and smoking ruins of occupied Berlin. His flight took him many months on foot, mostly by night; he had to swim the Elbe to reach Berchtesgaden, where his wife was living. There he was denounced by his own countrymen, arrested by heavily armed military police, subjected to endless interrogation and passed from one prison camp to another.

In the Ludwigsburg-Ossweil Camp where I was held in custody until October 1947, I came to know Kempka, a quiet, unassuming, extremely reserved man. In his concise, soberly written book, *I Cremated Adolf Hitler*, published in 1950 (whose sensational title was not thought up by him, but chosen without his prior knowledge by the publishers), Kempka restricted himself to a narrative covering a relatively short space of time, without any comment or value judgment on his part, giving prominence naturally to the burning of the body of the former Führer.

Soon after the first air attacks on Berlin, work was begun on subterranean constructions beneath the Reich Chancellery. Three years of intensive labour by night and day resulted in a multiform bunker complex so large that, in case of need, up to three thousand people could be accommodated. Those who have seen scale drawings of the Führer's bunker could easily have been misled into thinking that it was only a comparatively small enclave within the multi-storied labyrinth of passages, rooms, bomb-proof chambers, kitchens, cellars, store rooms, offices, hospitals, bedrooms and engine rooms deep beneath the surface. There were even garages for eighty vehicles, underground barracks, armouries, radio stations and so on.

When the announcement of the transfer of the Führer's head-quarters was received by the authorities concerned, the whole base sprang into operation immediately, complete with provisions for several months and with hundreds of kilometres of telephone cable to enable communications with command posts both within Berlin and outside the capital to be maintained.

For the time being, however, ministers and their staffs continued to function above ground in offices which, for the most part, were still laboriously kept going. On 23 April, however, the position worsened to such an extent that Goebbels, with his wife and children, moved over to a bunker under the Reich Chancellery. The Minister and his family occupied three small rooms in the so-called Old Bunker, not in Hitler's bunker itself. The Old Bunker originated from 1938 when the Reich Chancellery was rebuilt. Its roof had at first been only two and a half metres in depth, but during the last year of the war the floor of the banqueting hall of the Chancellery overhead had been raised by a further one and a half metres, so the bunker was well protected by a roof four metres deep.

The Old Bunker consisted of eight small rooms arranged in two sets of four each side of a central passage. Three were used for the lighting and heating plant, bathroom, lavatory and kitchen; two others served as store and lumber rooms. Thus only three rooms were available as living rooms. The Old Bunker had two exits; one led direct to the dining room of the Chancellery, the other to the garden. It was connected by a narrow passage and flight of steps with the Führer's own bunker, which itself communicated by means of a corridor with the so-called Voss Bunker, where the watch, an emergency hospital and offices were located.

A series of gas-proof conduits shut off the labyrinthine passages and well-stocked store rooms of this ghostly underworld from one another and from the surface. The system of bunkers was fully independent of the outside world. It had its own electrical generating plant, water pump and air-conditioning system, as well as radio rooms, communication centre and offices, and so many varied technical, hygienic and medical installations of all kinds that it is not possible to enumerate them all. The whole complex resembled a super-submarine lying securely at anchor, deep beneath Berlin.

On 13 March 1945 my father had had his last interview with the Dictator of the Third Reich, by now becoming increasingly deranged.

I spoke with Adolf Hitler for the last time when he summoned me to his office in the Reich Chancellery to congratulate me on my sixty-fifth birthday, which happened to coincide with the anniversary of my twenty-five years' unbroken service as Chief of the Presidential Chancellery. He struck me that day as an old man on the verge of complete collapse. His face wore a hectic flush, his eyes flickered; waving his arms wildly about, he shuffled up and down his spacious office. After courteously expressing his good wishes he handed me, with trembling hands, an inscribed photograph of himself as a souvenir, then began abruptly to shout in a hoarse voice: 'I'll fight to the death! I will never give in, never ... What do they take me for, if they think I would give in? I fight on until they are ready for a reasonable peace!' He went on and on, repeating time after time: 'I'll never give in, never!' The painful scene was brought to an end by the entry of an aide to announce that an air raid was imminent and that the military conference about to be held would take place in the bunker, instead of in the Führer's suite. I came away convinced that the fate of the German people in this, the final phase of the war, lay in the hands of a Head of State suffering from a complete mental breakdown.

On 20 April, Göring and Ribbentrop took their leave of the Führer. Both were convinced that the proper performance of their duties called for their presence outside Berlin. Hitler did not gainsay them and allowed them to depart.

Julius Schaub, Hitler's personal adjutant and constant companion for more than twenty-five years, described the scene to me later. 'My paladins forsake me,' said Hitler sadly, 'me, the Leader of the Party and their organization.' He slowly contemplated one by one the few ministers and secretaries of State who had turned up for the conference. 'Only Dr Goebbels, Group Leader Bormann and the civil servants remain – the old permanent officials with their traditional loyalty.'

Among the latter were Reich Transport Minister Dr Dorpmüller, Secretary of State Dr Lammers, Head of the Reich Chancellor's Department, and my father, Minister of State Dr Otto Meissner, Head of the Presidential Chancery, who in normal circumstances would have been about to retire by this time. Hitler advised them all to leave Berlin without delay while it was still possible, and betake themselves to Flensburg, to Grand Admiral Dönitz, who, on Hitler's instructions, was about to form a successor government, however short-lived it might prove to be.

My father, anxious not to go down in history as a deserter, requested that the order be given in writing and, in accordance with these instructions and accompanied by two colleagues, he left the capital during the night of 21-22 April. A gap near Nauen still existed in the Soviet stranglehold around Berlin and, in spite of fire from the many low-flying enemy planes and bomb craters, they were able to report to Admiral Dönitz the next afternoon.

Hitler himself, no longer capable of governing, gave the further order that all remaining personnel who could be spared should also leave Berlin. This chiefly affected the secretaries and other women employees. Until midday on 25 April it was still possible, by means of one of the last planes from Tempelhof Airport, flying close to the ground, to reach an objective in the West. Hitler's two chief secretaries, Frau Junge and Frau Christians remained behind, as well as his personal dietician, Fräulein Manziali.

On that same day Hitler once more offered to arrange for Magda Goebbels and her children to get away. He considered that the possibility would only exist for a very short space of time. Magda refused the offer. Hitler persisted, repeating in moving terms his wish that the mother and her six children should be saved. But she would not give in. 'My Führer,' she declared firmly, 'our decision is made. We stay here.'

The next morning the first shells from the Soviet artillery struck the Reich Chancellery. The blockade of Berlin was more or less accomplished, and the capital of the Reich had finally become a beleagured citadel. The trap was sprung; at dawn on 25 April the last German plane, with Hitler's adjutant, Julius Schaub, on board, took off from Gatow Airport. The Russian infantry was already entrenched there, on the outskirts of the airport.

Erich Kempka, with more than three armoured cars at his disposal, went to Magda and begged her to take this last chance of escape. He hoped to get her and the six children to Gatow, even though the road thither was already under fire, and to hold the necessary places in the waiting plane for another hour. As he described later in his book, and recounted to me in the internment camp, he was sure that she breathed a sigh of relief. She seemed to hesitate, to be on the point of seizing this opportunity of deliverance. But Goebbels had come quietly up behind her and overheard the conversation. He said that while his wife and children were naturally free to get away from the otherwise certain end in the bunker, he himself would stay on and die with the Führer. 'That,' said Magda immediately, once more sure of herself, 'goes for me too. The children and I stay here, thank you very much all the same, dear Mr Kempka!'

In the very last few days something happened that nobody had even dreamed remotely possible. On 26 April a plane actually reached the beleaguered, severely battered centre of Berlin, a two-seater mini-plane, a Fieseler-Storch. The intrepid hero of this final phase of the Second World War was, strangely enough, a woman, the test pilot Hanna Reitsch. She, alone of all German women, had had the distinction of being awarded the Iron Cross First Class. On take-off it had, in fact, been General Ritter von Greim, who was sitting at the controls. Von Greim had just been appointed Commander-in-Chief of the Luftwaffe, although now only a remnant still existed, in succession to the 'traitor' Reich Marshal Herman Göring.

Between Gatow and the Brandenburg Gate, caught by Russian gunfire, the General had been wounded in both legs, temporarily lost consciousness and slumped to the floor. Hanna Reitsch, sitting behind him, seized the control column and manipulated the machine so skilfully that the Storch landed safely on the Charlottenburg Chaussée, between the Victory Column and the Brandenburg Gate. On no other spot would it have been possible to do so. General Ritter von Greim was immediately carried into the bunker and there treated by army surgeon Dr Stumpfegger. Hanna Reitsch was received by the Führer straightaway.

She was astonished at Hitler's appearance. A complete wreck, a worn-out trembling old man with a bent back, was all that remained of the one-time ruler of the Greater German Reich who had been feared by the whole world. Nevertheless he spoke clearly and coherently, congratulating her on her amazing achievement. He said that, in spite of everything, there was still some courage and loyalty left in the world, above all where German women were concerned. He was undoubtedly thinking of Eva Braun, who had turned up a few weeks previously at the Führer Bunker from the safety of Munich, to see the end with her friend and ostensible lover.

As Hanna Reitsch explained to me eight years later, she was firmly convinced by this late encounter with Hitler that, even in the highly unlikely event of Berlin being liberated, he himself was past saving. He looked as though he would be dead within a week from complete mental and physical exhaustion.

In her book* Hanna Reitsch described her stay in the Goebbels' bunker:

When my services as nurse to Field Marshal von Greim were not required, I devoted myself to the Goebbels children. Shortly after I had been greeted by Hitler, Frau Goebbels took me to her room one floor up, to clean myself up after my flight.

As I entered the room, the faces of six lovely children between the ages of four and thirteen greeted me with lively curiosity from their air raid shelter bunks. Their childish imaginations were fired by the fact that I could fly, and whilst I, still overwhelmed by the experiences of the last few hours, washed myself, their little mouths prattled away questioning me so insistently that, whether I would or no, I was drawn into their colourful little world. From then on, I had to join them at every mealtime, describe the various countries and people I had seen, tell them all about my flights, or recount the fairy tales they liked to hear. Each one of the children exerted charm in his or her own innately subtle and revealing way. The love of the little siblings for one another was quite touching to see.

I taught them to sing part songs and to yodel in Tyrolean fashion, which they quickly picked up. The thunder and crash of enemy gunfire did not worry them, since they believed in their innocent way what they had previously been told – that Uncle Führer was defeating the enemy. When on one occasion the youngest child became uneasy, she was soon comforted by the older ones. This peaceful picture, unchanging as hour by hour the tension mounted, became for me in the days I spent in the bunker, the source of the deepest anguish. At times it was almost more than I could bear.

**The Sky my kingdom*, translated by Lawrence Wilson, London 1955.

Morgen früh, wenn Gott will,★
Wirst Du wieder geweckt ...

I sang with them at bedtime. *Would* they wake up again in the morning?

Already during my first night in the bunker [26-27 April], Russian shells began to fall on the Reich Chancellery. Above us the thunder of increasingly powerful artillery fire continued unchecked. The shattering impact of the gunfire sent showers of plaster swirling down from the walls even of those nethermost rooms. Sleep was out of the question; everybody remained on the alert. I did not doubt that the end was fast approaching. The others felt so too. This perception had an enervating effect on the beleaguered company and paradoxically enough seemed to engender a false evocation of hope which commonsense rejected.

The tight little clique around Hitler, living wholly cut off from the events taking place in the world above, in the desperate struggle for what was still left of Berlin and the rest of Germany, and in spite of all indications to the contrary, fostered time and again hopes of deliverance. These hopes were nourished, it is true, by rumours and reports getting through to the bunker from time to time, giving rise to concepts which, considering the true position, were but a grotesque distortion of the reality. One such rumour was that Fegelein, the long-standing liaison officer between Hitler and Himmler, brother-in-law of Eva Braun, suspected of intending to abscond, was believed to have been shot on Hitler's orders. At times like these, I felt completely out of my depth. We lost all hope of ever seeing the light of day again ....

On the second day of our stay in the bunker, Hitler sent for me to go to his study. He stood before me, an old man, a shade more livid, more withdrawn, with a ravaged look on his face. He handed me two small phials of poison so that, as he said, Greim and I should have freedom of choice at any time. He added that, together with Eva Braun, he too intended to take his life.

By a supreme miracle, Hanna Reitsch and Field Marshal von Greim, dragging himself along on crutches, were rescued by a two-seater Arado, which, in spite of direct fire from Soviet infantry, screaming shells and the bomb craters in the Charlottenburg Chaussée, took off and disappeared into a layer of cloud, succeeding in reaching the still unoccupied part of the country. In her bag Hanna Reitsch carried a letter from Magda Goebbels to prisoner-of-war Harold Quandt.

Hanna Reitsch is probably the most authentic and best informed witness as to the atmosphere and events in the bunker right up to 28 April 1945, just before the end. What she has reported, gives in many

★*When morning comes and God is willing*
We shall awaken once again

(Translator's note)

respects a completely different picture from that drawn by writers who were not there, and from so-called documentary reports on television. Although those responsible always declare in their preamble that they have closely questioned all the surviving witnesses, none has questioned Hanna Reitsch who, during those eventful days, was actually present at such close quarters with Hitler, Goebbels, Magda Goebbels, Martin Bormann and others. A great many of the statements and stories concocted about the final days under the Reich Chancellery contain many contradictions, but I follow in the main descriptions of those who remained behind in the maze of bunkers until the last moments, until after the suicide of Hitler, Eva Braun and Joseph and Magda Goebbels.

Above ground in Berlin incredible things were happening. So much had been destroyed; some 150,000 civilians had died and an estimated 30,000 soldiers had been wounded or had died of their wounds. Yet wherever there was no fighting, wherever the Russians had not yet arrived – in fact even where they had broken through – tramcars were still running here and there, the underground and State railways still operated, food supplies kept up, queues straggled outside the shops, people still cycled to their badly bombed places of work, those who owned radios could still get the news. It was even possible in unoccupied portions of the city to telephone to places where the Russians were already in control.

According to a great many reports about the final collapse of the Third Reich it would seem that Hitler went on believing against all rational judgment that a change for the better was still possible. Incredibly he continued to hope that daily, even hourly, the long-expected conflict between West and East would at last break out, which must mean deliverance. For a time he also thought that the army under General Wenck stationed near Potsdam would relieve Berlin and so liberate him. Many years later, I met General Wenck, whose name at the time was on everybody's lips. I questioned him about his 'ghost' army and he laughingly explained that it existed largely in Hitler's imagination. It was not until the military conference on 22 April that Hitler seemed at last to grasp that he and the National Socialist movement had absolutely nothing more to hope for. It was only then that he himself despairingly uttered the truth: 'The war is lost.'

Joseph Goebbels, of course, had known it for a long time. For some years past, he had seen more and more clearly the mistakes that Hitler was making. He also saw how deluded were those leaders of the Third Reich who were still naïve enough to think they could save themselves by forsaking the bunker and quitting Berlin, and scoffed at all their efforts. Above all he scoffed at the feverish attempts of Himmler and Göring during the final fourteen days, in complete ignorance of the situation, to enter into discussions with the enemy.

Goebbels knew full well that they would all die. And seeing with such absolute certainty that this would happen he, the born propagandist, decided to stage his own death and invest it with mythical significance. Dr Joseph Goebbels would remain faithful, even beyond the grave, to his oft-applied principle of misrepresenting defeat as victory.

Goebbels did not suggest to Magda that she and the children should die with him; she acted of her own free will. Of course he should have withstood any decision to kill on the part of Magda. He had always exercised such power over her that he could quite well have got her away by pleading or promising to follow her to Bavaria. But he left her and the six children to themselves. Presumably the couple had already decided at the beginning of March, perhaps even earlier, to die together. One wonders whether, during those fateful days, Magda might have reminded her husband of her strong, possibly decisive belief in the teachings of Buddhism – or whether indeed she ever spoke to him about it at all. In any case her firm belief in reincarnation must be the explanation of such a wholly unnatural act as the killing of her own children.

Frau K., the children's governess until 23 April when the Goebbels family moved into the bunker, was aware of Magda's Buddhist beliefs, but she regarded them as an inclination, a preference rather than a true adherence. She nevertheless felt that this made the decision to bring about the children's deaths more understandable, even perhaps excusable. According to Buddhist teaching, it was precisely because Helga, Hilde, Helmut, Holde, Hedda and Heide were still innocent children that they were guaranteed rebirth in more favourable conditions than in the life which had run its course. The circumstances in which the soul finds rebirth are determined by its moral conduct in the previous existence. Thus an evil-doer could possibly be reborn into the world as a rat or an earthworm; young children, however, would not have committed any sins for which, on rebirth; they would have to atone. Magda indeed once remarked to Ello that she wished to offer the children a new and better chance in life and for this they would first have to die.

Since Joseph Goebbels could no longer go on living, his wife would die too, taking the children with her; in this way he thought his name would live for ever. His final act of propaganda would ensure that he would go down in history as a shining example of a worthy man of honour, loyal to the Führer and the people. On the afternoon of 29 April, Goebbels wrote out his valedictory statement, to be added as an appendix to Hitler's political testament. It was not intended for the day on which it was written, nor indeed for the day on which it would be published; it was addressed to posterity and ran as follows:

The Führer has commanded me, should the defence of the Capital of the Reich collapse, to leave Berlin. For the first time in my life I must categorically refuse to comply with an order from my Führer. My wife and children join me in this refusal. If I were to do otherwise, for the rest of my life I would regard myself as a dishonourable traitor and a vile blackguard and would lose my self-respect as well as the self-respect of my fellow citizens.

In the frenzy of betrayal in which in these critical days the Führer is engulfed, there must at least still be some who loyally and unconditionally stand by him unto death. It is my belief that in this way I also render the best service in my power to the German people, since in the grave times which lie ahead, examples will be more important than men. Men will always be found to point the way to freedom for the nation. But a regeneration of our national life would not be possible unless modelled on the basis of an example clearly understood by each and every one.

For these reasons I, together with my wife and on behalf of my children, who are still too young to speak for themselves but who, if they were old enough, would associate themselves unreservedly with this decision, hereby express my firm resolve never to forsake the capital of the Reich even if it falls, but rather at the side of the Führer to end a life which for me personally would have no further value if not spent in his service, ready to be risked for his sake.

(Signed) Dr Goebbels

Given in Berlin, 29.4.45   5.30 p.m.

This declaration seems to have failed in its purpose, however. Even in those days the phrases used had lost their meaning, and they were certainly more likely to put off than make an appeal to coming generations.

It is not possible to reconstruct with any degree of clarity the events which now took place in the bunkers. The published accounts of those final days are based on reports by the few who survived the fall of the Reich Chancellery, but hardly any of the survivors had been at really close quarters with the Goebbels family. Most were not even in the *Führerbunker* but in the large so-called Voss Bunker, and only came into the Old Bunker or the *Führerbunker*, if at all, to carry out duties of a brief nature. None was able subsequently to establish any chronology, or even to name particular days or give dates; below ground night and day were indistinguishable. Moreover, for other reasons, many of the statements which are seized upon today are pure invention, contradictory and by no means clear.

In some cases the interrogation of survivors was carried out soon after the collapse by members of the victors' army, or by the prosecuting tribunal at Nuremberg. It is understandable therefore that those questioned should have endeavoured to exonerate themselves, or to lay the blame on the dead, in order to protect the living. Many also saw no reason why they should enlighten their interrogators as to what really did take place in those last days, and often gave deliberately incomplete replies, none at all, or misleading ones. Others are said to have replied that their experiences were much too bizarre to be imparted to others for their purposes, and withheld them for later use.

Only fragmentary information is available about Magda's last days and hours. She seldom left the Old Bunker, whereas Goebbels spent most of his time with Hitler and kept up his activities until the last few moments. With grotesque pertinacity, he continued to publish a news-sheet, the *Panzerbär*, the last National Socialist news-sheet from the beleaguered capital, just as he had published some twenty years previously the first Nazi manifesto, the *Angriff*. One wonders what Goebbels really thought it could do.

His ministry continued to function in the cellars beneath the Wilhelmsplatz, as well as under his shattered palace. In the end, the Minister was no longer able to go across to his colleagues there, nor were his staff able to visit him, but right up to the last minute they could communicate with each other by radio and telephone.

When on 2 May the Russians broke into the cellars of the Ministry for Information and Propaganda, they found the Minister's staff still at their desks; the Promi was absolutely the last authority in Berlin still functioning. It was not until automatic pistols were aimed across the desks that the typewriters became silent. Hans Fritsche,* the

---

*Herr Fritsche, at first taken to Moscow to the Ljubjanska Prison, was among those prosecuted by the Nuremberg War Crimes Tribunal, but was later pronounced not guilty, in company with Dr Hjalmar Schacht and Franz von Papen. During June and July 1947 I shared my cell in the witness's wing with him. We published a daily news-sheet in

(continued overleaf)

radio commentator of the Third Reich, was still carrying on a business conversation when the telephone receiver was struck from his hand by a Russian soldier.

For days now the children in the bunker had been becoming increasingly restless. For Magda the agonizing moment had arrived to face the ordeal which lay ineluctably before her.

'Mummy, Mummy, must we really die soon?' Helga, the thirteen-year-old, kept plaintively demanding, as the bunker shuddered beneath the impact of the remorseless Russian shelling.

'The gunfire,' explained Magda to the child, 'only sounds so dreadful because the rescuers, the brave German soldiers, are getting so close.'

But the precocious little girl no longer believed what her mother said in such a listless tone. 'Mummy, can't we get out of here? I don't want to die – are we really going to die?'

Magda kept herself occupied all the time. She had expected the end to come sooner and had only brought with her a very few things for herself and the children. So she was continually washing things out, sewing on buttons, mending clothes and cooking for them all. The little ones had each been allowed to bring along one toy, with which they played in the narrow centre gangway of the bunker. Once a day they all trooped through the maze of passages to see Uncle Adolf, to say 'good-day' to him and to stroke his little dog Blondi, who had just had some puppies. After Hitler had cheerfully greeted them all and said a few words to each, they went back to their own bunker playing 'follow my leader' through the maze of underground passages. Magda's children, while deep underground and so near to death, remained as graceful, lovely and well looked-after as ever. Even old campaigners had to turn their heads when they saw the doomed little flock running about in the tunnels. Those rough old men, their own deaths staring them in the face, must have asked themselves why any parents should wish to sacrifice their innocent children. Indeed one wonders what Magda would have said had she felt called upon to give some explanation. In any case it was now too late to do anything about it.

The park in which the Minister's palace stood was once more

typescript under American auspices for the prisoners. We called it the *Neueste Nürnberger Nachrichten* (Nuremberg Express) and gleaned our material from American newspapers distributed to us. The commentaries written by Fritsche and myself, partly critical in tone, were never censored or suppressed.

running wild; the building was plundered time and again, mostly by his own people. The household staff dragged whatever they could get away with and made off with it through the tunnels underground, or picked their way through the ruins overhead. Those who were able to dive into an air raid shelter, or into the dwelling of a relative which still remained standing, or even into that of a stranger, had a chance of surviving the inferno which Berlin had now become. Grey-haired storm-troopers, the last of the call-up, turned up at the Goebbels' city palace and disappeared again, many heavily laden. Nobody in authority bothered any more about the valuables which had been left behind, nor about the paintings in the air raid shelter which had once belonged to the national museums.

The Russians had established themselves for weeks past in the castle of Lanke, and by now had also reached Schwanenwerder. In both residences, once so luxuriously appointed, not a single thing remained in place.

By 22 April, immediately after the blockade of Berlin was complete, Hitler's personal adjutant, Julius Schaub, was burning his master's private files in a bomb crater in the garden. Magda, taking advantage of a pause in the artillery fire, had gone up into the open for a breath of fresh air, when she came face to face with Eva Braun. The two women stood in silence watching the flames engulf the papers, turning them into charred fragments. Both knew the end had come. Never before had Hitler allowed himself to be parted from these papers; their significance had often been the subject of whispered conjecture, but nothing definite had ever become known, not even to Goebbels. It was hinted that they described successful inventions by German scientists, which were to be decisive in obtaining new sources of energy, or in the application of atomic weapons and other hitherto neglected natural resources. But Julius Schaub seemed to have no idea whatsoever about their significance. As far as he could see whilst burning them, the papers were all in Hitler's own handwriting, the files having been put together by Hitler himself; presumably he had begun them in the early days, long before the seizure of power. If those documents had only survived, historians might have found it easier to penetrate the mysterious depths of Hitler's personality. It is not known to this day, for example, what aroused in him the murderous hatred of Jews which led to the blood of millions being shed.

Eva Braun stood weeping at the door of the bunker; Magda, betraying no emotion whatever, withdrew once more below ground. As Schaub later told me, as far as he was aware Magda and Eva did not exchange a single word.

On Saturday, 28 April, Hitler called those of his close colleagues who still remained behind into his study and told them he was going to kill himself. He recommended all of them to make the same choice. Without exception they all declared their willingness to end their own lives, to die with their Führer, whereupon Hitler distributed capsules of swift-acting cyanide. Few of them had really made up their minds, however; most of them endeavoured after Hitler's death to make a dash for freedom, although only about a quarter of them succeeded in doing so.

During the night of Sunday 28–29 April, Hitler married Eva Braun; for the last day of her life she thus became Frau Adolf Hitler. Joseph Goebbels was best man. Fourteen years earlier, Hitler had been Joseph's best man when he married Magda at the Severin estate belonging to Günther Quandt. A small reception was held after the brief ceremony, which was performed by a hastily summoned registrar, who trembled nervously throughout. Champagne was passed round and even Hitler, total abstainer as he was, drank a glass. Everybody shook hands with the bridal pair, but nobody could bring themselves to wish them luck. Instead they discussed the various ways of committing suicide. Cyanide was by far the most favoured method, as being supposedly the quickest and surest way to end life. Nearly all of them were by then equipped with cyanide.

Hitler now dictated two wills, a political one and a personal one. In the personal one he bequeathed his collection of paintings to the Party; in the event that the Party no longer existed, then to the German State. In his political testament he called upon his colleagues, Goebbels included, to leave Berlin and save their lives.

Later that same day a second wedding took place, in fact a double wedding. Two young girls braved almost certain death to forge their way through the ruins, the bombing and the gunfire, to reach the bunker where their fiancés were on guard duty. They wished to be married hastily, before the end. As it was no longer possible to get hold of another registrar, Dr Werner Naumann, Secretary of State, as a qualified lawyer, performed the ceremony. In the prevailing circumstances such marriages were deemed legally binding. A few hours before the break-out, after the deaths of Hitler and Goebbels, the last wedding of all took place, performed by Erich Kempka, as the bridgegroom's superior officer. The bride, who had been severely wounded, lay on a stretcher and was given pain-killing drugs during the ceremony.

It is not known if any of these three bridal pairs survived the end in the bunker.

Soviet artillery had moved up to within a thousand metres of the Reich Chancellery. A sudden onslaught of heavy firing shook the floor and walls of the bunker. The children were terrified. 'Why don't we run away?' they demanded.

'Why should we run away?' asked their mother. 'Isn't it good to be here with Uncle Führer?' The children were pacified once more; they did indeed find it good with Uncle Führer. Just then he was being particularly nice to them, and, besides, there was the little dog Blondi with her funny little puppies. Only Helga kept on saying all the time that she did not want to die.

Shortly before his death, Hitler appointed a fresh cabinet. Himmler, Göring and Ribbentrop were removed as traitors. Instead of a Führer there was again to be a President of the Reich: Grand Admiral of the Fleet Dönitz, at that time living in Flensburg. Dr Joseph Goebbels was appointed Chancellor of the Reich. In accordance with Hitler's decree, the legality of which in the prevailing circumstances is open to question, Goebbels was the last of the chancellors of the Third German Reich; Otto von Bismarck was the first.

Goebbels was Reich Chancellor only for a day, with authority extending over less than a square kilometre in the centre of Berlin. Nevertheless for him it signified a triumph, his ultimate victory. The appointment as chancellor filled Joseph Goebbels with unbounded satisfaction. The lame, once starving, destitute scholar from Rheydt had, at the end of his life, become the successor to Prince Otto von Bismarck, outstripping all his rivals in the final round. Adolf Hitler had thrust them away from him, branding them as traitors. In the opinion of the egocentric Goebbels, those faint-hearted incompetents had forfeited the respect of posterity.

Goebbels was not so stupid as to think that his appointment as chancellor still had any practical meaning, however. Only for him was it of real significance. As a born propagandist he saw that he still had one more task to perform, namely to promote his own fame for posterity (whereby he greatly over-estimated posterity's likely interest). For Goebbels it was of the greatest importance that the old paladins of the Third Reich, the co-founders of the National Socialist movement, should at the eleventh hour be officially proscribed, as had happened previously with Strasser, Röhm and Hess. Of the hierarchy of the Third Reich, now agonizing in its final convulsions, only Joseph Goebbels, the most loyal of them all, remained. Since he must carry this rôle through to its logical conclusion, death was imperative, death by his own hand; according to his own conviction, a hero's death.

The last day of his life saw the culmination of his ambition. Death was not too great a price to pay for that. The fact that he was taking his wife and their children with him cast an aura over his final abnegation and constituted a fitting consummation. Accompanied by his family, he would yield up his life undefeated.

In the early morning of 30 April, Hitler and his wife took their leave of all the faithful who had stayed behind with them in the bunker. If on the previous day Joseph Goebbels had experienced the proudest moments of his life, today an unprecedented honour awaited Magda. As Hitler stood before her to shake her hand for the last time, he gave her a long and searching look, his chalk-white, wrinkled face convulsively twitching. Suddenly, to the astonishment of all those around him, with a deft movement he removed the gold Party badge from his field grey coat and fastened it to the lapels of Magda's jacket. She, usually so self-controlled, outwardly so cool, burst into tears. In spite of all the faults she had perceived in the Führer, in spite of much disillusionment attributable to him, this spontaneous gesture on the part of the doomed Hitler signified for her the highest honour any woman could receive. In her eyes no war hero, however meritorious, had ever been so uniquely decorated as Magda Goebbels, by the man who had both founded the Greater German Reich and brought about its catastrophic downfall.

Hitler and Eva then withdrew. But several hours were still to elapse before they died.

Hitler had definitely made up his mind to commit suicide. But that of itself was not enough. He had to ensure that nothing, absolutely nothing, of his and Eva's bodies would be left to be desecrated by the victors. It would be the height of infamy were his head to be preserved in spirit and put on show for men to gape at, or his brain to be dissected by foreign professors and analysed in long-winded reports. What had they not done with Benito Mussolini and his beloved? Their mutilated bodies had been hung upside down at a Milan petrol station, spat on by angry women. He was not going to let that happen to his and Eva's mortal remains.★

His personal adjutant, S.S. Major Otto Günsche, was given the instructions to pour 100 litres of petrol over them, so that they would be completely incinerated; nothing was to be left. Erich Kempka and perhaps others would assist him.

The Soviet army was standing at the Potsdam Bridge, at the Belle Alliance Platz, and at the Anhalt and Friedrichstrasse railway stations, all within ten minutes' walk away. Soviet shells continued to burst relentlessly on the massive heap of ruins which had once been the Reich Chancellery. Underground the concrete walls shuddered and the plaster dust eddied gently in the air. Reich Chancellor Dr Goebbels, Magda and the children stayed in their own bunker awaiting news of the deaths of Adolf and Eva Hitler. What they talked about and how they kept the children quiet no one knows; they were quite alone.

At midday on 30 April, Hitler held a farewell lunch, his wife, the two secretaries, Frau Junge and Frau Christians, and Fräulein Manziali, his cook for many years, all at the same table. Hitler chatted in a light, carefree spirit, with never a word about what was going on all around them. It was still some hours before Hitler died. Twice he appeared outside his suite, shook hands all round once more, asked for something to eat and shuffled back again.

Towards six o'clock on 30 April 1945, Kempka faced his chief in Hitler's sitting room for the last time. 'He was completely done in,' reported Kempka later. 'He had already switched off and his whole body was shaking like a leaf.' Finally the door was shut. Hitler shot himself through the mouth. At the same time he is thought to have bitten on a cyanide capsule. Eva Braun poisoned herself, presumably a few moments earlier. Near her was a lady's pistol with the safety catch released, but it was not fired.

Major Otto Günsche, standing outside the door, heard the shot and immediately afterwards entered to find the two dead bodies, dripping blood, leaning against each other on the sofa.

Günsche asked Erich Kempka for two hundred litres of petrol. It was not easily to be had. Several men set off, not very hopefully, to hunt against time for fuel, risking being blown to pieces by

---

★The announcement of Mussolini's death and the desecration of the corpses was one of the last pieces of news to reach the bunker beneath the Reich Chancellery from the outside world.

exploding shells. But in spite of everything the impossible was achieved: six or seven cans of petrol were placed at the doors of the bunker, with more in reserve. Otto Günsche dragged Hitler's body up the twenty steps, while Martin Bormann took hold of the dead Eva. Erich Kempka, well aware how deeply Eva Braun despised Bormann, pulled her body sharply away from him without a word and carried it up himself. Dr Goebbels, Stumpfegger, Bormann and others followed.

There in the open, right in front of the bunker exit, Günsche and Kempka laid the bodies in a bomb crater. What then transpired is best described by Erich Kempka:

All around us the Russian shells were exploding as if the artillery at that moment had deliberately stepped up their firing on the garden of the Reich Chancellery and the *Führerbunker*. I was hurled back into the bunker, losing my breath. I kept still for a moment, waiting for the next shell to burst, then seizing a can of petrol I ran out of the bunker and placed it alongside the bodies. Bending down quickly, I placed Hitler's left arm closer to his body; wisps of his disordered hair blew eerily against my cheek. Shells were bursting immediately outside; shrapnel buzzed and whistled all around us; dirt and filth showered down upon our heads. We waited agitatedly until the explosions eased a little, so as to be able to pour the petrol over the bodies. Near me, Günsche and Linge were helping to carry out the same last duties for Hitler and his wife, whose clothes fluttered sadly in the wind until soaked by petrol.

Time and again we were showered by the churned up earth; more than once we stumbled back into the bunker to get fresh cans of petrol. Dr Goebbels, Bormann and Dr Stumpfegger stood mutely watching in the doorway near us as we carried out this gruesome task. Not one of them at that moment dared to leave the door of the bunker. Outside all hell was let loose.

How were we going to set the fuel alight? 'Here are some rags,' I shouted excitedly. It was the work of a moment to raise the lid of a can and soak the material. 'A match, quick! Give me a match!' Dr Goebbels tore a box out of his pocket and threw it to me. In a flash a bright flame shot sky high, gurgling and seething, whilst at the same time black smoke rose towards heaven and hung like a pall in the sky. Dr Goebbels, Bormann, Dr Stumpfegger, Linge and I stood transfixed, blinking at the fearful spectacle. Again and again the remains of the still only partially charred corpses had to be dowsed with petrol. From about two o'clock in the afternoon until seven in the evening the burning continued.

Later, under cover of darkness, the remains were gathered into a sack and buried in loose earth close to the wall of Erich Kempka's house, directly opposite the Führer's bunker. Russian assault troops had already reached the Potsdamer Platz. From there to the ruined Reich Chancellery it would normally take five minutes. The remnants of the German defence forces – veteran infantrymen, paratroopers, members of the Hitler Youth, ill-equipped members of the Volkssturm, Hitler's personal bodyguard – withdrew step by step.

Among the fighters in the ruins were eighty Latvian volunteers under the command of S.S. Second Lieutenant Neiland, as well as a relic of the Denmark Regiment and a few men from the Netherlands Brigade. Even more surprising was the bitter resistance put up by the French Division Charlemagne, who had been fighting on the now dead Hitler's side. No more than a hundred, or at the most two hundred of them had survived. They had nothing more to hope for, since in liberated France, if they ever got there, they would face court martial and execution as traitors. Yet these veteran French soldiers were some of the last defenders of the German capital. Since the order from General Weidling to capitulate failed to reach them, they held out right up to midday on 3 May.

In other sections of the bunker complex, there were at this stage about three hundred wounded crowded together in a very small space. They were being looked after by Dr Stumpfegger and Professor Hase, himself a wounded man, as well as possible in the circumstances. Everything depended on supplies of light, water and, above all, ventilation being maintained. The operating machinery was located in the deepest part of the bunkers, but only one technician was still available to work the plant, mechanical engineer Hentschel, a technician in the old Reich Chancellery since the early days of the Weimar period. Hentschel had seen many chancellors come and go, and now too Hitler. Surprisingly he was not a member of the Party, although he was employed by the Reich Chancellery, but he was a loyal and dutiful worker.

After the burning of Hitler's body, Reich Chancellor Dr Goebbels summoned all the remaining Party leaders and army commanders to a conference – the only conference which he, as chancellor, conducted. It was agreed, according to a later court hearing, that General Krebs should be authorized to go to the Soviet commander-in-chief, Schukow, carrying a white flag. General Krebs was to offer to surrender Berlin conditionally upon the defenders being allowed to go free. Early next morning Krebs returned with a negative reply. Freedom for the defenders was out of the question – as Goebbels must very well have known. Schukow merely guaranteed that wounded and prisoners would receive the treatment laid down by the Geneva Convention – though in fact the Russians did nothing of the sort in a great many cases. A large number of survivors, particularly those from the *Führerbunker*, were treated as political prisoners and given sentences of twenty-five years' imprisonment; many were detained until 1957. Of all those imprisoned, only about two-thirds finally returned home. Among those who perished in Soviet prisons was General Weidling, Commander-in-Chief for Berlin, who capitulated on 2 May.

Those who still remained in the bunker in the night of 30 April–1 May decided to make a break-out attempt the following day, at about nine o'clock in the evening.

A little later, Chancellor Goebbels said to General Krebs, who wished to place one of the armoured cars at the disposal of Magda and the children, 'We no longer want to go on living.' Such a late attempt had in any case only a very remote chance of success. Yet only a week earlier, Magda could have flown out with the children, the planes which took off at that time reaching Munich or Flensburg unscathed.

Much has been written about the tragic deaths of the children by poisoning, but little is known of the actual details. The children died from a poison injection just as the marriage of the badly wounded girl with the bunker guard was being performed by Erich Kempka. As Dr Stumpfegger told Kempka and others several hours later, Magda approached him asking for his help in ending the children's lives. But Stumpfegger, who had children of a similar age himself, and was moreover thoroughly aware that legally he would be committing murder, refused to carry out Magda's desperate wish. Among the refugees crowded together in the bunker there happened to be a country doctor from the enemy-occupied eastern region, though how or why he came to be there is not known. He is said to have carried out the fearful task and then disappeared straightaway among the crowd of strangers. Even Ello Quandt never knew whether the children had met their fate in the way described by Magda in the sanatorium at Dresden, namely by being given a sleeping tablet and then the fatal Evipan injection. It may well have happened quite otherwise.

At about seven o'clock in the evening of 1 May, at almost the exact hour when in the days before the war Joseph Goebbels used to deliver the traditional May Day speech to the German workers, to be followed by the magnificent firework display in the Berlin amusement park, the new Reich Chancellor's adjutant, Günther Schwägermann, knocked on the door of the bunker. He said that the breakout was timed for nine o'clock; he still did not know, or would not believe, that his chief would remain with his family in the bunker. Only then did Goebbels reveal that he and his wife were going to kill themselves, and he asked Schwägermann to see to the burning of their remains. He did not mention the children. Magda instructed him further to give her love to her son Harold. (This officer successfully evaded the Russian onslaught, escaping through old underground passages and flooded cellars, until he finally reached the West; he was then able to deliver Magda's message.)

On 28 April Magda had given Hanna Reitsch a letter for Harold which, after many vicissitudes, came eventually into his hands. In this letter Magda returned to the idealistic hopes which she had entertained many years before in connection with Hitler and his movement. Magda did not give her son the same reasons why she and the children had to die with 'Papa' as she had confided to her friend in that last conversation in Dresden. The letter expounded a faith which – unless appearances were deceptive – she had for years no longer found tenable:

My dearest son,
We have now been for some six days here in the Führerbunker, Papa, your little brother and sisters and myself, in order to end our National Socialist life in the only possible honourable way. I do not know whether you will ever receive this letter; but there must still surely be some good soul who will help me to send these my last greetings to you. You must know that I have remained at Papa's side against his will, that the Führer last Sunday wished to help me to get away from here. But you know your Mother – we share the same blood – I did not even consider it. Our glorious ideals of Nazism have been destroyed and with them everything in my life that has been beautiful, admirable, noble and good.

The world which will come after the Führer and National Socialism will not be worth living in. Therefore I have brought the children over here with me. They would have been too handicapped in the days that lie ahead and a merciful God will forgive me for taking it on myself to save them.

You will go on living – and I have only one plea to make to you. Never, never forget that you are German; never do anything that is dishonourable, and make quite sure that through your life our dying will not have been in vain.

The children are wonderful. They do everything for themselves in these more than primitive conditions. Whether or not they have to sleep on the floor, are able to wash or have enough to eat, there is never a word of complaining or any tears. When bombs shake the bunker, the bigger ones comfort the little ones. Their presence here is an added blessing in that now and again they even manage to bring a smile to the Führer's face.

Yesterday evening the Führer took off his gold Party badge and fastened it to my jacket. I am proud and happy. May God give me the strength to do my last, most difficult duty. We now have only one resolve – to remain true to death to the Führer. That we can end our lives together with him is a blessing for which we had never dared to hope.

Harold, my dear child, I bequeath to you the best thing that I have learned from life – be true, true to yourself, true to others, true to your country, in every way, always, in everything.
[fresh sheet]

To start a new page is difficult. Who knows if I can fill it? But I want to give you so much love, so much strength, and to spare you any sorrow over our loss. Be proud of us and try to hold us in proud and joyful remembrance. Everybody has to die at some time, and is it not better to live a brief, good, honourable and courageous life than a long one under shameful conditions?

This letter must go ... Hanna Reitsch is taking it with her. She is flying out again!

I embrace you with all my deepest, my most heartfelt motherly love

My beloved son
Live for Germany!
Your Mother

Leaning on the arm of her husband, Magda, came out of the room in which lay her dead children; neither spoke a word. After the children's death she suddenly seemed to age; drawn and haggard, with red-rimmed eyes and stooping badly, she dragged herself wearily about the bunker.

The clock showed 8.45 [wrote Erich Kempka]. Preparations for burning the bodies of Dr Goebbels and his wife had been made, he himself personally having given the necessary instructions. All those who wished to take part in the break-out, whether military, refugees or relatives, were separated into various groups. About thirty women were allocated to the group under my command. I went once more into the *Führerbunker*, to take my leave of Dr Goebbels and his wife. Although their children had only died such a short time ago, both seemed calm and composed.

At nine o'clock on the evening of 1 May 1945, Joseph and Magda Goebbels slowly climbed the concrete steps leading to the garden. They wished to spare others the trouble of carrying their bodies up. At the door of the bunker stood Captain Schwägermann and

Goebbels' chauffeur Rach, who had been with him for many years. The cans of petrol to be used for burning the bodies were beside them on the ground.

The Goebbels passed them without a word, slowly going some metres into the semi-darkness. A shot was heard. Goebbels had turned his gun on himself. Magda bit on a poison capsule and sank lifeless to the ground. A few seconds later there was another shot – fired by a soldier who was carrying out the explicit orders of the chief of the Promi, who wished to ensure that he was really dead.

26

Aftermath

The Soviet artillery kept up its remorseless fire. Time was running out; it was too late now to bother about burning the bodies completely, as barely half an hour was left in which to get away from the death trap. General Krebs and Burgdorf and Ambassador Walter Havel were among those who shot themselves in that labyrinth of subterranean rooms. Shots could be heard too in the *Führerbunker,* but who they were who chose this way out is not known.

Just as little is known about the many who, either in groups or entirely on their own, attempted the break-out. Erich Kempka led one group of about a hundred; another was headed by Brigadier Möhnke. Reich Leader Martin Bormann, Secretary of State Dr Naumann, Dr Stumpfegger, Hitler's last adjutant, Günsche, his valet Linge, Goebbels' latest adjutant, Schwägermann, Frau Junge, Frau Christians, and Fräulein Manziali all tried to get through the blazing ruins, braving the ceaseless fire of the Soviet bombardment. The parties separated, dispersing into the tunnels of the underground, climbing over the dead and dying, wading thigh-deep through turgid water, to emerge eventually into the open and look for new hiding places in ruined cellars.

Kempka and his group reached the massive heap of ruins near the Weidendamm Bridge. Infantry fire from all directions made it impossible to go on. Suddenly, as if by a miracle, three of the heaviest type of German armoured vehicles, remnant of a tank company of the S.S. North Division, surged up ahead of them. They had been given orders to strike out for the north and if possible to reach 'Reichspresident' Grand Admiral Dönitz in Flensburg – a hopeless undertaking if ever there was one.

Kempka succeeded in inducing the commander of the three tanks rolling slowly along to give protective cover to the men and women who huddled closely behind. For about a hundred metres all went well, until the vehicle in front of Kempka was hit by an armour-piercing shell, which caused it to explode, flinging Martin Bormann, Dr Stumpfegger and Kempka himself through the air with terrific force. When some time later Kempka came to, confused and half-blinded, he managed to stagger, more by luck than judgment, into a store room of the Friedrichstrasse railway station. There a teeming throng of Jugoslav women workers, who had been transported to the Reich as forced labour, came to his help in a most moving way, providing him with a mechanic's grease-stained overalls, so that he would be taken for a forced labour worker by the Soviet authorities. Although suffering badly from his experiences, he was thus able to struggle through finally to the West.

Earlier, in the mad confusion round the station, he had run into Dr Naumann, the woman dentist Dr Hausermann and Goebbels' adjutant Schwägermann, all of whom had abandoned the *Führerbunker* barely a quarter of an hour after him. They told him how they had seen the apparently lifeless bodies of Martin Bormann and Dr Stumpfegger lying where they had been hurled by the force of the exploding tank, but because of their urgent need to press on they had not stopped to investigate.

As far as it is possible to judge, Bormann, one of the most hated leaders of the Third Reich, responsible for countless infamous deeds, could not have survived. The fact that he was wearing the heavily gold-bedecked uniform of a leader of the National Socialist German Workers' Party makes it even more unlikely. Although the legend persists to this day that Bormann actually did escape from the inferno, those who were there at the time of the break-out consider this to be quite inconceivable.

Among the few who did succeed in getting through to the West were Erich Kempka, Günther Schwägermann, Dr Werner Naumann, Frau Traudl Junge and Frau Christians; Fräulein Manziali was missing, presumed dead. Lieutenant Colonel Otto Günsche, Brigadier Möhnke, Flight Captain Baur and many others were imprisoned by the Russians and remained for up to twelve years in Siberian or similar prison camps, returning eventually to the homeland. Certainly more than half, probably as many as two-thirds, of those involved in the break-out perished.

In the *Führerbunker* only the dead remained behind. In the area which for some six weeks had served as a hospital, some three hundred wounded still lived, among them many women and children. Old Dr Hase, limping about on crutches, was the only doctor there, trying his best to give medical aid, assisted by self-sacrificing nurses who had voluntarily remained behind in the bunker. The majority of the wounded who survived those days and nights owed it largely to Chief Engineer Hentschel, who ensured that the lights continued to burn, apparatus to function, hot and cold water to flow from the taps and above all fresh air to stream through the ventilators. Hentschel stayed by the vital machinery until the Russians arrived. He even continued to do so until all the wounded had been evacuated. What happened to him afterwards I do not know. He was a hero, deserving a monument to his memory, though he himself would undoubtedly have been the last to think so.

The first Russians to arrive at the bunker were, according to reports, not soldiers but a group of women doctors who, after a rapid survey, made off with the clothes, underwear and cosmetics which Magda and Eva had left behind. After them came Russian officers, but opinions differ, even in official reports, as to who was the first to discover or enter the *Führerbunker*. The official reports do state, however, that they were astounded at the sight of the six children; in their little white beds, their faces peaceful and relaxed, they looked as if they were still sleeping.

Hans Fritsche, the leading radio commentator of the Third Reich, was, as a Soviet prisoner, confronted the following day with the dead body of his former chief.* He was able to identify beyond any doubt the doctor and his wife, as their bodies had only been partially consumed by the fire. Photographs exist of the remains of Magda and Joseph Goebbels as they were found thirty-six hours after their deaths.

In the morning of 8 May these half-burnt remains were brought to the mortuary of the Buchau Cemetery in Berlin and an inquest was held by a team of Russian doctors. Nothing is known in the West of the outcome, let alone the ultimate fate of the bodies. What was done with the dead children and where they were buried, their grand-

---

*Hans Fritsche gave me a detailed account of this tragic and deeply moving experience during the weeks we spent together in the wing of the Nuremberg U.S. military prison where witnesses were held.

mother, Frau Behrend, could never find out, although she repeatedly questioned the authorities.

From all that we know of Magda and her Buddhist beliefs, she most probably went to her death in the certainty that for her, and particularly for the children, a new and better life would immediately begin.

What Goebbels himself thought about death and the hereafter no one knows. Many, if not the majority, of his contemporaries would have consigned him to hell by the fastest route. But whoever thought thereby that he, in that dark and torrid abyss, would suffer eternal torment must surely be mistaken. If there is a hell and its ruler incarnate, Goebbels would presumably have been greeted warmly as a kinsman. A place at the devil's table must long since have been kept for the monster who so richly deserved it, right next to the Prince of Darkness himself.

Biographical Notes

AUGUST, Wilhelm, Prince of Prussia (1887–1949).
Fourth son of Kaiser Wilhelm II; early member of the S.A.

BLOMBERG, Werner von (1878–1946).
1929 major-general; 1933 Minister of Defence; 1935 Minister for War; 1938 dismissed.

BORMANN, Martin (1900–45).
Reichsleiter, head of Party Chancellery, designated minister in Hitler's will. Probably killed escaping from Berlin.

BRÜCKNER, Wilhelm (b.1884).
Until October 1919 in Volunteer Corps Epp; 1923 N.S.D.A.P., S.A. regimental leader in Münich; 1930 adjutant to Hitler, S.A.; 1936 member of Reichstag; 1941 lieutenant-colonel in German army.

BRÜNING, Heinrich (b.1885 in Münster, d.1970).
Doctor of political economy; in First World War captain of a machine gun company. 1920–30 managing director of the General Association of Christian Trade Unions; from 1924 member of the Centre Party in the Reichstag. Recognized tax and finance expert. 1929 president of the Centre Party; March 1930 Reich Chancellor of the Presidential Cabinet, relying on the confidence of the Reich President; resigned end May 1932. From May 1933 chairman of the Centre Party; after its dissolution in July 1933 went to U.S.A., returning in 1950 for a short period to Germany.

DIETRICH, Sepp (1892–1966).
First World War vice-sergeant major; 1919 in charge of Bavarian State Police; 1923 relieved of his duties (Hitler revolt); 1928 N.S.D.A.P., forwarding clerk in party publishers Eher, founder member of S.S. in southern Bavaria; 1931 S.S. group leader, helped form Hitler's bodyguard 'Berlin Escort'; from September 1933 Hitler's bodyguard; 1934 directed executions in Röhm putsch; 1944 S.S. general and colonel-general of Waffen S.S. July 1946 arrested, sentenced to life imprisonment for shooting S.A. leaders 1934.

DÖNITZ, Karl (b.1891).

Grand Admiral, Commander-in-Chief of the Navy; designated Reich President in Hitler's will, after Hitler's death set up rump government at Flensburg-Mürwik; sentenced at Nuremberg to ten years' imprisonment, which he served in Spandau Jail; released October 1956.

DORPMÜLLER, Julius Heinrich (1869–1945).

Engineer; 1922 President German Railways Board; 1926 Chairman German Railways; 1937–45 Reich Minister of Transport.

ERNST, Karl (b. 1904 in Berlin, d.1934 in Lichterfelde).

Lift operator and hotel page. Typical Berlin youth of postwar years, came into early contact with National Socialism, probably through Captain Ernst Röhm. Founded one of the first S.A. homes in Ross-strasse in centre of Berlin. S.A. group leader at age thirty with rank of general. On 30 June 1934 on honeymoon trip to Madeira taken off ship in Bremen, conveyed to Berlin and shot by S.S.

FRICK, Wilhelm (1877—1946).

Studied law in Munich, Göttingen and Berlin; 1901 doctorate in Heidelberg. Authority. Thereafter Chief Constable, Munich, head of Political Police Department; together with Munich police chief Pohner early supporter of Authority. Thereafter Chief Constable, Munich, Head of Political Police Department; together with Munich police chief Pohner early supporter of N.S.D.A.P. After Hitler revolt (9 November 1923) sentenced to imprisonment in fortress, but evaded it through election as member of Reichstag for the substitute organization for the suppressed N.S.D.A.P. 1928 national leader of National Socialist Reichstag fraction; 1926–January 1930 and 1932–30 January 1933 Official Insurance Administrator, Munich; 1930–31 Minister for the Interior and Minister for Education, Thüringia; 30 January 1933 Reich Minister for the Interior; 1934 also Prussian Minister for the Interior (until 1943); 30 January 1934 Reorganisation law; 15 September 1935 Nüremberg laws were passed under his auspices; General Authority for Supreme Administration of Reich. From 1943 Reich Minister without Portfolio; Reich Protector for Bohemia and Moravia. On 1 October 1946 condemned to death by International Military Tribunal.

GÖRING, Hermann (b.1893, Rosenheim, Bavaria, d.1946).

Son of a senior official in the Colonial Service from a Westphalian family. Age nineteen lieutenant; airman in First World War; 1918 led the famous Richthofen fighter wing and was awarded the 'Pour le mérite'. 1922 member of the N.S.D.A.P.; slightly wounded at the revolt at the Feldherrnhalle (1923), fled to Austria and lived for next few years in Italy and Sweden; 1928 member of Reichstag. April 1935 married actress Emmy Sonnemann. End April 1945 condemned to death by Hitler because he wished to negotiate capitulation. Freed by Luftwaffe unit and arrested by American military authorities. Tried by Military Tribunal at Nuremberg and, unlike many of the other accused, defended his actions. Condemned to death by the court, he committed suicide the night before he was due for execution.

HANKE, Carl (1903–45).

Miller; from 1931 full-time functionary in N.S.D.A.P.; 1932 member of

Reichstag. Adjutant and personal assistant to Gauleiter Joseph Goebbels (Berlin). 1933–41 in Reich Ministry for Information and Propaganda (finally as Secretary of State); January 1941 Gauleiter and Lieutenant of County of Lower Silesia. Designated in Hitler's will as successor to Himmler. July 1945 presumably shot by Czech partisans.

HELLDORF, Wolf Heinrich, Duke of (b.1896 in Merseburg d.1944).

Officer in First World War, then fighter in Volunteer Corps; 1928–30 Manager of a stud farm. 1931 S.A. leader Berlin-Brandenburg. 1932 arranged the first anti-semitic persecutions which provoked Hindenburg's disgust. 1933 police chief of Potsdam and member of Reichstag; 1935 police chief of Berlin. In this position Helldorf protected many Jews in a remarkable way and enabled a number to emigrate; 1944 one of the leaders of the conspiracy against Hitler. Executed.

HIMMLER, Heinrich (b.1900 in Munich, d.1945).

Primary school, then grammar school in Munich and Landshut. 1918 Officer cadet (senior) in II Bavarian Infantry Regiment. 1924 qualified agriculturist; 1928 set up a chicken farm near Munich. After Goebbels' appointment as Gauleiter of Berlin became secretary to Gregor Strasser. 1930 Member of Reichstag. March 1933 leader of S.S., police chief of Munich; soon after Commander Political Police in Bavaria and other provinces. His finest hour at the time of the Röhm purge 1934. July 1934 appointed Reich Leader of S.S. directly responsible to Hitler. In course of time built up the S.S. as the most feared body of troops; 1944 Commander-in-Chief of Reserve Army; end of year Chief of Army Equipment. Disguised as a soldier sought to escape in May 1945, was recognized and committed suicide.

LAMMERS, Hans-Heinrich (1879–1962).

1922 head of section in Ministry of the Interior; 1932 police administrator; 1933 secretary of State and chief of Reich Chancellery; 1939 executive member of Council of Ministers for the Defence of the Reich (the signatory of the edict of 1 September 1939); April 1940 member of the Academy of German Law; leader of National Association of German Boards of Administration. On 11 April 1949 sentenced to twenty years' imprisonment for war crimes by the Military Tribunal in Nuremberg. 1951 released.

LEY, Robert (1890–1945).

Chemist, airman in First World War; 1921 chemist with I.–G. Farbenindustrie in Leverkusen; 1925 N.S.D.A.P., Gauleiter in Rhineland; 1928 member of Prussian State Diet; 1931 Reich Inspector of the Political Organization; November 1932 Chief Organizer of N.S.D.A.P.; May 1933 leader of the German Labour Front; September 1935 member of Prussian Council of State; Member of German Law Academy. 1945 committed suicide.

NAUMANN, Dr Werner.

Secretary of State in Reich Ministry for Information and Propaganda. Lives in West Germany.

PAPEN, Franz von (b.1879, d.?)

Adroit German diplomat, former General Staff officer; scion of Westphalian noble family, unsuccessful Catholic centrist politician, but appointed Chancellor June 1932; resigned November 1932; January 1933 Vice-Chancellor (under Adolf Hitler) and Premier of Prussia; August 1934 Minister to Austria; February 1942 dismissed by Hitler. Acquitted at Nuremberg 1946.

RÖHM, Ernst (b. 1887 Munich, d. 1934).
Wounded in the face at the Front in the First World War. 1919 joined Epp Corps of Volunteers, same year came to know Hitler and became his intimate friend. 1924 sentenced to fifteen months' imprisonment for participating in the 1923 Hitler revolt; on release stood aloof for one year; 1929 went to Bolivia to reorganize the Bolivian army. Recalled by Hitler and 1931 took over the leadership of the S.A., revealing his genius for organization, creating within twelve months an army of 500,000 S.A.; 1933 Reich Minister without Portfolio. 30 June 1934 shot in Munich by Hitler's orders, presumably because he planned a revolt and was guilty of moral depravity.

ROSENBERG, Alfred (1893–1946).
1921 chief editor of *Völkischer Beobachter*. Author inter alia of *The Myth of the Twentieth Century* (1930). 1933 head of the Foreign Affairs Office of the N.S.D.A.P.; 1941 Reich Minister for Occupied Territories in the East; executed in Nuremberg.

RUST, Bernhard (1883–1945).
1922 member of the People's Movement; member of the N.S.D.A.P.; March 1925 Gauleiter (Hannover); February 1933 Prussian Minister for Science, Art and Education; September 1933 Prussian Councillor of State; 1934 *Obergruppenführer* (lieutenant-general). Committed suicide.

SCHACHT, H.G. Hjalmar (b.1877 in Tingleff, Schleswig, d.1970).
1916 director of National bank; 1923 National Currency Commissioner; until 1930 president of the Reichsbank, and again after 1933. After 1937 in opposition to Hitler's rearmament policy. Interned 1944 on Hitler's orders, later arrested by the Western Allies, tried by the Nuremberg War Crimes Tribunal and acquitted. Thereafter spent a further two years in a denazification prison camp. Later founded a private bank and published several books. Lived after the war in Düsseldorf and Munich.

SCHAUB, Julius (b.1898).
Druggist; member of the N.S.D.A.P. and S.S.; 1936 member of Reichstag, S.S. *Obergruppenführer* (lieutenant-general); Hitler's escort and driver to 1945. Destroyed Hitler's private files in Berchtesgaden and Munich. Verdict of guilty by the court.

SCHWERIN VON KROSIGK, Lutz, Duke of (1887–1977).
1932–45 Reich Finance Minister, confirmed in that appointment in Hitler's will. 1945 head of the caretaker government in the Wilhelmstrasse; sentenced to ten years' imprisonment; 1951 released from Landsberg; 1951–71 departmental head of Bonn Institute of Finance and Taxation.

STRASSER, Gregor (b.1892 in Geisenfeld, d.1934).
Apothecary; formed N.S.D.A.P. 1923; arrested 1923 for participation in Hitler revolt and sentenced to eighteen months' imprisonment. Released autumn 1924 on election to Bavarian Parliament. Until Hitler's release in 1924 together with von Graefe and General Ludendorff he led the National Socialist Freedom

Party, cloak for the suppressed N.S.D.A.P.; 1924 member of the Reichstag. Moved to Berlin and founded with his brother Otto the North German N.S.D.A.P. Hitler barred from public speaking and agitating in Prussia for twelve months. Otto Strasser resigned 1930 from the Party, Gregor remained a member. June 1932 Gregor Strasser appointed Party Organizer-in-Chief, thus becoming most powerful man in N.S.D.A.P. next to Hitler. After resigning his various posts in December 1932 withdrew from politics altogether. On 30 June 1944 murdered by order of his former secretary, *Reichsführer* S.S. Himmler. Hitler presumed not to have ordered the murder, Himmler having exceeded his authority, but Himmler was never called to account.

STRASSER, Otto (b.1897 in Windsheim, d.1974 in Munich).

Sided with the rebels in the Kapp revolt. 1924 member of N.S.D.A.P.; 1930 resigned and founded the National Socialist Revolutionary Party (known as the 'Black Front', not because of their black shirts, but because they operated underground – 'black'), banned 1933. Founded in Prague the newspaper *Germany Awake* and operated an anti-Nazi radio station, whose head, Formis, was murdered on Czech soil by German agents. 1940 emigrated to Canada via Portugal; returned to Germany in 1954.

STREICHER, Julius (1885–1946).

1925 Gauleiter of Franconia (dismissed 1940); 1923 founded the anti-semitic weekly *Der Stürmer*, remaining editor until 1945. Executed at Nuremberg.

TERBOVEN, Josef (1898–1945).

Bank clerk, N.S.D.A.P.; 1930 member of the Reichstag, 1933 *Gauleiter* (Essen); February 1935 President of Province of the Rhine; September 1939 Reich Defence Commissioner for Defence Area VI; April 1940–45 Reich Commissioner for Occupied Norway; S.A. *Obergruppenführer* (lieutenant-general). Committed suicide.

TODT, Fritz (1891–1942).

Engineer; 1922 N.S.D.A.P.; 1931 S.A. 1933 Expert in charge of all military construction; general inspector for German roads and for water and energy; head of 'Todt Organization'; commissioner for building and architecture under the Four-Year Plan; 1938 in charge of West wall construction; 1940 Reich Minister for Armaments and Munitions.

WAGNER, Robert (1895–1946).

Until 1924 in the German National Defence Force; March 1925 N.S.D.A.P. Gauleiter (Baden); May 1933 Keeper of Free State of Baden; 1933 member of Reichstag; 1940 Gauleiter of Baden-Alsace; 1946 condemned and executed by order of French court.

WESSEL, Horst (b.1907 in Bielefeld, d.1930 in Berlin).

Clergyman's son; 1926 law student; member of the N.S.D.A.P.; leader of S.A. Detachment 34 (Ben-Friedrichshain). Wessel wrote what came to be the second national anthem, the *Horst-Wessel-Lied*, based on an old communist fighting chorus. Lived with a Berlin prostitute whose protector murdered him out of jealousy. After his death through Dr Goebbels' propaganda, he was built up as a national hero, a victim of murder by the communists, a martyr of the movement, but during his lifetime he was only one among many S.A. detachment leaders.

Bibliography

Wilfried Bade, *Joseph Goebbels*, Lubeck 1933

Joseph Goebbels, *Wetterleuchten*, Munich 1933

Joseph Goebbels, *My Part in Germany's Fight*, translated by Dr Kurt Fiedler, London 1935

Joseph Goebbels, *Von Kaiserhof zur Reichskanzlei*, Munich 1934

Jürgen Hagemann, *Die Presselenkung im Dritten Reich*, Bonn 1970

Ernst Hanfstaengl, *Zwischen Weissem und Braunem Haus*, Munich 1970

Helmut Heiber, *Joseph Goebbels*, Berlin 1962

Helmut Heiber, *Joseph Goebbels und seine Redakteure, Einige Bemerkungen zu einer neuen Biographie*, in VFZ 9, 1961, 66–75

Erich Kempka, *Ich habe Hitler verbrannt*, 1950

Erich Kempka, *Die letzten Tage mit Adolf Hitler*, Oldenburg 1975

Ernst Kohn-Bramsted, *Goebbels and National Socialist Propaganda, 1925–1945*, London 1965

Roger Manvell and Heinrich Fraenkel, *Doctor Goebbels: his life and death*, London 1960

Otto Meissner, *Staatssekretär*, Hamburg 1950

Hans-Otto Meissner, *Die Machtergreifung*, Hamburg 1958

Hans-Dieter Müller, *Der Junge Goebbels, Zur ideologischen Entwicklung eines politschen Propagandisten*, Freiburg i.Br. 1973 (Maschinenschr. vervielf.)

Wilfred von Oven, *Mit Goebbels bis zum Ende*, Bd 1,2, Buenos Aires, 1 1949

Viktor Reimann, *Dr Joseph Goebbels*, Vienna, Munich, Zurich 1971

Hanna Reitsch, *The Sky my Kingdom*, translated by Lawrence Wilson, London 1955

Curt Riess, *Joseph Goebbels, A Biography*, London 1949

Friedrich Christian Prinz zu Schaumburg-Lippe, *Dr Goebbels: Ein Porträt des Propagandaministers*, Wiesbaden, 1963

André Scherer, Joseph Goebbels, in: Rev Hist. 2 Guerre Mond. 5 1955, H 19, 34–40

Rudolf Semmler, *Goebbels, the man next to Hitler*, London 1947

BIBLIOGRAPHY

Werner Stephan, *Joseph Goebbels, Dämon einer Diktatur*, Stuttgart 1949
Walter Stoeckel, *Erinnerungen*, Munich 1966
Anneliese Uhlig, *Rosenkavaliers Kind*, Munich 1977
The Goebbels Diaries: the last days, introduced and annotated by Hugh Trevor-Roper; translated from the German by Richard Barry, London 1978

Index

Aachen Cathedral, 165, 166
Abyssinia, Emperor of, *see* Victor Emmanuel III
Adlon Hotel, Berlin, 199
Admiralty Palace, 37, 38
Africa, 226
Agriculture, Ministry of, 115, 138
Alamein, El, 224
Albertus Magnus Society, 18, 19, 25, 38
Alma Mater, 24, 25, 127, 128, 213
Alsace, 83, 232
America, North, 57, 58, 61, 77, 163, 164, 208
American Embassy, 148
American Military Tribunal, Nuremberg, 7
American troops, 117, 238, 239
Anast, Café, 242
Andergast, Maria, 130
Anglo-American authorities, 232
Angriff, Der, 85, 127, 261
Anhalt Railway Station, Berlin, 20, 94, 106, 267
Anka, 24
Anti-Comintern Pact, 101
Anti-German propaganda, 227, 228
Anti-Semitic, anti-Semitism, 31, 72, 127, 128
Arado aeroplane, 257
Ardennes offensive, 251
Arendt, Benno von, 149, 179, 180
Armour Meat Canning Co., 58
Arndt Grammar School, Berlin-Dahlem, 56
Artistes' Club, Berlin, 149, 150, 201
Asahi Shimbun, 83
Atlantic coast, 232
August Wilhelm, Prince, 86, 165

Baarova,Lida, 130, 174–182 *passim,* 186–191 *passim,* 195, 198, 199, 205, 210
Babelsberg, 38, 44, 46, 47, 57, 59, 65–6, 150, 173, 176, 199
Baden-Baden, 15n
Baedeker, 34
Baldur (yacht), 177, 179
Baltic, 134
Bamberg, 54
Baur, Captain, 275
Bavaria, 259
Bavarian countryside, 231
Bayreuth, 91
B.D.M. (Bund deutscher Mädchen), *see* League of German Maidens
Beer Hall, Munich, 219, 220
Beer Hall Putsch, *see* Munich Revolt
Behrend, Frau (mother of Magda Goebbels who reverted from her married name of Friedländer to her maiden name at Joseph Goebbels'

request), 8, 13, 14, 16, 20, 21, 30, 36, 45, 64, 65, 90, 92, 93, 96, 103, 174n, 202, 205, 247, 250, 276
Belgians, 20, 21
Belgium, 16, 17
Belle Alliance Platz, Berlin, 267
Bellevue Hotel, Dresden, 238, 242
Benedictines, 147
Benfer, Friedrich, 172
Berchtesgaden, 251
Berengaria, 58
Berghof, Berchtesgaden, 203, 221
Berlin, 8, 10, 11, 27–29, 31–34, 36, 37, 44, 53, 55–57, 60–62, 68, 70–72, 74–79, 86, 88–90, 92, 94, 97, 99, 106, 108, 111, 113–115, 117, 119, 127–129, 132, 135–137, 139, 148, 150, 153, 162, 171, 175, 178, 194, 200, 210, 216, 225, 231, 237, 238, 243, 247–250, 252–255, 257–259, 263, 264, 265
Berlin amusement park, 271
Berlin Castle, 22
Berlin-Dahlem, 108
Berlin dialect, 228
Berlin Olympic Games, 1936, 152, 153, 175, 204
Berlin, Red, 203
Berliner Tageblatt, 25
Bernhard, Prince of The Netherlands, 153
Biennale, Venice, 155
Bismarck, Prince Otto von, 265
Blitzkrieg, 219, 227
Blomberg, General Werner von, 123
Blondi (Adolf Hitler's pet dog), 262, 265
Bogensee, 133, 136, 137, 248
Bolshevism, 232, 241
Bonn, 24
Boris, Czar of Bulgaria, 136
Bormann, Martin, 204, 219, 220, 254, 258, 268, 274, 275
Boston, 58
Bouhler, Frau Heli, 120
Bouhler, Philip, *Reichsleiter,* 120, 123, 168
Brandenburg Gate, 109, 255
Brandenburg Mark, 31, 65
Braun, Eva, *see* Hitler, Eva
Breslau, 234, 235, 237, 246
Breslau, Castle of, 205, 234
Brindisi, 59
Bristol, Hotel, 92
British Broadcasting Corporation, 227
British Embassy, Berlin, 114, 115
Brown Shirts, *see* S.A. (Sturm-abteilung)
Bruckmann, Frau, 90
Brückner, Wilhelm (adjutant), 96, 99, 158, 204
Brunswick and Lüneberg, Grand Duke of, 153
Brussels, 16, 20, 21, 168
Buchau Cemetery, 276

Buddha, Buddhism, 11, 12, 21, 45, 70, 141, 214, 259, 277
Buffalo, 58
Bülowstrasse, 13
Burgdorf, General, 274
Bürgerbrau, 55

Cabaret of the Comedians, 188
Caesar, Julius, 18
Campaign Publishers, *see Kampfverlag*
Caribbean, the, 58
Caroline Islands, 100
Casanova, 170
Cassel, 28
Catholic Church, 16, 18, 19, 21, 25, 31, 45, 85, 147
Centre for German Art, 155
Charell's Revue, 37
Charlemagne, French Division, 269
Charles II, King of England, 173
Charlottenburg Chaussée, Berlin, 255, 257
Chemin des Dames, *see* Verdun, Battle of
Chicago, 58
Christ, Jesus, 70
Christians, Frau Gerda (secretary to Adolf Hitler), 254, 274, 275
Churchill, Winston, 146, 223
Cicero, 18
Ciro's Club, 201
Cologne, 24, 63
Communists, Communism, 11, 41, 55, 68, 74, 84, 86, 92, 112, 113, 137, 227
Continent, the, 185
Court of Protection for Wards, 125
Crete, 145, 210
Crown Circus, *see* Zirkus Krone
Crown Prince of Germany, 165
Crystal Night, 72
Cuba, 58
Cunctator Maximus, 167
Cuno, Chancellor, 49
Czech partisans, 235
Czechoslovakia, 123, 210

Dagover, Lil, 130
Denmark, 209
Denmark Regiment, 269
Dietrich, Sepp, Colonel-General (Commander of Hitler's S.S. Bodyguard), 97, 122
Dirksen, Her Excellency Frau von, 86, 90, 249
Dirksen, His Excellency Dr Herbert von, 90
Dix, Dr Rudolf (Berlin lawyer), 196
Dönitz, Grand Admiral Karl, 225n, 234, 235, 254, 265, 274
Donna Rachele Mussolini, *see* Mussolini
Dorpmüller, Dr (Ing) Julius Heinrich

(Reich Transport Minister), 123, 254
Dostoyevsky, 40
Dreesen, Hotel, 64
Dresden, 228, 237, 239, 242, 243, 246, 270, 271
Dreyfus affair, 182
Dunkirk, 223
Düsseldorf, 50

East Prussia, 221
Eastern and Western allied powers, 232
Ebermeyer, Dr Erich, 9
Ebert, Frau, 168n
Ebert, Friedrich (Reich President), 7, 8, 49, 115, 168
Ebertstrasse, Friedrich, 115
Education and Cultural Affairs, Prussian Ministry of, 111, 112
Egypt, 58, 59, 226
Elbe, eastern, 57
Elbe, River, 239, 242, 251
Elberfeld, 49
Enabling Act (23 March, 1933), 114
'Engelchen', 99, 102, 132, 233
England, English, 59, 136, 146, 167, 171, 206, 208, 216, 223, 227, 242
English army, 206, 226, 239
English history, 223
English press, 218
Epp, Ritter von, 96
'Ernest', 62, 63, 65, 76–8, 81, 82, 84, 87, 88, 247
Ernst, Karl (Group Leader S.A.), 113
Etruscan tombs, 34
Europe, 17, 54, 100, 136, 185, 217, 232, 241
Evipan injection, 243, 270

Fairbanks, Douglas, 148
Fascist Organization, 159
Fatherland, see German Reich
Faust, 46, 217
Federal Republic, 38
Fedem, mit fremden, see Mit fremden Fedem
Fegelein, Hermann (S.S. Cavalry leader), 204, 257
Feldberger Hof, Hotel, 119
Felderrnhalle (Hall of the Field Marshals), 51, 71, 83, 155
Fieseler-Storch aeroplane, 255
First World War, 19, 83, 207
Flensburg, 225n, 231, 232, 235, 254, 265, 270, 274
Florence, 34, 87
Florida, 58
Foreign Office, German, 8, 149, 172, 209
France, French, 17, 48–50, 83, 138, 146, 167, 171, 206, 208, 227
Franck, Carl, 98n
Franco, General Francisco, 169n
François-Poncet, André (French Ambassador), 147
Frankenallee, 46, 57, 65, 96
Frankfurt, 24
Franz Josef, Emperor of Austria-Hungary, 165
Frau K., Governess to Dr Joseph Goebbels' children, 245–250, 259
Frederica, Queen of Greece, 153
Frederick the Great, 116, 224
Frederick Wilhelm III, 152
Freiburg, 24
French army, 206
French Division Charlemagne, see Charlemagne
Frick, Frau, 122
Frick, Dr, Wilhelm (Minister of the Interior), 107, 111, 122
Friedländer, Frau, see Behrend, Frau
Friedländer, Herr, 14, 16, 20, 21, 30, 127
Friedländer, Magda, see Goebbels, Magda
Friedrich Wilhelm III, 152
Friedrichstrasse railway station, Berlin,

267, 275
Fritsch, Willy, 130
Fritsche, Hans, 261n, 262n, 276
Fröhlich, Gustav, 175–177
Führer Bunker, 252, 253, 256, 261, 269, 270, 271, 274, 275, 276
Führer Corps, 127

Gastein, Bad, 204
Gatow Airport, Berlin, 104, 255
Gauleiter, see Goebbels, Dr Joseph
Gautama, see Buddha
Gebühr, Otto, 144
Geneva Convention, 270
German armament production, 229
German army, 207, 210, 220, 230, 248, 251, 262
German cities, 229, 231
German defence forces, 269
German dialect, 227
German divorce court, 192
German 'economic miracle', 38, 229
German economy, 128
German film industry, 137
German folklore, 238
German Foreign Office, see Foreign Office, Germany
German National Party, 41, 49
German nobility, 233
German offensive, the, 219
German people, 11, 206, 208, 209, 215, 217, 219, 223, 224, 227, 228, 238, 239, 241, 253, 260
German press, 209
German Reich, Greater German Reich, 8, 11, 19, 20, 51, 52, 68, 73, 93, 100, 109, 114, 165, 187, 194, 207, 208, 216, 217, 227, 230, 231, 239, 256, 258, 266
German scientists, 263
German women, 140, 255, 256
German youth, 143
Germany, 17, 25, 52, 54, 61, 86, 92, 93, 127, 130, 140, 144, 174, 176, 177, 181, 184, 189, 194, 195, 198, 199, 205, 207, 208, 211, 214, 215, 217, 218, 220, 223, 226, 230, 232, 233
Germany, Imperial, 188
Gestapo, 193, 231
Gigli, Benjamin, 168
Gish, Lilian, 148
Gloria Palast, 184
Godesberg, 21, 34, 64, 76
Godesberger Hof, 34
Goebbels, Friedrich (father of Dr Joseph Goebbels), 15, 39, 48
Goebbels, Hans (brother of Dr Joseph Goebbels), 48, 103, 116
Goebbels, Hedda, 142, 143, 158, 175, 256, 257, 259, 262, 270, 272, 276
Goebbels, Heide, 142, 209, 256, 257, 259, 262, 270, 272, 276
Goebbels, Helga, 142, 102, 103, 134, 142, 144, 244, 248–250, 256, 257, 259, 262, 265, 270, 272, 276
Goebbels, Helmut, 142, 244–246, 248, 250, 256, 257, 259, 262, 270, 272, 276
Goebbels, Hilda, 126, 134, 142, 256, 257, 259, 262, 270, 272, 276
Goebbels, Holde, 142, 143, 144, 256, 257, 259, 262, 270, 272, 276
Goebbels (Paul), Joseph Dr:
  personal life: birth, family background, 14–16
  early life and education, 17–20
  student and doctorate, 23, 24, 38, 39
  appearance and physique, 40, 73, 74, 79, 84, 85, 90, 109, 119, 145, 177, 245
  character, 40, 42, 52, 69, 72, 73, 93, 94, 104, 109, 124, 126, 132, 144–148, 160–163, 170, 195, 198, 202, 214, 223, 230, 236, 238, 245, 246, 259, 261
  engagement and marriage to Magda Quandt née Ritschel, 44, 77, 79,

81–87, 89–97 passim
  as husband, 11–13, 98–100, 102, 104, 108, 112, 126, 132, 136, 141, 144, 145, 170, 172–181 passim, 184–191 passim, 193, 196, 197, 200, 202–205, 209, 212–215, 228, 229, 231, 233, 234, 237, 240, 247, 252, 255, 260, 270, 272
  and divorce from Magda, 181, 185, 186, 187, 189, 192–197 passim, 205
  as father, 102, 103, 126, 143, 144, 147, 189–191, 193, 196, 200, 202, 203, 209, 231, 237, 243–246, 252, 255, 260
  as stepfather, 97, 124, 125, 143, 210, 226
  as son-in-law, 103, 205, 247
  as property owner, 114–117, 132–138, 207, 210, 225, 263
  social attitudes, 119, 120, 124, 130, 136, 149, 150, 198, 200, 207
  political life: entry into politics, 41, 42, 48, 49
  as political speaker, 49–54, 79, 93
  becomes Gauleiter N.S.D.A.P., Berlin, 55
  as Gauleiter, 68–74
  engages Magda Quandt as assistant, 82, 83
  Reichstag fire, 113
  as member of Reichstag, 70, 93
  as Propaganda Leader and Minister, 72–74, 83–86, 93, 94, 98, 104, 111–114, 117, 118, 122, 126–128, 136, 137, 144, 148, 155, 163–164, 172, 198, 209, 212, 224, 230, 238
  as Reich Chancellor, 265, 266, 267, 269, 270, 271
  control of arts and letters, 118, 119, 130, 148, 150, 155, 164
  as Plenipotentiary for Total Prosecution of War, 229, 230, 240
  persecution of Jews, 25, 72, 73, 127, 128, 200, 233
  relations with Hitler, 51, 54, 55, 71, 72, 91, 94–98, 100, 101, 104–107, 111–114, 123, 124, 126, 133–135, 173, 184, 193–197, 199, 203–208, 213, 218–220, 226–229, 254, 260, 261, 263–5
  attitude to masses, 69, 112, 117, 145, 163, 185, 216, 223, 231, 236
  attitude to and relations with members of Nazi hierarchy, colleagues and staff, 69, 70, 72, 83, 117–123, 132, 133, 162, 173, 183, 187, 188, 189, 194, 198, 202, 205, 219, 236, 237, 245, 246, 261, 265
  attitude to money and financial resources, 84, 85, 90, 97, 99, 115, 116, 131–133, 135–138, 163
  attitude to war, 164, 206, 223, 226, 227, 230, 238, 258, 259
  and so-called wonder weapons, 217, 231, 232
  relations with the press, 70, 72, 83, 85, 113, 128, 147, 150, 163, 173, 209, 223, 238, 261
  scandalous behaviour as Minister, 129, 130, 149–155, 170–174, 176, 181, 183, 184, 186, 189, 190, 192–194, 198, 205, 211, 214, 215
  achievements, 94, 98, 107, 109, 114, 216, 217, 229, 238, 239
  downfall, 174, 194, 200
  valedictory statement, 258
  suicide, 258, 259, 271, 272, 276, 277
Goebbels, Katharina Maria (mother of Dr Joseph Goebbels), 17, 39, 48, 49, 116
Goebbels, Konrad (brother of Dr Joseph Goebbels), 15, 48, 103, 116
Goebbels, Magda (Maria Magdalena, née Ritschel), adopted Friedländer, divorced wife of Günther Quandt,

married Dr Joseph Goebbels 1933: 8–12 passim,
childhood and education, 13, 16, 20–21, 36
betrothal and marriage to Günther Quandt, 27–32, 34
as fiancée and wife to Günther Quandt, 32–38, 42–46, 56, 61–64, 125, 140, 142
appearance, manner and attributes, 27, 32–33, 36, 37, 43–45, 59, 61, 62, 200, 202, 203, 209, 240, 266, 272
health, 42, 58, 59, 76, 77, 102, 108, 141, 202, 211, 213, 228, 234
basic character, 33, 44, 77, 102, 116, 139, 190, 207, 211, 224, 246
religious beliefs and adherence, 11, 12, 21, 31, 45, 243, 259
as mother, 42, 61, 102, 103, 125, 142, 143, 160, 189, 202, 205, 210, 226, 241, 242, 243, 245, 246, 248, 252, 255, 257, 262, 271, 272
as stepmother, 35, 36, 44, 59, 60
as foster mother, 42–44
as employer and housewife, 35, 36, 44, 46, 47, 61, 97, 98, 116, 131, 138, 139, 207, 244, 246, 247, 262
social life, 56, 61, 76–78, 119, 120, 130, 138, 154, 155, 177, 198, 200, 203, 207
attitude to sport, country life, 57, 78, 141, 201
financial affairs, 29, 38, 46, 61, 62, 64, 65, 67, 75, 76, 79, 92, 97, 99, 131, 138, 196, 205
as member of N.S.D.A.P. and early involvement with Joseph Goebbels, 79–93 passim
as wife to Joseph Goebbels, 93–100 passim, 102, 104, 108, 109, 112, 114, 116, 117, 119, 120, 122, 125–128, 130, 132, 135, 136, 138, 140, 144, 145, 162, 164, 183–191 passim, 196, 197, 200, 202–205, 209, 212, 213, 215, 229, 230, 233, 234, 237, 241, 242, 252, 255, 259, 270–273
189–191, 192–197 passim, 205, 211
attitude to his infidelities, 129, 130, 171–173, 175–181 passim, 211, 214
suicide, 241–243, 258, 259, 270–273, 276, 277
relations with Hitler, 80, 91, 95–98, 100, 111, 112, 122, 124, 134, 140, 141, 158, 159, 166, 184, 193, 195–197 passim, 203–205, 207, 210, 219, 221, 222, 228, 242, 254, 263, 266, 267, 268, 271
and Eva Braun, 157, 158, 222, 263, 264
attitudes to politics, 75, 78, 79, 140
party allegiance, 11, 140, 158, 207, 222, 241, 242, 271
relations with party leaders and wives, 207
extra-marital affaires, 62
with Karl Hanke, 182–184, 187–190, 200–202, 204, 234, 236, 237
with Werner Naumann, 236, 237
Goebbels, Maria (sister of Dr Joseph Goebbels), 15, 48, 103, 124, 131, 132, 185
Goering, Frau Emmy (née Sonnemann), 121, 126, 166
Goering, Hermann (Reich Marshal, Commander-in-Chief Luftwaffe), 51, 52, 97, 98, 106, 107, 109, 111, 113, 120, 121, 126, 133, 138, 145, 153, 155, 170, 199, 202, 216, 219, 253, 255, 259, 269
Goeringstrasse, Hermann, Berlin, 116, 143
Goethe, Johann Wolfgang von, 18, 51, 217
Goslar, 22, 27–29, 36

Gothic script, 218
Granzow, Walter, 57, 95, 96
Graubünden, 58
Great War, see First World War
Greece, 144
Greim, Field Marshal Robert Ritter von, 255–257
Gretchen (Faust), 46
Gritzbach, Colonel (adjutant to Hermann Goering), 199
Grosser Stern, 214
Grunewald, 214
Grunewald, Lake, 202
Guelphs of Hanover, 166
Gundelfinger, Friedrich, see below Gundolf
Gundolf, Friedrich, 25
Günsche, S.S. Lt-Colonel Otto (adjutant), 204, 267, 268, 274, 275

Hague, The, 168
Hamburg, 224
Hamlet, 73
Hanfstaengl, Ernest (Putzi), 8, 97, 99, 100
Hanke, Karl (Adjutant and personal assistant to Dr Joseph Goebbels), 96, 118, 124, 132, 136, 141, 162, 163, 182–184, 187–190, 192–195, 198–205 passim, 234–237
Hapsburg monarchy, 166
Hase, Professor, 269, 276
Hauptmann, Gerhard (writer), 239
Hausermann, Dr, 275
Havel, Lake, 35, 104, 133, 134, 136, 152, 154, 177, 249
Havel, Walter, Ambassador, 274
Hedemannstrasse, Berlin, 81, 82, 86
Heidelberg, 23, 24, 25, 27, 85, 127
Heiligendamm, 134
Heine, Heinrich, 25, 128
Helldorff, Count Wolf Heinrich von (Chief of Police, Berlin), 113
Henkell, 108, 122
Hentschel (mechanical engineer), 269, 276
Hess, Rudolf, 51, 52, 107, 121, 170, 216, 217, 266
Himmler, Frau Margarete, 121
Himmler, Heinrich (Reichsleiter S.S.), 53, 97, 98, 121, 127, 133, 153, 170, 198, 210, 216, 219, 257, 259, 265
Hindenburg, Major Oskar von 108
Hindenburg, General Field Marshal Paul von, 7, 8, 104, 105, 108, 110, 123, 124
Hitler, Adolf, 1889–1945 (Reich Chancellor), 7, 9, 11, 41, 42, 48
first attempt (1923) to seize government, 51
prison and release, 51–53
refoundation of N.S.D.A.P., 53, 54
elections, 71, 74, 94, 104–108, 112–114
as Chancellor, 108, 109–112, 124, 125
as Dictator, 114, 124, 222, 253, 254, 256
personality and physique, 99, 100, 124, 145, 160, 222, 253, 256, 257, 262, 266, 267
social attitudes, 149, 153, 155, 157, 160, 222, 223
Röhm revolt, 133, 134
assassination plots against, 99, 133, 134, 221, 228, 230
relations with Joseph Goebbels, 41, 42, 48, 51, 54, 55, 71, 72, 91, 94–98, 106, 107, 111–114, 122, 124, 126, 128, 133–135, 145, 173, 184, 193–197, 199, 203, 205, 218–220, 227, 247, 254, 260–265
relations with Magda Goebbels, 80, 91, 95–97, 99, 100, 112, 124, 134, 140, 141, 158, 159, 166, 184, 192, 193, 195–197, 203–205, 210, 219, 221, 222, 247, 254, 263, 266, 272
relations with children, 103, 126, 160,

195, 197, 208, 250, 256, 262, 265, 272
and with ministers and Party leaders, 157, 159, 166, 193, 201, 202, 216, 253, 254, 264–266
and monarchies, 165–168
as Leader and Supreme Judicial Authority, 192, 196, 264
political standing outside Germany, see N.S.D.A.P. international attitude towards
political ideas and strategy, 100, 106, 158, 159, 165, 166
and divorce, 192n, 193–197 passim, 204, 205
conduct of war, 100, 208, 209, 221, 232, 251, 258
invades Poland, 207
declares war on Soviet Union, 212
testament, 234, 260, 264
suicide, 257, 258, 264, 266, 267, 268
Adolf Hitler, the Man (proposed biography by Joseph Goebbels), 203
Hitler, Eva (née Braun), 9, 157, 158, 167, 222, 256–258, 263, 264, 266–268, 276
Hitler Jugend (Hitler Youth), 50, 83, 96, 97, 124, 143, 159, 165
Hoffman and Campe, Hamburg, 9
Hohenstaufen castles, 34
Hohenzollerns, 86, 165
Holland, 17
Holzhausen (Goslar), 22
Hommel, Professor, 150
Hoover (nephew of Herbert, former President of U.S.A.), 61, 77
Hoover moratorium, 73n
Horcher's Restaurant, Berlin, 67
Hundred Year Pact (with Russia), 216
I Cremated Adolf Hitler, 252
Iliad, The, 18
Imperator, 58
Imperial Germany, see Germany, Imperial
Information and Propaganda, Ministry for, 10, 114, 117, 118, 125, 136, 199, 217, 231, 261
Italian court, 10
Italian language, 167
Italian partner, 167
Italian people, 155
Italy, 34, 87, 101, 144, 226
Italy, Crown Princess of, 155
Iron Cross award, 229, 255

January 1933 – The Story of a Coup d'Etat, 9
Japan, 11, 100, 101
Jena, 106
Jesus Christ, 50, 70
Jews, 14, 16, 25, 40, 72n, 73, 127, 128, 133, 194, 200n, 233, 242, 263
Jewish film producer, 194
Jewry, German, 127, 128
Jugend, Hitler, see Hitler Youth
Jugo, Jenny, 130, 172
Juliana, Queen of The Netherlands, 153
Junge, Frau Traudl (chief secretary to Adolf Hitler), 254, 267, 274, 275
Jungvolk, see German Youth
Kaiser Wilhelm II, 86, 115, 165, 222
Kaiserhof Hotel, 89–91, 99, 108, 109, 118, 135, 147
Kaiserhof underground station, 118
Kampfverlag (Campaign Publishing House), 53
Karajan, Herbert von, 238
Karinhall, 120
Katyn, Poland, 218
K.D.F. (Kraft durch Freude), see Strength through Joy
Keitel, Field Marshal Wilhelm, 206
Kempka, Erich, 9, 204, 251, 252, 255, 264, 267, 268, 270, 274, 275
Kerrl, Hans, Dr (Minister for Church affairs), 123

INDEX

Kimmich, Herr (film producer), 132, 185
Kimmich, Maria (née Goebbels), *see* Goebbels, Maria
Knittel, John (Swiss writer), 150
Kochler, Dr, 62
Kohnen (Jewish couturier), 200n
Kolmorgen Grammar School, 20, 21
Königsberger Klops mit Kartoffelpürée, 38
K.P.D., *see* Communist Party
Krebs, General Hans, 269, 270, 274
Kremlin, 218
Kurfürstendamm, 184

Labour Front, 98
Labour Services, 83
Lammers, Dr Hans Heinrich, Secretary of State, 254
Landsberg fortress, 51, 52, 71
Lanke Castle Estate am Bogensee, 133, 136–138, 143, 150, 162, 190, 211, 213, 226, 231, 244, 246–248, 263
Lanke primary school, 244
Latin, 146, 218
Latvian volunteers, 269
League of German Maidens (B.D.M.), 124, 140, 143, 159
Lebensborn (Fount of Life), 159
Le Bon (writer), 40
Lee, Ivy, 163, 164
Leipzigerplatz, Berlin, 120
Lenin, Nicolai, 54
Leopold Palace, 114, 117, 207, 224, 244, 250, 263
L'Etat c'est moi, 222
Ley, Lore, 166
Ley, Dr Robert, 98, 122, 166
Linge, Heinz (valet to Adolf Hitler), 204, 268, 274
Lippe Detmold, 107, 108
Ljubjanska prison, 261n
London, 8, 57, 59, 60, 168, 208, 217, 218, 232
Lord Mayor (Berlin), 111
Louis XIV, 135, 173, 222
Louis, Joe, 145
Louise, Queen, 152, 153
Ludendorff, General Erich, 51, 52
Ludwigsburg-Ossweil prison camp, 9, 252
Luftwaffe, 98, 126, 216, 219
Luxemburg, 17

Mahomet, 70
Manziali, Fräulein (dietician to Adolf Hitler), 254, 267, 274, 275
Mariana Islands, 100
Mary, the Virgin, 17
Massimo, Prince (Governor of Rome), 167
Mecklenburg, province of, 35, 95, 96
Mediaeval war lords, 238
Mein Kampf, 52, 80, 89, 91
Meissner, Dr Hans Otto, 9
Meissner, Dr Otto (Chief of Presidential Chancery), 7, 110, 123, 133, 225n, 253, 254
Meissner, Frau (née Roos, wife of Dr Otto), 8, 132, 133, 225n, 228
Mensch und Arbeit Verlag, Munich, 28
'Mephisto', 218
Mexico, Mexico City, 58
Meyer's Encyclopaedia, 18
Michael (Autobiography of Dr Joseph Goebbels), 23, 40, 50
Milan, 8, 266
Ministry for Agriculture, *see* Agriculture, Ministry for
Ministry for Information and Propaganda, *see* Information and Propaganda, Ministry for
Mit fremden Federn (In Borrowed Plumes), 72
Möhnke, Brigadier Wilhelm, 274, 275
Molotov (Soviet Prime Minister), 225
Mommsen, *see Roman History, Works on*

Monte Cassino, 210
Morell, Dr Theodor (Hitler's physician), 195, 204
Moscow, 8, 54, 219, 261n
Müller, Renate, 130
Munich, 8, 24, 40, 42, 45, 48, 51–55, 90, 106, 155, 256, 270
Munich Revolt, 51, 220n
Mussolini, Benito (Il Duce), 10, 83, 153, 159, 166, 168, 266
Mussolini, Donna Rachele, 166

Naples, 59
Napoleon, 173
National Polish Government, 218
National Socialism (*see also* N.S.D.A.P. ethos below), 194, 195, 233
National Socialist Gauleitung Headquarters, 81
National Socialist German Workers' ('Nazi') Party (N.S.D.A.P.), 7, 10, 11, 42, 48, 51–55, 68, 70–74, 79, 80, 82, 83, 86, 105, 149, 164, 187, 195, 233, 238, 264, 275;
  election campaigns, 71, 74, 93, 94, 104–108, 112–114
  terror tactics, 68, 84, 107, 113, 114, 125–128, 149, 161, 162, 172, 176, 177, 184, 196, 199, 230, 232, 233, 242
  international attitude towards, 90, 91, 94, 128
  Party ethos, objectives, 11, 50, 71, 94, 95, 108, 109, 110, 112, 118, 124, 147, 185
Party funds, 91, 92, 106, 107
National Socialist lawyers, 98
National Socialist (Nazi) leaders, 8, 10, 206, 227, 241, 265, 266
National Socialist movement, 185, 266
National Socialist régime, 188
National Socialist State, 227
National Socialist Women's Organization (Berlin West End), 80, 81
Nauen, 254
Nauheim, Bad, 58, 59, 251
Naumann (writer), 72
Naumann, Dr Werner (Secretary of State, Ministry for Information and Propaganda), 163, 210, 236, 237, 264, 274, 275
Navarro, Ramon, 148
Neiland, S.S. Second Lieutenant, 269
Netherlands Brigade, 269
Neueste Nürnberg Nachrichten (Nuremberg Express), 262n
New Babelsberg, *see* Babelsberg
New York, 61
Niagara, 58
Nice, 31
Nil, Maréchal, roses, 28
Norway, 171, 209
Nostradamus, 217, 218
Nuremberg, 7, 122, 158, 261
Nuremberg U.S. Military Prison, 276n
Nuremberg War Crimes Tribunal, 261n
Nymphenburg Castle Park, 155

Obersalzburg, 194
Officer Corps, 123
Old Bunker, 252, 253, 261
Ondra, Anny, 180

Palestine, 58
Panzerbär, 261
Papen, Franz von (Vice Chancellor and Prussian Premier), 106, 108, 110, 123, 261n
Paris, 57, 60, 76, 138, 208, 217
Paris Conference, 1929, 73
Paris, the occupation of, 199
Partner to the Devil, 9
Peacock Island, 152
People's Freedom Party, 52, 53

Pharus Assembly Rooms, 68
Phèdre (Racine), 10
Philadelphia, 58
'Phoney war', 209
Pickford, Mary, 148
Pioneers (German Youth Organization), 152
Plenipotentiary for Total Prosecution of War, *see* Dr Joseph Goebbels
Plötzensee Jail, 223
Poland, 208
Polish campaign, 207, 209, 218, 227, 234
Potsdam, 258
Potsdamer Bridge, 267
Potsdamer Platz, 269
Prague, 175, 210, 235
Presidential Chancery, 7
Prinz Eugenstrasse (Rheydt), 15
Pritzwalk, 32
'Promi' *see* Information and Propaganda, Ministry for
Propaganda, Ministry for, *see* Information and Propaganda, Ministry for
Protestant, Protestantism, 31, 45
Prussia, Commissioner for, 108
Prussia, Kings of, 109, 114
Prussia, Princess of, 131
Prussian Junkers, School of, 165
Prussian people, 224

Quandt, Eleonore (Ello), 8, 32, 44, 45, 63, 69–71, 77, 85, 87, 90, 93, 96, 103, 108, 109, 124, 127, 129, 138–142, 159, 160–162, 171, 173, 174–181 *passim*, 183–189 *passim*, 191, 194, 198n, 200, 201, 203, 206, 208, 211–213, 220–222, 228, 230–233, 237–243 *passim*, 247, 259, 270
Quandt, Günther, 8
  as suitor, 27–31
  background and personality, 28, 31, 32, 34, 37, 38, 64
  status and wealth, 30, 31, 36–38, 44, 77
  social attitude, 31, 36, 56
  religious belief, 31, 45
  as fiancé and husband, 31–37, 42–47, 57, 61–67, 76, 81, 86, 87, 89, 90–96, 125, 126, 243, 264
  as father, 42, 56, 57, 60, 96, 97, 125, 210
  and foster father, 42, 43
  attitude to and relationship with Nazi Party, 81, 87, 89–92, 95, 125, 140
Quandt, Harold, 28, 42, 44, 56, 61, 62, 66, 67, 75, 76, 87, 91, 92, 96, 97, 124, 125, 134, 143, 210, 226, 242, 257, 271, 272
Quandt, Hellmuth, 30, 35, 56, 58, 59–62, 142
Quandt, Herbert, 28, 30, 35, 44, 56, 57, 61, 62, 142
Quandt, Magda, *see* Goebbels, Magda
Quandt, Frau Toni, 32
Quandt, Werner, 32, 45
Quirinal, 167

Rach (chauffeur to Dr Joseph Goebbels), 273
Rapallo, Treaty of, 40
Rath, Ernst vom (attaché), 50
Rathenau-Villa, 149
Rathenau, Walter (German Foreign Minister), 40
Reich, The, 230
Reich Chancellery, 99, 100, 108, 109, 114, 115, 117, 120, 135, 251–254, 257, 258, 260, 265, 267, 267n, 268, 269
Reich Chancellor, 7, 8, 108, 109, 112, 125
Reich, German, *see* German Reich
Reich Government, 50, 51, 122, 231
Reich Ministry for Information and Propaganda, *see* Information and

INDEX

Propaganda, Ministry for
Reich President, 105, 108
Reich Presidential Palace, 8
Reich Presidential Secretariat, 7
Reich Propaganda Leader, see Goebbels,
    Dr Joseph
Reich, Third, see Third Reich
Reich, Thousand Year, see Third Reich
Reichsbank, 52
Reichskanzlerplatz, 46, 66, 75, 80, 96,
    98, 116, 130, 158
Reichstag, Berlin, 52, 70, 71, 93, 94,
    105, 108, 113, 114
Reichswehr, 123
Reitsch, Hanna, 255–258 passim, 271,
    272
Remer, Major, 229
Rhenish, 15, 62
Rheydt, 15, 17, 20, 23, 38, 39, 48, 50,
    74, 116, 117, 120, 238, 265
Rhine, Rhineland, 13, 49, 53, 64
Ribbentrop, Joaquim von, 108, 121, 122,
    153, 206, 216, 219, 253, 265
Riefenstahl, Leni, 97, 130, 204
Riess, Curt, 15n
Ritschel, Dr, 13, 14, 16, 20, 21, 30, 31,
    65, 90, 96
Ritschel, Frau, see Behrend, Frau,
    mother of Magda Goebbels
Ritschel, Maria Magdalena, see
    Goebbels, Magda
Riviera, the, 59
Röhm, Ernst, 97, 98, 122, 133, 134, 266
Röhm Revolt, 133, 134, 153
Romagna, the, 166
Roman History, Works on, 18
Romantic Movement, the, 25
Romatzki, Couturier, 158
Rome, 10, 166, 167, 168
Rommel, Field Marshal Erwin, 50, 150,
    210
Roos, Hans, see Meissner, Dr Hans Otto
Rosenberg, Alfred, 73, 80
Rübenach, Graf Eltz von (Minister for
    Postal Services), 123
Ruhr, the, 48, 49, 50
Russia, see U.S.S.R.
Russian Amry, 225n, 231, 232, 239, 244,
    248–250, 254, 255, 257, 258, 261, 265,
    267, 274
Russians, 218
Russian flags, 216
Russian winter, 220, 227
Rust, Bernhard, 111

S.A. (Sturm-Abteilung, Assault
    Detachment, Storm Troopers or
    Brown Shirts), 78, 98, 104, 122, 128,
    133, 165
S.S. (Schutzstaffel, Guards), 97, 98, 113,
    121, 122, 126, 146, 153, 154, 159, 165,
    199, 221, 227
S.S. North Division, 274
Sacré Coeur Convent, Vilvorde, see
    Ursuline Convent
St Moritz, 87
Salzburg Festival, 204
Scandinavia, 168
Schacht, Dr Hjalmar, H.G., 53, 108, 123
    261n
Schaub, Julius, 8, 96, 100, 195, 206, 254,
    255, 263, 264
Schaumburg-Lippe, Prince Christian
    von, 86, 131
Schierke, Harz, 29
Schimmelmann, Graf (adjutant to Adolf
    Hitler), 95
Schinkel (architect), 114
Schlageter, Leo, 49, 50
Schleicher, General Kurt von, 106
Schlesien, Gauleiter of see Karl Hanke
Schliersee, 225n
Schloss Bellevue, 225n
Schmeling, Max, 145
Schmundt, Colonel, 221

Schreck, Julius, 251
Schroeder, Baron Kurt von, 108
'Schrumpf-Germane', see Goebbels, Joseph
Schukow, Soviet Commander-in-Chief,
    269–70
Schulze, Herr (Principal Assistant
    Secretary, Ministry for Trade and
    Industry), 42
Schulze children (Carola and two
    brothers), 42, 43, 44, 56, 61, 62
Schütz, Wilhelm von, 25
Schwägermann, Captain Günther,
    Adjutant, 246, 271, 273, 274, 275
Schwanenwerder Peninsula, 133–136,
    138, 143, 150, 162, 172, 175–178, 184,
    186, 188, 189, 191, 196, 200, 202, 203,
    205, 208, 211–213, 218, 220, 223, 226,
    231, 244, 248–250, 263
Schwerin von Krosigk, Graf Lutz (Reich
    Minister of Finance), 123, 137
Second World War, 38, 115, 164, 206,
    227, 255
Severin Estate, Parchim, Mecklenburg,
    57, 90, 95, 96, 264
Silesian engine driver, 188
Skagerratplatz, 149
Sky my Kingdom, The (Hanna Reitsch),
    257
Slavs, 219
Sleczak, Gretl, 130
Social Democratic Party, Social
    Democrats (S.P.D.), see below,
    S.P.D.
Sonnemann, Emmy, see Goering, Emmy
South Sea Islands, 100
Soviet army, see Russian army
Soviet Government, 218, 275
Soviet prisons, 270, 275
Soviet Union, see Union of Soviet
    Socialist Republics
S.P.D. (German Social Democratic
    Party), 114
Spain, 169
Spartacists, 22 (see also Communists in
    Germany)
Speer, Albert, 127
Sportplast, Berlin, 78, 82
Stadt der Bewegung, see Munich
Stalin, Joseph, 212, 216, 218, 219, 230
Stalingrad, 216, 224, 227
Stalinism, 219
State Opera House, Berlin, 113
State Theatre, 154
Stauffenberg, Colonel Count Claus von,
    230
Steglitz, 74, 96
Stolberg, Fürst, Hotel, 29
Storm Troopers, Berlin, see S.S.
Strasbourg, Alsace, 8
Strasser, Gregor, 53, 54, 71, 106, 107,
    266
Strasser, Otto, 53
Streicher, Julius, 122, 159
Strength through Joy (Kraft durch
    Freude, K.d.F.), 126, 140
Stumpfegger, Dr Ludwig (army
    surgeon), 255, 268–270, 274, 275
Stunde der Versuchung (Temptation's
    Hour), 175
Stürmer, Der, 159
Supreme Command (German Army),
    209, 251
Sweden, 52
Switzerland, 99, 214, 243

Tank Corps (German), 8
Tannenberg, see Paul von Hindenburg
Tasso (Goethe), 51
Tattersalls, 201
Tempelhof Airport, Berlin, 254
Terboven, Reich Commissioner for
    Norway, 170, 171
Teutonic Order, 165
Third Reich (Thousand Year Reich), 9,
    10, 123, 125, 127, 146, 149, 155, 163,

165, 166, 168, 176, 192, 200, 216, 218,
    225, 229–232, 249, 258, 259, 262, 276
Thompson, Dorothy, 163
Thuringia, 106
Times, The, 83
Todt, Doctor Fritz, 127
Tokyo, 8, 195
Trigeminus facial muscle, 141, 228
Trinity College, Cambridge, 8

U.F.A. (German Film Organization),
    173, 175
Ukraine, the, 216
Uhlig, Anneliese, 172
Umberto, Crown Prince (of Italy), 150
Umbria, Italy, 34
Unter den Linden, 109
Unoccupied Germany, 231, 257
Ursuline Convent, Vilvorde, 10, 16
Union of Soviet Socialist Republics, 54,
    72, 212, 216, 219, 227, 232, 241

Valkyrie, The (Wagner), 113
Vansittart, Lord (Secretary of State,
    British Foreign Office), 136
Venice, 131, 155
Verdun, Battle of, 21, 23
Versailles, Treaty of, 11, 40, 49
Verschovensky, Peter Stepanovitsch, 40
Via Mala, 150
Victor Emmanuel III, King of Italy, 166,
    168
Victoria Louise, Duchess, 163
Victory Column, 255
Vilvorde, Ursuline Convent of, see
    Ursuline
Virgil, 18
Völkische Beobachter, 159
Volksgericht (People's Court), 140
Volksturm, 269
Voltaire, 9
Voss Bunker, 253, 261

Wagner, Gauleiter Adolf, 155
Wagner, Winifred, 90
Waldberg von, Professor, 25
'Walter', 22, 23
Wandlitz, 143
Wannsee, 135
Wannsee Golf Club, 77
Washington, 232
Weber, Christian, 155, 156
Wegener, Paul, 174
Wehrmacht, see German Army
Weidendamm Bridge, Berlin, 274
Weidling, General, 269–70
Weimar Republic, 113, 115, 168n, 269
Weisser Hirsch Sanatorium, Dresden,
    228, 237, 239, 242, 246
Wenck, General Walther, 258
Wessel, Horst, 50
West End Hospital, Berlin, 77
Western Allied Powers, 232, 239, 240
Western Democracies, Western Powers,
    208, 227, 232
Wilhelmstrasse, Berlin, 8, 109, 114, 115,
    117, 129, 133, 143, 162, 199, 207, 224
Windsor, Duke and Duchess of, 136
Werewolf Underground Movement,
    238n, 239
Wittelsbach monarchy, Bavaria, 166
Wittstock, 32
Wolff, Theodor, 25
World Film Festival, Venice, 155
Wurzburg, 24

Young, Dr Owen (American financial
    authority), 73n
Young Plan, 73n, 74

Zarathustra, 70
Ziegenberg, near Bad Nauheim, 251
Zirkus Krone, 41, 42, 51
Zoological Gardens, 115, 201, 225n
Zossen bei Jüterbog, 251